Art and the Greek City State

An Interpretive Archaeology

Widely known as an innovative figure in contemporary archaeology, Michael Shanks has written a challenging contribution to recent debates on the emergence of the Greek city states in the first millennium BC. He interprets the art and archaeological remains of Korinth to elicit connections between new urban environments, foreign trade, warfare and the ideology of male sovereignty. Adopting an interdisciplinary perspective, which draws on an anthropologically informed archaeology, ancient history, art history, material culture studies and structural approaches to the classics, his book raises significant questions about the links between design and manufacture, political and social structure, and culture and ideology in the ancient Greek world.

MICHAEL SHANKS is Professor of Classics at Stanford University, and Associate Professor, Institute of Archaeology, Göteborg University. His publications include *Reconstructing Archaeology* (1992), *Social Theory and Archaeology* (1987) and *Classical Archaeology of Greece* (1996).

NEW STUDIES IN ARCHAEOLOGY

Series editor
Clive Gamble, *University of Southampton*
Colin Renfrew, *University of Cambridge*

Archaeology has made enormous advances recently, both in the volume of discoveries and in its character as an intellectual discipline: new techniques have helped to further the range and rigour of inquiry, and encouraged inter-disciplinary communication.

The aim of this series is to make available to a wider audience the results of these developments. The coverage is worldwide and extends from the earliest hunting and gathering societies to historical archaeology.

For a list of titles in the series please see the end of the book.

MICHAEL SHANKS

Art and the Greek City State

An interpretive archaeology

PUBLISHED BY THE PRESS SYNDICATE OF THE UNIVERSITY OF CAMBRIDGE
The Pitt Building, Trumpington Street, Cambridge CB2 1RP, United Kingdom

CAMBRIDGE UNIVERSITY PRESS
The Edinburgh Building, Cambridge, CB2 2RU, United Kingdom   http://www.cup.cam.ac.uk
40 West 20th Street, New York, NY 10011-4211, USA   http://www.cup.org
10 Stamford Road, Oakleigh, Melbourne 3166, Australia

© Michael Shanks 1999

First published 1999

Printed in the United Kingdom at the University Press, Cambridge

Typeset in Plantin 10/13pt [VN]

A catalogue record for this book is available from the British Library

Shanks, Michael.
Art and the Greek city state: an interpretive archaeology/Michael Shanks.
     p.   cm. – (New studies in archaeology)
Includes bibliographical references and index.
ISBN 0 521 56117 5
1. Corinth (Greece) – Antiquities. 2. Greece – Civilization – To 146 BC. 3. City-states – Greece. 4. Social archaeology – Greece – Corinth. 5. Art – Greece – Corinth. 6. Archaeology – Methodology. I. Title. II. Series.
DF221.C6S53 1998
938′.7   98-7923 CIP

ISBN 0 521 56117 5 hardback

CONTENTS

ILLUSTRATIONS

Unless otherwise stated, all illustrations were prepared in their final form by Shanks (see also the remarks on illustration in the Introduction, pages 7–8).

TABLES

This book is about the design of a culture and way of life in times of great change some two and half millennia ago. It deals with the remains of archaic Greece, the end of a 'dark age' in the eighth and seventh centuries BC, the emergence of the city state, colonial settlement outside Greece and the spread of Greek goods and influences abroad. Bearing radical cultural, social and political change, these times must feature in any understanding of the mature classical city state – the *polis*. Written sources are partial and fragmentary; most documentary material is archaeological. Attempt is made to develop narrative and interpretation appropriate to the character of the sources – this book is as much about relationships with the material ruin of times past as it is an account of what may have happened in Korinth, a city state at the forefront of the changes. Through interdisciplinary approaches to material culture and design this book is about what may be done with archaeological sources, the sorts of narrative that may be constructed. In this it is a work of art history as much as archaeology.

The book adopts traditional focus upon a category of material culture, a type of pottery conventionally classified *protokorinthian* and considered of fine artistic quality. The prefix *proto-* is used to indicate that the style prefigures pots produced later and called of *ripe* Korinthian style; the terms belong to a particular conception of the character of art and design history. This is challenged in the book. Different angles are offered on the significance of material culture in the early polis as style and design are related to society and social change, to human agency and ideology. It is this contextualisation that makes the conventional terminologies inappropriate and so they hardly appear in the book.

Nevertheless it is suggested that the arguments and methodology hold considerable implications for the classification and interpretation of pottery and other objects typical of archaeological interest. The book can also be read as a large-scale empirical exploration of the theoretical issues which have been the focus of considerable debate in anthropological archaeology since the late 1970s. While its particular academic context is one of an increasing number of interdisciplinary studies informed by anthropology, archaeological theory and art history, the label *interpretive archaeology* is one which may be attached to the book.

Various influences will be clear. Ian Hodder's contextual archaeology and the work of Anthony Snodgrass are very much in evidence; I studied under both these innovative scholars. Some lines of argument are in the tradition of Moses Finley, and I have found stimulating the French school of classical studies, after Vernant, Gernet and Schnapp. In material culture studies Bruno Latour and his colleagues have transformed my thinking. Further in the background is a long-running debate in Marxism about the interpretation of culture; for archaeology I may mention Randall McGuire's fine book, *A Marxist Archaeology* (1992) which explores Marxism as a relational philosophy. The project of weaving together fragmentary sources in a way which respects their character and the loss inherent in historical science is epitomised for me in the melancholic Marxism of Walter Benjamin and his great unfinished *Passagen-Werk* (1982) which aimed to fashion a history of nineteenth-century Paris, like Korinth, another great city in times of radical change.

I began my archaeological researches and writing with prehistoric themes of death and mortuary ritual, moving to contribute particularly to the development of archaeological theory – reflection upon modes of thought and interpretation appropriate to the remains of past societies. Foregrounded is the creative role of the archaeologist, constructing knowledges of the past, and I consider archaeology to be as much about its discourse as about its object. A result of a traditional education in classical languages (and having taught the same in high schools) was my encounter with a *discipline* as well as a *topic*. Hence this book on the early polis is accompanied by another, *Classical Archaeology of Greece* (Shanks 1996a), which deals with the *discourse* of classical archaeology. While the two works complement each other, the intention is not to produce any sort of definitive statement or judgement, but rather to sketch a field of possibility. Here I join others in confronting archaeology and art history with a revised set of intellectual and cultural reference points, renegotiating academic interests in these postmodern times.

Anthony Snodgrass, Alain Schnapp, Ian Hodder and Colin Renfrew have given great practical and moral support to my researches. Although I did not realise it at the time, my thinking was to take a new turn after a seminar week in June 1992 on the sociology of techniques at Les Treilles, Provence, courtesy of Anne Gruner Schlumberger. I thank Bruno Latour for the invitation to attend. With respect to ceramic design I have learned much from students and staff of Newcastle and Cardiff Colleges of Art and Carmarthen College of Technology and Art with whom I have worked on and off since 1988. I make special mention of ceramic artists Mick Casson and above all my partner Helen. I cherish links with the creativity of art workers and makers; she has transformed my thinking about design.

Research for the book was carried out in Cambridge, and I thank the Master and Fellows of my college Peterhouse for tremendous support, especially Philip Pattenden, Senior Tutor. Some library work was undertaken in the British School at Athens. I made visits to museums and major collections in Boston (May 1990), the British Museum (October 1990), Athens (July 1990 and April 1991), Korinth (May 1991), Naples (May 1991), Syracuse (June 1991), and Paris (March 1992). I particularly thank the staff of the Museo Nazionale, Naples, the Museo Paolo D'Orsi, Syracuse, and the Museum of Fine Arts, Boston for help and cooperation. Quentin Drew of the Computer Unit, Department of Archaeology, University of Wales, Lampeter helped with some of the work on the illustrations. Figure 1.1 is reproduced with permission of the Boston Museum of Fine Arts, parts of Figures 3.3, 3.24 and 3.30 are courtesy of the British Museum.

Work for the book has spanned over seven years, during which time I have explored ideas with the seminar and lecture audiences of many universities in Europe and the United States. Reactions have varied from warm support and constructive comment to aggressive dismissal and virulent opposition, but the point is that so many people have listened, and this is an appreciated luxury. I do not forget the infrastructures of privilege which have enabled this work.

My project has received funding from Peterhouse, Cambridge, the Maison des Sciences de l'Homme, Paris, the British Academy, the Pantyfedwen Fund and the Department of Archaeology in my college in Wales, Saint David's, now the University of Wales, Lampeter. I thank them all.

Maison Suger, *Paris, 1992*
Lôn, *Bwlchllan, 1996*

INTRODUCTION: THE SETTING AND ARGUMENT

A narrative setting

We have heard of Korinth, city on the isthmus joining central Greece with the Peloponnese to the south. Korinth figures in biblical and ancient histories of Greece and Rome. Proverbially wealthy and always known to the Greeks as a commercial centre (Thukydides 1.13.5), the place is described by Homer (*Iliad* 2,570) as *aphneios* (rich). For Pindar (*Olympian* 13.4) it was *olbia* (blest with worldly goods), for Herodotos (3.52) *eudaimon* (fortunate).

Our knowledges are subject to the sources. Most physical traces of the city are Roman and later – history was obliterated in 146 BC by Roman general Mummius who sacked the city. Only snippets give glimpses which take us back earlier. Back in the eighth to sixth centuries BC of archaic times Korinth was at the forefront of those changes which are associated with the early years of the Greek city state, the polis. Here developed new architectures, including the monumental temple. Changes in the accoutrement of war (standardisation of the hoplite panoply) were focused upon the north-east Peloponnese; the most familiar helmet of the Greek heavy infantryman is, of course, known as Korinthian. From meagre traces of later historical writing it seems that Korinth was one of the first states to undergo something of a social revolution in the middle of the seventh century, as the power of the old and exclusive aristocratic big men was broken. They had been known for their interests abroad. Colonies out west were set up. Korinthian naval power came to be foremost in Greece.

Its sanctuary at Perachora, just across the gulf, was one of the richest in Greece in its day, outstripping even Delphi with its deposits of goods of local and foreign manufacture. Herodotos, writing in the middle of the fifth century BC, notes that the Korinthians despised craftsmen least (2.167.2), a phrase referring to the characteristic Greek attitude towards manufacture. From metal figurines to painted stucco and roof tiles, archaic Korinthians produced a distinctive range of products, including, most notably for the archaeologist, pottery.

Edward Dodwell had bought a pot of the distinctive style and fabric in 1805 (von Bothmer, 1987: 187), establishing Korinth as the site of manufacture of a style found across the Mediterranean from the eighth to sixth centuries BC. It was here that some potters began producing new vessel forms upon which were made experiments in painted design. From pots with very austere linear surface, multiple lines with only a narrow range of geometric decorative devices, there was a shift to smaller sized and miniature pots with floral devices and pattern and with figurative design – painted animals, birds, people and monstrous creatures. While most pots continued to be decorated geometrically as they had been for some generations, this time of experiment in the late eighth and early seventh centuries is taken now to mark a significant change; for early Hellenic archaeologists and art historians the change is from Geometric to orientalising style, a key phase in the development of Greek figurative art with its topic of the form of the body. The demand for figured fine ware from Korinth increased. Design evolved into a distinctive animal art of later Korinthian ceramics. The mode of painting caught on too. Potters, in Athens particularly, adopted the freehand style of painting with incised details; this is the basis of Athenian black figure pottery, with later red figure considered, of course, an acme of ancient Greek ceramic achievement.

'Orientalising', because contacts with the east are evidenced, whether fabrics brought to Korinth by a mercenary, or a Phoenician trader making a stopover to exchange and collect. Korinthian goods travelled. Pliny (*Natural History* 13.5) much later remarked that Korinthian perfume of lilies had been popular for a long while. From its harbour at Lechaion were shipped the distinctive small archaic *aryballoi* (perfume jars) and other vessels. They were taken to sanctuaries such as that of Hera Akraia at Perachora, to Delphi, Ithakan Aetos and the Samian Heraion as votive offerings and accompaniment to sacred rites. They reached the Greek colonies of southern Italy and Sicily in quantity, where they turn up particularly as grave goods. Some items of Korinthian make are found in most western Greek, and even some Phoenician and native non-Greek settlements of the seventh century BC and after.

Mobility and far-flung connections, social and political change, precocious manufacturing talent, and the polis: these are some features of Korinth in that 'Greek renaissance' of the eighth and seventh centuries BC.

A social archaeology

This book is a social archaeology, seeking to make sense of the design of Korinth, this 'capital city' of archaic Greece. Following the pioneering work of Anthony Snodgrass (esp. 1980a, 1987) and Ian Morris (esp. 1987) a break is made with the artifact-centred, descriptive and typological work of so much classical archaeology, the art histories of stylistic change and pot painter, the historical chronologies. An aim is to further establish the worth of archaeologically based accounts of social history. Attempt is also made to reconcile social archaeology (interpreting art style in relation to social and cultural strategies of potters, traders and consumers) with the aesthetic appreciation and idealist accounts of conventional art history (compare Whitley 1991b and 1993; for further context Shanks 1996a).

I draw on approaches to artifacts and society found in postprocessual or interpretive archaeology (particularly the work, for example, of Hodder, Miller, Tilley, Barrett; see Hodder, Shanks *et al.* 1995; Shanks 1992b; Shanks and Tilley 1992 for issues and bibliography). Emphasis is placed on the contexts of artifact design – placing archaeological finds in context of their production, exchange and consumption. There are also strong links with the iconology of French classical studies, after, for example, the classic volume *Cité des Images* (1984), investigating the structures of meaning, the *mentalités* to be found behind the visual arts.

Changes in art and design are related to social factors, to changing life-styles and ideologies, and to everyday life. The category 'Art' is here challenged and replaced somewhat by 'style' and 'design', but without, it is hoped, losing the facility of being able to distinguish between different qualities of design (between good and bad 'art'). Conventional typological nomenclatures are shown to be largely redundant in such an approach which situates art and design in social context.

It is held that understanding the archaic city state must involve locating structural changes within the local social and political strategies of the people of the time: aristocratic 'big men', soldiers, potters, sailors, traders and travellers, and other 'citizens' of the early polis of Korinth. Here the argument follows a major premise of much contemporary social and archaeological theory that social understanding must refer to the *agency* of social actors. A fundamental aspect of society is material culture: another premise is that any historical interpretation which fails to take into account the material dimension of society is inadequate. Goods and artifacts are not just resources or expressions of social relations, but actively help make society what it is; material culture is active.

Narrative textures and archaeologies of the ineffable

The necessity of translation

The sources – pots and wall foundations, hints in early lyric poetry, accounts of later Greek and Roman historians – are varied and fragmented. It will be seen that they do not cohere. Indeed an argument can be made that they should not be expected to cohere, because they are part of, they help construct a social world which is not singular but manifold (Shanks 1996a). The question is then begged: in working upon the sources, what sort of narrative or interpretive structure is appropriate? Should all be brought together in a clear and coherent narrative or analytical account of early Korinth?

Any adequate account of archaeological and historical sources, it is held here, must consider how they are constituted in social practice – what people do. This connects closely with the necessity of subjecting source materials to critique and interpretation, not accepting their apparent face value, for critique is about reading (social) interest and motivation in materials presented as without or with different interest.

And how is practice to be conceived? The social is experienced, felt, suffered, enjoyed. Institutional forms such as economy, religion, technology and the state, so often the main features of social histories, are the medium and the outcome of concrete sensuous human, or indeed inhuman, practice. Most importantly, practice should be considered multi-dimensionally, as *embodied*, that is, rooted in people's senses and sensibility as well as reasoning. Here must be stressed the importance of the concept of *lifeworld* – environments as lived and constituted in terms of five senses, not just discursive rationality, which is so usually taken to be the basis of an understanding of society. I use the term experience to refer to the embodied, lived character of practice. (These issues are discussed in Shanks 1992b, 1995a.)

Thus it is held that a task of the scholar of the humanities is to ground social reconstruction and understanding in a *sensorium*, a cultural array of the intellect and senses embodied in social practice. So much of this is ineffable (as what cannot be put into words, the unspeakable, the otherness of experience, alterity). So much is felt, left unsaid. Our sources speak only through an interpreter; they are in need of translation. The ineffable: because archaeological sources are material and are translated into image and text. The ineffable: because there is always more to say (about the site and the artifact, the textual fragment); the loss, decay, death. How many, which data points, in what way shall the item be classified? What is to be discarded, what more lost? We translate what is left so inadequately. The ineffable: because the social is embodied in the human senses. A subject of this book is the aesthetic, the evocations of Greek art. Is such a field to be separated from the social, from rational thought processes and analysis? Is art to be considered to belong with subjective response and sensuous perception? This book attempts to deny such distinctions between reasoning and perception or feeling.

So a task is set to attempt to get to grips with sources translated through lived experience, with experience a constituting part of social lifeworlds which are not singular and coherent, but multiple, contested, forever reinterpreted.

Translating textures

A well-established route for dealing with the ineffable and with varied sources is the presentation of historical and narrative *texture* or illustration. Detailed empirical material may be presented in apposition to analytical interpretation. However, my reading of social theory and philosophy indicates that the relationship of manifold social reality to its representation and interpretation is one which supports no easy resolution; the separation of raw material or data from interpretation is one stringently denied here. Instead a technique from the arts and film is adopted – collage, juxtaposing in parataxis, allowing the friction between fragments to generate insight (for definitions see Shanks 1992b, 1996b).

Accordingly, much of the book is designed as a textured collage characterised by thick description achieved through close empirical attention to the particularity of style and design and to the production and consumption of goods, coordinated also with reference to written sources and anthropological discussion. A primary aim is to relate macro- and micro-scales, moving to and fro between particular sources and wider themes and narratives.

An interpretive method is outlined in Chapter One. This discussion is intended as clarification in response to calls from colleagues, though it is one I would have preferred to emerge simply from my treatment of the sources. There is no intended *application* of theory (for example of material culture, society, or archaeology); the presentation does not take the form of theoretical critique and development followed by data exposition and then explanation. Instead the bulk of this book is an attempt to be more empirical, moving through interpreting accounts of the design and production of fine pottery in Korinth, the workshops and the changing character of the 'city', the society of the early city state, style and iconography, the sanctuaries where were dedicated many items produced in Korinth, travel, trade and exchange out to the new colonies of Italy where many Korinthian pots or local copies were deposited with the dead. Basically the technique is to follow association in exploring contexts appropriate to different source materials. Contexts are conceived as fluid and open to allow interpretive leaps; it is not considered valid to have contexts predefined according to date and place.

Evidence relating to the design, production, style and the consumption of Korinthian goods leads off into explorations of a constellation of fields:

> Early historical sources and social revolution in Korinth in the seventh century BC.
>
> Gender issues in the early city state: women constructed as other.
>
> Sovereignty and power of the (aristocratic) lord: the hero as individual; warrior 'castes' and war machines; warfare (and fighting in phalanx); discipline, drill and posture; armour and the armoured body; speed, war and the race; mercenaries; the symposion.
>
> Boats and travel.
>
> Animal imagery and body metaphor: lions and other animals in orientalising Greek art; the warrior as lion; monsters and myth; birds; panthers; faces, eyes and helmets.
>
> Flowers and perfume in the archaic Korinthian world.
>
> The (techniques of) manufacture of fine artifacts.
>
> The pottery craft and industry: organisation of production; understanding the technologies of firing, painting and decorating; the possible meaning of miniature wares.
>
> Town planning and temple architecture.

The creative process of interpretation consists in the careful structuring of this collage, (re)constructing what I term assemblages, the implicit or explicit links made evident or possible, the commentary and critique applied. The juxtapositions may thus create, in Walter Benjamin's phrase, *dialectical images*, where insight comes from the friction between positioned source materials, their translations and interpretations. This may require from the reader more of an active role than often found in expository texts.

Emergent narratives and an argument

Sometimes the impression is necessarily one of dislocation and an incessant need to (re)interpret – immersion in the shifting textures, but nevertheless various narratives do emerge. Ultimately a subject I present here is the forging of political discourses of sovereignty, discourses which are still effective today. This is not to imply that there are no other subjects of this history, that other narratives may not be at work; interpretive choice has inevitably been exercised in constructing the collage.

I connect the material culture of the late eighth and seventh centuries BC in Greece to political and social interests and strategies by a set of concepts refined from recent archaeology, material culture theory and social philosophy. These concepts include: style and stylistic repertoire, technology of power, translation of interests, ideology, design and agency. They are given definition and form throughout the book, but I may anticipate a little, if some lack of clarity is permissible.

Style is interpreted partly as a mode of communication (via methodologies developed through and after structuralism) and it is proposed, for example, that the new figurative imagery to be found particularly on pottery dealt with ideologies of self and identity *vis à vis* worlds of violence and animals. Materiality is considered a primary dimension of social experience; people in the early city state were reworking their lifeworld and the experiences it afforded. It is proposed that this reworking can be understood as involving a new technology of power, that is, new uses of wealth and resources in building environments, promoting new designs of goods and developing experiences such as trade and travel, all of which were partly means of facilitating the achievement of certain goals (hence the term technology of power). For example, a self-defining social elite channelled their wealth into new lifestyles, assemblages of goods and experiences which articulated displays of their sovereignty. They did this because older technologies of power were not working; legitimations of rank based on birth and tradition alone were weakening.

So the changes of the late eighth and seventh centuries are presented as ideological shifts; new richly textured ideologies (of lifestyle, narrative and social experience, and prominently focused upon gender) legitimated a particular distribution of wealth and power. However, there is no simple process of a dominant group imposing a new ideology upon subservient underclasses. Ideologies are always contested. It is also argued that fundamental to the working of power is the translation of interests. At a time when the old ways were not working as they had done, some sections of archaic Greek society translated their (strategic) aims and interests (political and personal) into lifestyles and newly articulated ideologies of sovereignty. Potters and other artisans in turn translated these into new artifacts, attending to such interest in new ways of living and behaving with new techniques and designs, relating demand and concern with new visual forms and life-styles to their own interests in making and finding an outlet for their goods.

Such processes of translation, interpretation or reworking of interest contain the possibility of perhaps profound unintended consequences; this is the contingency of history. It applies to Korinth. Created were new forms of belonging and identity (particularly citizenship) as older and restricted aristocratic ideologies opened up. Demand and design principles combined, through the agency of potters and others, to create the values and intricacies of archaic Greek art.

It is via such concepts and interpretations that items like the Korinthian perfume jars are related to society and historical change. They were part of a new visual lifeworld, part of attention to the body in new ways, part of new pottery techniques. The pots translate interests in a reworking of political discourse. It is in this way that artifacts and material culture forms are central to the changes in what is known as the polis.

The structure of the book

Five chapters follow the life-cycle of some artifacts made in Korinth in the late eighth and seventh centuries BC. A sixth rounds off with summary comment.

Chapter One deals with the questions of beginning. Methodology is raised and discussed as a theory of design is presented. Rather than define a method in advance of interpretation, a relational philosophy or outlook is sketched. The varied intellectual contexts include critical theory, Hegelian marxism, poststructuralism and constructivist thought. Taking an arbitrary beginning, a single Korinthian perfume jar, the task is set of following indeterminate association through the life-cycle of the artifact.

Chapter Two sets out with the workmanship of the artifact introduced in Chapter One. The social context of craft production in the early city state is explored. Several types of source and approach are juxtaposed: archaeological remains of archaic Korinth, centred upon a working sample of 2,000 ceramic vessels; traditional and processual archaeologies of art style and the building of the archaic city; attempts to write political histories of the eighth and seventh centuries BC; anthropological approaches and social histories; analyses of the discourses of the archaic state.

Chapter Three tackles art and style. Radical changes in pottery design are outlined, illustrated and discussed. The first part of the chapter is a collage or counterpoint of illustrated vessels, literary sources and anthropological discussion – routes into the archaic Greek imagination. Connections are followed into ideological worlds of animals, soldiers, violence, gender, personal identity, sovereignty, posture and techniques of the body. The second part of the chapter begins with a wider consideration of anthropologies of art and style, then an overview of Korinthian ceramic style is presented.

Chapter Four, *Perfume and Violence in a Sicilian cemetery*, deals with patterns of consumption in a statistical and qualitative interpretation of the contexts of deposition of the sample of 2,000 Korinthian pots. These artifacts are proposed as unalienated products, 'total social facts' in a repertoire of style, a set of resources drawn upon in social practices of cult, death and travel.

The shipping of goods out from Korinth, travel, trade and exchange is the topic of Chapter Five. Rather than traded as 'economic' goods, it is argued that Korinthian ceramics were part of a social construction of travel and attendant experiences explored in previous chapters. This argument is set in the context of long-standing discussions of the character of the ancient economy, anthropologies of travel, as well as more recent notions of the archaic Mediterranean 'world system'.

Chapter Six returns to the concept of ideology and Marxian ideas of material production to draw the book to a close with a sketch of contestation and strategic interest in the emerging states of archaic Greece.

A note on illustrations and references to ceramics

Many of the illustrations have been taken from older sources, adapted and altered through computer processing according to my own museum notes and drawings. The aim has been to indicate as clearly and accurately as possible the subject matter –

a surprisingly difficult task given the disparate location of many of the pots, marked differences in access and publication, and, not least, the miniature size of the perfume jars which feature most in this study. Given this aim, there are not many photographs and there is no consistency with respect to the depiction of the characteristic 'black figure' incision. Sources for each illustration are given, and location too (usually a museum, with accession number). Reference is made to standard catalogues simply for further description, bibliography and context; there is no intention to acknowledge the position taken by these works on design and iconography, though my debt to the great catalogues of Johansen (1923), Neeft (1987), Amyx (1988) and Benson (1989) will be clear.

A note on Greek texts
For early Greek poetry I have used the texts and translations of Davies (1991), Lattimore (1951, 1960, 1967), Lobel and Page (1955), West (1992, 1993), and the Oxford editions of Thukydides, Herodotos, Pindar and other authors. Supplementary use was made of the excellent Loeb edition of Greek lyric (Campbell, 1982–93). All translations are my own unless otherwise stated.

1

The design of archaic Korinth: the question of a beginning and an interpretive archaeology

This chapter deals with the interests which lie behind the book, the issue of where to begin, the object of interest (the design of archaic Korinth), how this may be understood (the methods of interpretive archaeology), and finally a sketch is made of some directions to be taken from the starting point adopted – a single perfume jar from the early seventh century BC.

Interests and discourse

Korinth and its material culture in the eighth and seventh centuries BC – why have I chosen to research and write upon this topic? Any answer to such a question must deal with interest and discourse.

The topic is at the margins of several (sub)disciplines and historical themes and narratives. There is the art history of orientalising style, first appearing in Korinth fully fledged within a generation at the end of the eighth century. The characteristic black figure incision was taken up in Athenian and Attic potteries, forming the basis of fine classical ceramics found in art museums the world over (see Cook 1972). Iconographers take up the figured designs as illustrations of myth and narrative (for example Fittschen 1969). In classical archaeology this style 'protokorinthian', with its distinctive aryballoi, is the basis for the relative and absolute chronologies of the century in most of the Mediterranean (after Payne 1931). An ancient historical interest lies in the emergence of the polis and the tyranny and social revolution in the middle of the seventh century (Salmon 1984 for Korinth).

These disciplines have become the subject of significant change of outlook, with new anthropologically informed approaches in ancient history and classical studies, critical approaches to early literatures, new social archaeologies and iconologies, art histories too, breaking the mould of the last two centuries. Detailed reference will be made to these later; here and for orientation, I cite discussion in my book *Classical Archaeology of Greece* (Shanks 1996a). This interdiscipliniarity makes of archaic Korinth a rich topic.

These are the interests of discourse. However, my interests do not lie in the fulfilment of any obligations or rites of passage in these disciplines (such as the filling of lacunae in empirical knowledge of the past). My interest is in the *constitution of an object*, how Korinth and its material culture, particularly its pottery, came and comes to be what it is. I consider early archaic Korinth as an artifact, in two senses. First, the material culture, the archaeological sources: presented is an interpretation of their *design*. In so doing it is necessary to consider style and design generally – a theory of design. Second it is considered how this Korinthian past itself is and may be designed – the category 'archaic Korinth' is treated as artifact. Hence this study is between disciplines, somewhat meta-disciplinary. There is also here a symmetry between past and present about which there will be more below.

A premise is that an artifact is always and necessarily an object of discourse. I do not mean by this a stronger (idealist) sense of the material past being created by the discourse of the present. I refer to the (unexceptional) argument that while the raw materiality of a Korinthian pot may have been given shape some time ago, and in this way be considered to *belong* to the past, the same pot can only be known, understood and described through discourses which are of the present. Its raw substance is meaningless. A Korinthian pot, any artifact, cannot exist for us without interest, even desire, sets of assumptions, categories valued, without questions and answers considered meaningful, forms of expression. Discourse (as a shorthand term for such a nexus) is a mode of production of the past; hence I refer to 'archaic Korinth' as artifact.

In foregrounding the constitution of the past in the present, a substantial part of this book is a presentation of what can be called an interpretive encounter with the material culture of Korinth and what it touches. I conceive this as the construction or crafting of an interpretation and understanding which can only be said to lie *between* past and present; the past is no more 'discovered' than its empirical form is invented (such 'constructivist' thought is dealt with below). Again, within the interstices.

I have described this awareness of the contemporary location of interpretation as unexceptional; why is it therefore necessary to raise the issues? Because the implications are beginning to re-emerge in classical studies. I have worked in the theory and philosophy of material culture, archaeological methodology, prehistory and modern material culture studies. The contrast between these, with their disciplinary introspection of the last two decades, and the discourse of early Hellenic studies is a sharp and fascinating one. The weight of classical discourse has obfuscated and acted against considering the constitution of the empirical object of study; it is already there, built by decades of research (Morris 1994). The sheer weight of remains stored in museums is there, *a posteriori*, the empirical past to be known, discovered. I anticipate eagerly the changes sweeping the field and alluded to above; this study, and its accompaniment (Shanks 1996a) will, I hope, contribute to the fervent debate (see also Dyson 1989, 1993; Fotiadis 1995; Morris 1994).

The question of a beginning and a problem of method
Thus my approach is an oblique one and rooted in personal circumstance. I have this topic, archaic Korinth, and a set of interests. But where do I begin? The introduction *here* of the personal may seem inappropriate because there are well-established methodologies and research strategies to follow, but I begin with a worry concerning the idea of methodology – that there can be independent and *a priori* specification of how to approach and deal with an empirical encounter. Essentially, the worry originates in an argument that methodology defines the object of study in advance.

To approach an empirical situation with a general method requires that the empirical is to fit the method. This assumes that the objects of archaeological study all have something in common, and this is what the archaeologist is interested in; idiosyncrasy or the particular is secondary. Is this reasonable?

The immediate context of this issue is the argument presented by myself and Tilley (1992: esp. Chapters 2 and 3) against what we termed 'positivist' archaeology, the scientific movement in archaeology, associated with new and processual archaeologies, which has proposed an independent and supposedly neutral way of building archaeological knowledge, one usually meant to be modelled upon the natural sciences. The classic opposition to such a primacy of method came from critical theory (see particularly the collection *The Positivist Dispute in German Sociology* (Adorno *et al.* 1976); and within, Adorno 1976a, 1976b; Habermas 1976; also Pollock 1976; more generally, Arato and Gebhardt 1978: Section 3). The matter is succinctly put in pointing out that method is indeed simply the act of questioning and no method can accordingly yield information that it does not ask for (through its very formulation). It should be acknowledged that method is best conceived as resting not upon methodological ideals, something which would entail a metaphysics of method, but upon the object world itself. A key question is therefore how to ensure an open encounter with an object of interest. So while method may be more or less flexible, I wish to raise the idea that method may also and alternatively be conceived as arising out of the empirical encounter, and not be the means whereby the empirical encounter is made. This is also, *a fortiori*, to reject an empiricist notion that there need be no method, only descriptive sensitivity.

An aryballos from Korinth: the beginning of an approach

I asked – is it reasonable to elide individual traits and categories of method? The word reasonable contains reference to both rationality and ethics. So consider now the past, the object of interest, as a partner in a dialogue, with method as encounter. Is it not reasonable to approach a meeting or encounter with an openness to possibility, an acceptance of fallibility? We reason in conversation, moving from initial statements towards a consensus (of sorts) which is better conceived here as being more than the sum of the initial positions. The Hegelian term *Aufhebung*, 'sublation' – cancellation and preservation – captures this movement. Reasoning here is not some absolute for which we can formulate rules and procedures (methodology). Method can impose unnecessary and possibly damaging constraints, preventing a recognition of the partner in the desire to follow the rules. Rationality is best conceived as a recognition of partiality; and an encounter depends in its nature on being open. Dialogue requires tact and judgement – these are ethically *reasonable*. I wish to explore this idea of methodological dialogue.

Essentially this is to propose learning the lessons of hermeneutics (for archaeology Shanks and Tilley 1992: Chapter 5; Johansen and Olsen 1992; Preucel 1991; Shanks and Hodder 1995). A topic is approached with interest and prejudgement (prejudice) and a dialogue followed of question and response, a spiral of interpretation of answers given to questions posed which draws the relationship forward. Details of a critical hermeneutics are less important here (for which see above and also Bleicher 1980, 1982; Ricoeur 1981; Warnke 1987) than pointing out some aspects of this metaphor of dialogue applied to the material past (discussion also in Shanks 1992b *passim*, 1994). It may appear absurd to hold that the material past, inert and dead, could be conceived to partake in anything like a dialogue. But it is quite feasible to treat the results of scientific experiment as a response to hypotheses posed; problem orientation, involving questions and answers is a major feature of the scientific method of processual archaeology (Binford 1972, 1983; Watson, LeBlanc and Redman 1971). But, as I have maintained, dialogue entails an ethics of relationship and respect which goes beyond such methodological rules. What I wish to stress is a need to be sensitive to the independence of the material past, for this is the basis of critique of the present.

So rather than beginning with a methodology, I begin more simply and empirically, with a Korinthian pot (Fig. 1.1), its character (as pottery), and, of course, its insertion in various discourses, the things that have been said and written about it.

Design in the material world: understanding an artifact
There now follows a discussion of artifacts and style, design and interpretation. The aim is to consider the character of archaeological sources and what may be made of them.

What is illustrated in Fig. 1.1? It appears upon a shelf in a museum of 'fine art' (Boston, Massachusetts). It is small, 7.5 centimetres high, and carries upon its surface two friezes of finely drawn animals, birds and human figures. With the size and shape, the hard, smooth, pale clay fabric, the incised and painted decoration, its subject matter and style indicate that the pot is Korinthian and of the seventh century BC. Specifically it is of the art style or industry *proto*-korinthian, so named because it prefigures *ripe* Korinthian of the late seventh century and after. The depicted monster, stand with bowl, animals and floral ornament mark it distinctively as orientalising, making reference to eastern design. It has been attributed by Dunbabin and Robertson (1953: 176), Amyx (1988: 23–4) and Benson (1989: 44) to the so-called 'Ajax Painter', on the basis, mainly, of style of figuration and subject matter. Such attribution allows fine-grained dating (according to estimates of rates of stylistic change between fixed points supplied by stratigraphical associations in dated colonial foundations). The scene is considered to illustrate either Zeus and Typhon, Zeus and Kronos, or Zeus and a centaur (discussion: Fittschen 1969: 113–14, 119f; Shanks 1992a: 18–20). The Ajax Painter is so named (since, at the latest, Johansen 1923: 144) because a scene reckoned to be of the death of Ajax appears upon another aryballos in Berlin's Pergamonmuseum (inventory 3319; Amyx 1988: 23). This 'artist' is considered to have produced key pieces in the evolution of protokorinthian style. The violence of the scene certainly seems to invoke an heroic ethos characteristic of dark age and archaic Greek figurative design (for example, Boardman 1983: 23–33; Snodgrass 1980a: 65–78, 1980b, 1987: 158–69) further discussion Chapter 3, Part 1).

The shape and size mark the pot as what is conventionally termed an aryballos, an oil jar. The small size of such aryballoi means that they held only little oil. It may be

Figure 1.1 An aryballos in the Boston Museum of Fine Arts. Numbered 95.12. Recorded as from Korinth. Catharine Page Perkins Collection.

supposed therefore that the oil was special, expensive, or rare, probably perfumed. This was a perfume jar for full discussion see pp. 172–5, in Chapter Four. Mention has already been made of the context of trade/export of such wares from an early city state to colonies abroad.

In answer to the question of what the pot is, conventional discourse produces such a description. This is quite valid, but in a limited way. Here I wish to delve behind such description into the assumptions made concerning the interpretation of material culture. Specifically the following will be discussed:

particularity and its relationship to classification;
the motivation of style (why potters make in certain ways and not others);
materiality (acted upon by potters);

social structure and its influences on production;
style itself and how the concept is best conceived and used;
temporality, that the pot survives to be interpreted by contemporary scholars.

I begin by identifying some questions.

Particularity

Traditional classical archaeology seems to focus on the particularity of this aryballos, attributing it to a style, identifying its date to within a decade through stylistic comparison, appreciating its relation to the development of style, recognising its subject matter, and even the mark of its maker. However, in all of this the pot is subsumed beneath some thing other than itself: it requires relating to chronology, style and artisan's workshop, and the sense of its figured decoration is found in the body of Greek myth. Though the terms of close description, both analytic and evaluative, seem to represent direct and intimate contact, not merely empirical but also affective and aesthetic, the aryballos is epiphenomenon. It *represents* some thing else, which is often general and abstract.

Also those approaches to style which would place the pottery in social or cultural context (of trade and export, or ideologies, for example) can make the particular artifact as epiphenomenal. Artifacts are taken to *signify* cultural belonging (Korinthian or Greek); pots are considered as *representing* social interaction (trade and colonisation); style is *explained* by its social function, expressing the heroic or epic temper of contemporary society. The artifact becomes a by-product of social practice or cultural outlook. The primary determining forces are style, artist, culture, society; the artifact expresses, reflects, signifies, or engages with the 'something else' which gives it significance or meaning.

This is an observation that is valid of many archaeological treatments of material culture, and indeed those found in cognate disciplines. Here are some examples from classical archaeology (more generally see Conkey 1990; Hodder 1991).

Artifacts may be conceived as signifiers, carrying meanings, belonging not singly to an artifact, but inhering within sets of signifying artifacts, structures of difference (for example Hoffman's structuralist analysis of Attic askoi, 1977).

Artifacts may be conceived as a surface upon which is written a cultural (or other) text. The many iconological studies of black and red figure illustration, seeking mythological or political meaning, may be referenced here (for example, the work of Schefold on Greek art generally, 1966 and 1992).

Artifacts may be conceived as icons, carrying a particular meaning. This may be date or ethnicity (for example Coldstream on Geometric pottery, 1968 and 1983). Boardman (1983: 15–24) has interpreted elements of geometric pottery from Argos as icons of the city and its people (images of horses, fish, water and water-birds).

Patterns of artifacts may be held to reflect social practices, interactions or social structures. Whitley (1991b) has related differences in Geometric pottery style and the use of pots to social class in Athens. Morgan and Whitelaw (1991) have explained variability in the decoration of pottery found in settlements of the plain of Argos in terms of changing political relationships, with pottery conceived as an index of interaction.

None of these conceptions is exclusive of the others.

I am asking whether the relation between this particular aryballos and that other which is to give it meaning (date, style, social structure) is necessarily one of representation. Let me move on with a simple, perhaps naive, question. Can the particular pot only be understood through the general (categories of description, whatever is conceived as going beyond the artifact)? Consider the role of the interpreter.

The role of the interpreter

Close empirical description, definition of attributes and consequent classification would seem to belong with the artifact itself. They do not. They are but a gloss upon it. Description necessarily derives from operations carried out upon the pot. These operations to achieve description, such as measurement or optical scrutiny, are the interpreter's own and not of the pot itself, as are the terms and language of description, the purposes of classification. For the most part this is all taken not to matter. How can these things not be as they are? – they are the condition of any interpretation. Quite. But the question of the artifact remains: what is beneath the descriptive attribute?

There is an associated hermeneutic problem: is explanation and interpretation of the artifact in Figure 1.1 to be in the terms of its maker and their times, or in those of the interpreter? Is a mix possible or a problem? Beard (1991) has provided a programmatic call for an empathetic approach to Greek vase-painting understanding in terms of the viewer. Should the terms of explanation be neutral and not specific to an historical context? The distinction, in an awkward anthropological terminology, is that between 'emic' and 'etic' (Harris 1968, 1977; also Melas 1989), between empathy and objectivism (Wylie 1989a, 1989b, 1991). This is the old debate about forms of explanation or understanding appropriate to the humanities and social sciences with their historical and cultural objects of interest, and whether they should be distinct from the physical and natural sciences (Hollis 1977; von Wright 1971; see also comments and references to the dispute over positivism mentioned on page 11).

Society and the motivation of style

To hold that the artifact's style represents something else implies that whatever is represented exists somehow prior to the pot. (Analogous argument is about the possibility of pictorial or iconic *illustration* of, for example, a person upon a pot's surface.) Possible corollaries of such a function of expression are that society exists prior to the pot, that there is a realm of 'real' society and a subordinate field of representation. What people do is separated from what they make or draw. 'Real' people and their 'real' social relations come first. Perhaps style is held to represent social structure (as in the idea of a status symbol). But where is this structure? Is it the *logic* of what people do? Does it exist in the mind of the potter? The potter creates the artifact and the pot signifies their unconscious social structures?

The relationship is between the pot and some 'other' – its maker, and/or that which it signifies. Separated are fields of contingency and determinacy – the unreal and real, the dependent and the determinate. How are these to be distinguished? Is a pot less real than a thought? Style and culture are identified with the potter, the social subject, in that their meaning is to be found there. Or style and culture are conceived as descriptive, a set of attributes, a collection of types of object: culture and style are identified with the object. Mysteries remain of the meaning and genesis of materiality (the real), and of the meaning and origin of society and its structure. These often somehow exist prior to the potter and the pot. Where do they come from?

I have marked a distinction between the particular artifact and general categories to which it is referred. Why do people make the particular pots they do? This is a question of the motivation of style, or more abstractly, the variability of variability. How do social forces or structures impose upon the action of the potter? If style or society achieve expression in the artifact, how does this work through the individual potter, through the potter's particular encounter with clay? How does art style, such as protokorinthian, reveal itself in the act of the potter? Four sources of motivation may be invoked:

> the mind of the potter (unconscious or conscious);
> time or temporality (history, the weight of tradition, future destiny);
> social structure (the force of the norm);
> nature or the environment (determining social responses).

The individual potter may be conceived as being socialised, receiving the rules, values, dispositions of 'society' as they grow into their society; these then appear in the things made by the potter. More actively, the Ajax Painter is conceived as struggling creatively with the depiction of action and event in a painting upon a pot, struggling to change the traditions and conventions of ceramic art, pushing style forward (Benson 1995: 163–6). The issue is that of agency, the power of the individual to act and change, and the degree to which this is regulated, curtailed, determined (Anderson 1980: Last 1995: 148–53). The conventional choices are between

> voluntarism (the power of the agent's will);
> idealism (the primacy of the cognitive, of the intellect, or of abstract principles);
> determinism (a primacy of society or the environment).

(For further discussion see Shanks and Tilley 1992: 119–29; Giddens 1984; Hollis 1977).

Temporality

When the artifact is considered as representative, referring to something else, analysis of style becomes a search for pattern (which represents), or involves a symptomatic logic, finding *traces* of that other which is desired – the person of the maker, the artistic hand, the date, the society. It is a desire for that other which, in fact, can never now be had – the dead and lost artisan, the society no more. There are considered absent origins to which the artifact must be referred to achieve meaning. Time has passed; the person is torn away. In filling this absence, the pot is referred to that which is desired by the interpreting archaeologist. The desire is here given shape by our discourse; date, mark of maker, society are required. The pot duly delivers, but is this not possibly on condition of its loss, a loss often disguised by an assertion of explanatory scope, by the text or subjective self of the archaeologist or connoisseur? The terms of classification and aesthetic apperception which claim communion with the past, intimate knowledge, have their source in the discourse and sensibilities of the archaeologist.

I have indicated that if the pot is treated as a relay or device to get the interpreting present to something else, there is a need to explain the materiality of the pot. A related question concerns time or temporality (Shanks 1992c). If the meaning of the pot is found in some thing else (myth, the mind of potter, society), and in some thing else *then* in the seventh century BC, what becomes of the pot *now*? The thing remains, the aryballos in the museum case, worn, scratched, surviving in its materiality, its particularity. What becomes of this material resistance to the death, loss and decay which have overtaken so much to which it apparently refers?

These are not questions incidental to interpretation, for they concern the character of archaeological sources.

What is this pot? – the fallacy of representation
What is this artifact in Figure 1.1? My response has been to unpack the question. Issues of style and design, interpretation and temporality have been shown to involve relationships between the following: the particular and the general; potter and artifact; individuals and their society; agency and social structure; empathy and indifference or objectivity. Artifacts are clearly about their social contexts of production and use; they carry meanings, help create meanings. It is quite legitimate that these may appear in archaeological accounts through reference to social structures and the agency of makers and users, through analytical stance or aesthetic response. However, I have outlined at length a series of issues which need careful resolution. It is important to be clear about what it is that we are trying to understand – archaeological sources, material cultural remains. Failure to do so can lead to the problems, unresolved questions and conceptual dead ends of what I term a *fallacy of representation*, which is to hold that artifacts somehow represent what discourse desires to discover – past artists and artisans, their societies and cultures.

The intellectual contexts of this concept are varied and complex. There is the wide philosophical problem of representation which took a particular, and for the position I adopt here influential, turn in western Marxist debates about modernist aesthetics, the relation of cultural production to society more generally (Bloch *et al.* 1977; Lunn 1985). Mention should be made of poststructuralist critiques of *logocentrism*, the notion that meaning and reference can be anchored to some fixed point or principle (*logos*), some primary and underlying order such as reason or 'reality', with language, meaning and the 'real world' following a traditional order of priorities, from reality through secondary perception by mind, expression in speech and representation in written signs or figures (Derrida 1974; Leitch 1983; Ryan 1982 on links with Marxism relevant to discussion here; for archaeology, Yates 1990). Photographer and critic Victor Burgin (1982) has presented the argument for a fallacy of representation in relation to photography, making a stand against a reification or fetishisation of the photographic image (as somehow objective representation with a priviliged relation to 'reality') and for an emphasis on the practice that constitutes photographic objects – photowork. This closely connects with the position taken here.

Social structure and design: the primacy of production

Let me now deal directly with the questions I have raised. To avoid the intractable separation of the real and the represented I suggest that (material) culture be accepted as *production* or *design*. 'Works of art' are works indeed, and not self-contained or transcendent entities, but products of specific historical practices (Shanks and Tilley 1992: esp. 146–55).

The pot is *both* signifier and signified. An artifact operates in both ways. The pot is both of the potter and their society, and is also of the social object environment within which the potter works. The pot, maker, society and other contexts cannot be separated because they exist together in the act of production. The pot *is* the act of (raw) material taken and transformed, expression of potter (more or less), and an object of culture and style which opposes the potter who made it, those who take and use it. The artifact as signifier and signified is the creation of a social form, and then its distribution/exchange, and consumption. Consumption refers to both simple use of an artifact, and also the use of the object world to create other cultural artifacts: aryballoi were taken from Korinth to be placed in sanctuaries and cemeteries, helping to create the artifact of religious devotion, the experience of travel and burial in an early colony. Nor does it end with discard from a temple or deposition in the ground: the aryballos was collected and sold in the nineteenth century, has come to signify so much through the practices of discourse and metanarrative. I will say more of this *continuity* below.

Concomitantly, the style of an artifact is not an expression or an attribute. Style is the means by which objects are constituted as social forms. Style is the *mode* of transformation of material into social form, the way that a social group constructs its social reality; it is the way something is done (Hodder 1990). Styles, genres, rules of design and aesthetic codes are always already established, confronting the artist–worker, and so delimiting and constraining the modes in which style may appear. Style is thus situated practice, and the worker–artist is the locus where technological, stylistic and social propriety are interpreted in the production of ideas and other cultural artifacts. Nor is culture an assemblage of objects or things done: culture is a *process* of constructing identity and values.

Just as the artifact cannot be separated from its mode of production, the potter cannot be separated from their object environment (the world of things produced). There is no *a priori* 'potter subject' who acts in society. The primacy of production involves a dialectic between potter and pot, social subject and object world. Neither are separable unities. They exist in their process of transformation or becoming: the potter becoming subject self in their (social) practice; the pot becoming what it is in (life)cycles of production, exchange and consumption.

The refusal to separate real and represented on the grounds that the signifying pot is a material form as much as it is representing means an artifact is as much a social actor or agent as its maker (for analogous argument: Callon 1986; Latour 1988b; Law 1987, 1991). This is the argument for active material culture. Artifacts help to form the society and makers who produced and consume them.

Asserting the primacy of production is simply saying that people, pot and society have to be made; they are not 'given'. So there is no context (such as society), or subject of history (such as individual artist) which is necessary, can be pre-defined, and which may be conceived as supplying meaning and significance to the pot (arguing to the same end but from different premises, Bapty and Yates 1990: passim).

This is to deny the absolute reality of 'society' as *sui generis*. Society and social relationships do not exist in-themselves, as detached realities. I am happy here to follow Marx's appropriation of Hegel in arguing that society is in a continuous process of self-creation through people producing, making or attaching themselves to forms outside themselves (see Ollman's reading 1977). This is objectification and self-alienation: people making things which appear then as objects and forms separate from them. These productions may achieve various degrees of autonomy from the people who made them (alienation may be rupture, estrangement and reification), but the consumption, use and reappropriation of things produced is the condition of history: people eat food produced, use languages and live with institutions, use pots and live with their imagery. The process of reappropriation and consumption may remain incomplete as people can fail to overcome the alienation and estrangement of those objects and forms which remain autonomous and even determining forces. This is one of the operations of ideology. For example, an artifact can become a commodity, part of an abstract(ed) order with separate logic and values opposing the individual. But the full process is one of *sublation*, taking those external forms back within oneself (the meaning of consumption) in further cultural production: artifacts, ideas, institutions are the basis of further construction of society and culture. And such sublation recognises that these things and forms consumed retain their identity and difference; they are not simple reflections of people's wishes, aims, purposes and thoughts, but have material, logical and temporal/historical autonomy.

The full implications of *sublation* for an understanding of the social construction of reality are brought out by Miller in his book *Material Culture and Mass Consumption* (1987). In Hegelian terms society is created through its own *negation*, as the object created by people stands opposite and alienated. In consumption, far from being simply a commodity consumed (a principle and experience which dominates today), the object 'confronts, criticises and finally may subjugate those abstractions in a process of human becoming'. That is, the commodity is product and symbol of abstract structures which deny people's creative involvement in production, and the object of consumption is, in contrast, a negation of the commodity (*ibid.*: 191–2). *Sublation* is argued as being 'the movement by which society reappropriates its own external form – that is, assimilates its own culture and uses it to develop itself as a social subject' (*ibid.*: 17). This enables Miller to write that the full process of objectification (the social subject projecting into the world) is one where the subject becomes at home with itself in its otherness.

Social structure, in such a position adopted here, is not a determinate given, but comes to be in people's practice. Social structure is both medium and outcome of people's practice; it is the condition whereby people can act, but only exists in those acts. This 'duality of structure' is central to what Giddens terms the process of structuration (Cloke 1991; Giddens 1984; Thompson 1989; for archaeology: Barrett 1988). In lacking any definable essence, and in coming to be only in particular acts, structure is not like a rule book or legal or ritual code, giving precise directions as to what people must do. Structure is better thought of as disposition and propriety, a sense of normative order; it provides a basis for the acting out of people's plans and social strategies according to their perspectives, interests and powers. Structure is a sense or feeling that something is 'right'; it is about feeling, comfort, *taste* (Miller 1987: 103f, after Bourdieu 1977, 1984; further discussion for archaeology: Shanks and Tilley 1987, 1992).

I suggest that structure in this sense has a great deal of obvious relevance to the understanding of artifact design. Material artifacts are not easily analysed as having fixed rules of use and meaning, as in a language. The object world 'does not lend itself to the earlier analyses of symbolism which identified distinct abstract signifiers and concrete signifieds, since it simultaneously operates at both levels. It cannot be broken up as though into grammatical sub-units, and as such it appears to have a particularly close relation to emotions, feelings and basic orientations to the world' (Miller 1987: 107). Just as structure is to do with feeling and sense of 'right', providing an environment of propriety, so too artifact design, transformation of material, is a lot to do with taste, choice of what is conceived appropriate – a central point made by designer David Pye (1978). The object world is constructed and manipulated around flexible feelings or dispositions to do with things appearing appropriate and proper, tasteful and becoming. Of course, these may be deliberately flouted in strategies of opposition, but they then still act as points of reference. Objects and artifacts provide an environment for action, frameworks which give cues as to what is right and appropriate to do; they can literally be a structure or medium and outcome of action (Miller 1987: 100–1; Giddens 1984: 73–92; Goffman 1975). This is a field permeated by uncertainty and interpretation. Technical manuals for artifact design are, like legal and ritual codes, formalised custom and taste, and may provide secure routes through interpretive uncertainty and choice. The connection between social structure, design, and indeed history, or any cultural artifact is, of course, not coincidental: all are cultural production.

This primacy of production thus also assumes a continuity to the artifact form (and indeed to social agents), from a material artifact such as this aryballos to something as conventionally immaterial as the *experience* of travel implied in the shipping of aryballoi out to the margins of a seventh-century Greek world. Both aryballos and experience are artifacts. This is because production is less about *being* than *becoming*.

A note on ideology

The potter/painter of this aryballos in Figure 1.1 has followed traditional manufacture and then painted a scene of violent encounter which may be interpreted as part of a new expression of an heroic ethos, an ideological system closely allied to the interests of an archaic aristocracy. The concept of ideology is vital, I argue, in understanding this interpretive act, when the worker takes material, propriety and taste, interest and purpose, and makes something else of them. For the artifact enfolds the interests and interpretive decisions of those who made it, and these may be ideological, bolstering inequality, reconciling social contradictions, working on social reality to make it more palatable.

Some remarks about this complex concept of ideology are appropriate here.

The concept of ideology has been found useful in a number of archaeological interpretations (for example Kristiansen 1984; Leone 1984; McGuire and Paynter 1991; Miller 1985a; Parker-Pearson 1984a, 1984b; Shennan 1982; Tilley 1984). But little reference has been made to the manifold nature of the concept; ideology is usually used to refer to a situation where social 'reality' is represented or misrepresented, in burial ritual, for example. The usage thereby falls within what I have termed the fallacy of representation.

For example, in his study of iron-age Attic burial, Morris (1987: esp. 37f) adopts a two-level model of social reality: social 'organisation', what people get up to, and social 'structure', a logic or patterning which is expressed in ritual. He mentions but bypasses the thesis developed by Bloch (1977: 280–1) that the order of ritual may be an ideological and therefore distorting one, with a pragmatic argument that 'ideologies are multi-layered, and difficult to grasp' (Morris 1987: 41), the character of archaeological data preclude their consideration, so they are best left alone, or considered only in theory (see also *ibid.*: 137; but compare his pragmatic use of the concept, p. 186). Morris adheres to a notion of ideology as above and secondary to social structure, a realm of ideas and world views. Again, this allows ideology to be ignored: actions and structure would appear to matter more. It is unfortunate that Morris follows only Abercrombie, Hill and Turner (Abercrombie, Hill and Turner 1980) in general discussion of the concept and the question of the nature of the social, its relationship with the archaeological record. There is so much more, as I hope to indicate.

Hodder has criticised the concept with justification because of the problems of distinguishing 'real' and 'represented' social relationships; indeed he has rightly questioned this division of the social (Hodder 1991: 64–70). And the concept has no place in his programme for a post-processual archaeology concerned with understanding the meaning of things (Hodder 1985: 9). Thomas (1990) has presented a similar critique, but with important remarks on how 'ideological' features of society and practice may be conceptualised, and with which I here broadly agree.

Whitley (1991b: 196–7; see also Whitley 1993) has criticised the use of the concept ideology in understanding style (his topic being the style of Attic geometric pottery in context of burial practices). 'To view material culture and, more importantly, prehistoric art as simply material ideology, the means through which a particular (and, of course, unjust) social order is naturalised . . . is to ignore aesthetics; that is, everything that makes the art of past societies interesting' (Whitley 1991: 196). Whitley presents ideology as a simple matter (in contrast to Morris) of the justification of an unjust social order: and such a concept, he claims, makes social analysis easier. More importantly he associates the use of the concept ideology (to relate style and social practice) with a 'pernicious' and 'perverse' anti-aestheticism and relativism which 'denies human sensuality and the value of the material world' (*ibid.*: 197; also Taylor and Whitley 1985). I hope to show that this need not be the case.

The term is indeed a complex and 'overdetermined' one, subject to all sorts of strategic and rhetorical uses: consider the entry on ideology in Williams' analytical cultural vocabulary *Keywords* (1976). The different uses and contestation over meaning itself implies that there is something to the concept. I suggest that the apparent complexity should not be avoided, nor should there be easy and formulaic applications (such as ideology is the distortion of reality which fools people into accepting the *status quo*). Such simplicity and formulaic analysis can itself be an ideological strategy, reducing particularity, making heterogeneity, difference and the possibility of alternatives marginal.

So it is important to note the considerable and sophisticated discussion of the concept of ideology as a counter to formulaic and rigid use of social theory in archaeology. Fine and comprehensive surveys are those of Larrain (1979 and 1983), Eagleton (1991), Thompson (1984, 1990). Most discussion has been within Western Marxism (Anderson 1976) – attempts to understand the cultural construction of later and contemporary capitalism, and indeed societies prior to capitalism. An attractive feature, one particularly relevant to archaeology, has been the argument that cultural production cannot be reduced to the economic. More recently, particularly with and after Althusser (1971, 1977; Althusser and Balibar 1970), have been efforts to integrate a psychology of socialisation (for Althusser through Lacan's concept of the 'imaginary'), that is to avoid reducing the individual to consciousness or social structures, but attempting to understand social practice and how people become social subjects or agents. Important here are the implications of Foucault's connections between self and knowledge constituted through discourse and technologies of power (Foucault 1980; and see Tilley 1990).

Given the apparent absence of the individual from archaeology, this is again of great interest.

The ideological may work in various ways (Shanks and Tilley 1987: 181, 1992: 130):

as simple political or social propaganda, a distortion of social reality;

as a universal in place of that which is partial, presenting interests which are partial
   as those of everyone;

as a natural and necessary order in place of that which is cultural and contingent;

as coherence, misrepresenting contradiction;

manipulating and referring to the past in making what is mutable appear permanent.

The ideological may well be associated with the propagation of 'false consciousness'
– mistaken views and ideas of the way things are. However, according to my
argument above concerning social structure and design, it is often much more,
referring to taste, propriety, sense of correctness in the way things are done and
appear. Thus it not only applies to the cognitive, but to style, practice and experience.

A major conclusion to Larrain's studies (1979, 1983) was that the significance and
power of the concept ideology lie in its critical edge. This is lost when the term is used
simply to refer to a body of ideas or beliefs held in common by a group of people. In
contrast to this *positive* use, ideology may also belong to a *negative* thinking, or
critique. Critique is to think according to the task at hand, shifting and adapting.
There is no methodology here, hence some of the problems with the concept
ideology. Critique is to do with the constraints to which people succumb in the
historical process of their self-formation, outlined above. These are questions of
people's identity, their subjectivity, power as people's ability to act and their subjection to power beyond them (see Calhoun 1995; Connerton 1976; Held 1980;
Kellner 1989 for introductions to a Marxian line of critical theory). This critical edge
which relates cultural production to power and interest foregrounds contestation:
ideologies are about constant reworking and manoeuvring.

So, ideology refers not simply to a set of ideas, or imaginary views of society, false,
distorting, or revealing. The endemic interpretability of social structure means
ideology works directly on the negotiated and constructed character of society in its
relationship with interests and people's (political) strategies. It is best thought of in
an adjectival way, as an aspect or dimension of practice and production: ideological
structures are those which have a particular relationship with power and interests,
serving, working in those ways I have outlined (containment and closure) to achieve
ends in line with the interests of some and not all.

Objects have a particular relation with time. They are a principal means of
referencing the past because of their (possible) durability, their life-cycle. Through
durability and continuity of use, or through a tradition of production, the object can
provide a medium wherein the transient present is brought into a much larger
temporal experience of past-present, cultural order re-enacting its own self-creation,
the particular practices of people in the present lost in the whole. This particular view
entails an ideology of denying or making natural that which is subject to change.
Alternatively, the fashionable artifact signifies the present (and/or) future, as the
value of an object is related to transient knowledge and cultural production. Here the
dynamic of production and design is tied to a system of emulation (Miller 1982,

1985a; discussion pp. 38–9), as artifacts associated with a valued sub-culture or disposition are followed by others in cycles of innovation by style-setting group and imitation elsewhere. Innovation and artifacts are thus involved in an ideological system of stabilising social difference (Miller 1987: 126).

Interpretive archaeology and relational philosophy

The previous sections dealt briefly with the character of design and production. I will now move to an archaeological ontology through an outline of a relational philosophy for an interpretive or contextual method.

Internal relations: multiplicity and the character of an artifact

This aryballos in Figure 1.1 only makes sense when related and compared to others. Its (unique) identity can only be appreciated when seen as *different* from others and from other things, qualities, experiences. Sense is also made of the aryballos by seeing that it is *similar* to others; the aryballos is classed (Ajax Painter, middle protokorinthian) of style and date. These are relations between the one and the many, the pot and its 'other'.

As I argued that the relation between the pot and its other cannot be separated (into potter and pot, culture and nature, material and (social) structure, for example), so I argue that the relation between the one and the many is as inseparable; or, rather, the (sometimes pragmatic and necessary) separation is not given but carried out under certain interests (analytical, for example). The relation is part of the character of an artifact. One aryballos and many other things – here the word 'many' is adjectival. I mean that the character of the artifact is *multiplicity* – that is, substantive.

I look at this aryballos in a Boston museum. I can attribute an identity and unity to it; it is not a stone or metal blade but a pot of a certain size, with decoration of a particular type, with colour and markings, a particular ceramic fabric. I can relate such attributes to styles of pottery (protokorinthian), to production centres, to places where such pots are found (Korinth). This is not what the pot *is*. Ontology (being) is in question. These attributes are not present *within* the pot, giving it an identity; they are an extra dimension. Its colour may bring me to think of flesh tone in a picture I know. Its painted strutting lion may remind me of my cat. The figures race round the pot like 'motorbikes round a wall of death', as someone once said of it to me. I may think of the first occasion I came across this pot, my mood or circumstance when I did so. Others may find different things through the aryballos. All is shifting. It would be better to talk of the piece of pot *becoming* rather than *being* something. It does not have (a unitary) identity and being, so much as difference and becoming. The pot *connects* and I am led into associations and periphrasis, metaphor (which asserts the identity of difference).

The pot is old. Is it the past? Does it bring the Greek past to me? Is it a sign of the past, its trace? Is the past its meaning? The past and the pot cannot, I am arguing, be reduced to promises of communion with a definitive or transcendent meaning. The meaning is here and dispersed elsewhere. The pot is always more. I may try to remove my feelings and perceptions and see through to what the pot actually is. But its existence is simply and grossly material, and even its chemical and physical composition lead me off into associations. It is always referred to something else; the pot is always somehow absent. Where do I begin? How do I know which lines of flight from the object, which deferrals to take? One answer is according to a law – being told the 'right' chains of relation. This is the operation of discourse in creating identities and knowledges. On another hand the (pot as) signifier may be subverted; instead of the sovereign signifying pot there are webs of difference – multiplicity.

The reality of the past is not simply its factuality, its raw existence as fact, as that which is there remaining after decay and loss, this aryballos. The reality of the pot is *realisation*, the process of it becoming other than itself. It is from the past, but here, changed, with us now, no longer what it was. This becoming-other-than-itself involves the intercession of subjectivity, of the perceiving, feeling, analysing archae-ologist, attending to interest. The pot is not defining itself as aryballos, as anything, but depends on its *relation* with me. The subjectivity of the interpreter is the form that the objective takes. It cannot speak for itself.

I am referring here to *relational thinking*. The background to this book is a body of thought focusing upon the character of relations and their importance to the identity of things. Hegel's idealism is one vital source (Marcuse 1955) running into Marx's dialectical materialism, where I follow the reading of Bertel Ollman (1971), see also McGuire (1992). Stress is placed upon the importance of internal relations. These are defined as intrinsic to the nature and identity of items they connect; external relations are those which could be removed without making any difference to what they connect (see Bradley 1930 for an argument for the universality of internal relations on the grounds that without relations nothing would be different from anything else). Structuralism and poststructuralism have emphasised the importance of structured context and webs of difference, other variants of relational thinking upon which I draw (Leitch 1983 for an introduction; Deleuze and Guattari 1988 for an application of the idea of connectivity I use).

The position taken here is that to know what something really is, what its concrete reality is, we have to get beyond its immediately given state, which is a tautology ('this pot is a pot'), and follow the process in which it becomes other, something else, as in the proposition 'the pot is yellow'. In the process of becoming yellow however, the pot still remains a pot. This is *sublation* – the dynamic of turning into something else and effecting reconciliation. I have already introduced the concept in relation to Marxian notions of production. Let me expand.

Sublate is the word usually used to translate the German *aufheben* (*Aufhebung* in its noun form) as used by Hegel. It is the central moment of dialectic. *Aufheben* is to take up, save, but also to cancel, terminate, annul, suspend. *Aufheben* is a term used of overcoming an opposition. I have already described sublation in the case of the pot and the other, for example, the opposition between potter (social subject) and object form. To sublate is not to find a middle way – a bit of both. It is to transcend or suspend the distinction without suppressing either element. Sublation contains a notion of preserving, and also of reconciliation. It means that artifact and potter lose

their immediacy, but are not destroyed by the loss; the loss of immediacy is mediation by the other. So in the sublated *relation* the artifact object is mediated by
subjective factors.

Relational thinking maintains that things, states (like presence), and concepts
(such as fact and objectivity) *exist* in their relation with other things, states and
concepts. So relations are not links between things which exist in themselves,
separate from the relations. Relations are internal.

Non-identity thinking

The concrete world is permeated by negativity, and identity is otherness. Another
name for this is *non-identity thinking* (Buck-Morss 1977). The identity of the pot,
conceived as a substantive multiplicity, is produced as a *supplement* (in Derridean sense
too: Derrida 1974: 141–64; Yates 1990: 215–25), an extra dimension. It is the 'other'
of which I was writing in the previous section. For Deleuze and Guattari (1988: 6, 17,
21) the artifact as multiplicity is characterised by 'n-i' dimensions, that is a set of 'n'
relations without a supplementary dimension of 'identity'; see Figure 1.2.

Abstract now comes to mean this aryballos devoid of (abstracted from) the
particular and negative otherness which gives it concrete form and which depends on
the mediation of my subjectivity. Common sense might have us believe that the pot is
concrete in itself, while following of the 'negations' of the piece of pot (tracing it
through its contexts, associations and relations) involves abstractions.

The artifact as assemblage

Clarke provided a classic definition of an archaeological assemblage: an associated
set of artifact types (Clarke 1968: Chapter 6). Here I am providing another use of the
word. The artifact, existing in these internal relations (with what might seem separate to its identity, beyond its unitary being), forms a multiplicity. The association and
displacement, as the artifact becomes what it is in our understanding, make of the
artifact itself an *assemblage*. Centrifugal and centripetal forces (of displacement and
association) make of the artifact an assemblage of particles of information and
connection. The forces are set in motion primarily through the intercession of the
investigating and interpreting archaeologist, their interests and desires. This means
that the artifact is defined more by what is conventionally conceived as the outside,
than by a set of 'internal' qualities or attributes (Fig. 1.3).

The creativity of interpretation

Just as the possible number of data points upon an artifact is infinite, so too the
internal relations of displacement and association are a threat of infinite dispersion. I
wrote above of the aryballos suggesting a line of investigation through the look of
animals, through pictorial flesh tones, through a dynamic of circular motion. Where
does it all end? I could say in an eventual loss of meaning, in absurdity, an existential
loss of sense in the raw materiality of the past (the question again of the raw substance
of the pot) and its dissolution in the present, in its material decay. This would be true,
but disingenuous. The artifact disperses as the interpreter follows lines of associ-

ation. These lines can be of various sorts: they may be of empirical association (as in conventional concept of assemblage), of conceptual alignment (circular motion), or of creative elaboration (drawing cats). Which interpretive line is adopted depends on the interest of the interpreter. The lines of displacement can be made to reconvene, forming a new unity. Deleuze and Guattari (1988) write of deterritorialisation and reterritorialisation: territorial unity dispersed and reconvened. How this occurs depends partly on what the interpreter wishes to make; it is a creative choice. I refer again to the primacy of (material) production. Dispersion and identity are matters of *design*. Choices are always already given to the interpreter; particular purposes and interests are already regarded as valuable (sense of chronometric date, operational qualities of measurement in asserting identity, the artifact's 'territory') and may be institutionalised; particular knowledges are pre-chosen. So usually the dispersion is curtailed or ends in those identities and narratives I have outlined for the aryballos of Figure 1.1 and which we know so well; this is the work of discourse. But it remains that this is work of production, and other 'artifacts' may be made. This is the craft of archaeology (Shanks 1992b; Shanks and McGuire 1996).

Much contemporary teaching of creativity in the fine and applied arts works with such notions, as I observed and experienced at Newcastle, Cardiff and Carmarthen Colleges of Art 1988–95. Dispersion away from an opening design brief and accepted solutions, dispersion through 'n' dimensions of elaboration and transformation, countered by convergence upon a viable production or artifact is a standard methodology. Clifford (1988) and Hebdige (1979), writing on native American and popular sub-cultural identity, provide analogies in (sub)cultural production – creative appropriation of material goods and reorganisation around constructed cultural identities.

Nor does the element of creativity necessarily involve a loss of the empirical. The facts of archaeological knowledge are created from observations of a reality, and, given an interest in 'knowledge', the archaeologist may be able to recognise that reality and master the technical aids that assist or allow us to observe it. But this does not mean giving absolute primacy to the object past. In the interplay between archaeological interpreter and object, both are partners in the final product. The archaeologist gains familiarity through working with the artifacts from the past, but they defy this familiarity through their resistance to classification and categorisation. The archaeological record can never quite be captured or pinned down – there is always more to say and do.

A conception of an artifact as assemblage brings problems to the notion that categories of evidence are 'given' or somehow self-evident. A relational stance holds that there are no natural units of data. I have been arguing that they are constructed. The concepts 'artifact' or 'aryballos', just like 'site' and 'region', are complex and determined, without unity or final all-purpose identity. The vectors of affiliation break away from the familiar.

There is nothing 'natural' or given about style, date and context of social structure. I would argue that their relation to the particularity of this aryballos is not a strong one, because so much is ignored. These conceived aspects of the pot are a part of the production of knowledges, part of discourse, and that is where they find their justification. This is not to deny the relative significance of date and style and such; they are vital to respectable, but *particular* interests in the past. Full use can alternatively be made of the variability and particularity apparent in artifacts such as this, rather than subsuming detail under high-level generalisations. I also suggest that the interests in or desires for lost potter and 'society' are perhaps inappropriate. As archaeologists we might rather accept the decay and loss of the past. This implies an obligation of restitution, the redeeming act of reconstruction.

So, this aryballos is cultural material over-worked with association and filiation. The question is not so much – what is it?, but – what is to be made of this aryballos?

Contextual archaeology

Context has long been recognised as vital in establishing an artifact's significance. It has rightly been stressed that context should be taken to refer not only to date, place and material location, but also to social context. 'Contextual archaeology' (Hodder 1987, 1991) makes much of associations, holding that meanings of things can only be ascertained if contexts of use are considered. I am arguing that these possible dimensions of context should indeed be noted, but *not* defined *a priori*. The artifact, as assemblage, may define its own context through the interpretive encounter (Shanks and Hodder 1995: 14–17). There need be no necessary or intrinsic context.

Constructing the past

In the background is a debate about the objectivity of archaeological (and other) accounts of the past. That the past can be separated from the present, as epistemological object from subject, that the object past is the *origin* of the meanings archaeologists deal in, has been seriously challenged. This is often known as the debate between processual and post-processual or interpretive archaeology, and is often (misleadingly) characterised as a polarisation of scientific research aiming at objective knowledge versus relativist interpretation in a postmodernist idiom (for such polarisation see, for example, Binford 1987; Bintliff 1993; Renfrew 1989; Trigger 1989, 1991). I will briefly attempt some clarification.

In tightly relating the observing archaeological subject and object past (the factual past imbued with the forms, meanings and significances of the archaeologist), past and present are no longer to be treated as separate temporal realms, but as informed by each other. (Hence my proposal of an interpretation *between* past and present.) The past exists as part of the present in terms of the aims, assumptions and conceptual frameworks of the archaeologist; and these may be political. But objectivity questioned (as a guide and aim in the production of the past) has prompted the fear of an incapacity to prefer one interpretation of the past to another – this is taken to be relativism, with each interpretation valid in terms of the subjectivity of each interpreter. Objectivity questioned may be taken to mean subjectivity unleashed. The past may even be open to political manipulation, if disinterested knowledge is discounted.

These issues have long been the subject of sociologies of knowledge. What has been termed the weak programme is a sociology of error, explaining why scientists get things wrong by finding some social source of distortion such as ideology or class interests. Sometimes it is a limited exercise of studying the general conditions for the growth of knowledge. This weak programme supports or excludes from its study notions of the rational origins of genuine knowledge. So, for archaeological examples, Nazi ideology is frequently seen as a distorting factor in racial theories of prehistory promoted by the likes of Gustav Kossina; Trigger (1984) has related the growth of archaeological knowledge to ideologies of nationalism, colonialism and imperialism.

In the last twenty years a stronger programme in the sociology of knowledge has developed, sometimes associated with the term 'constructivist philosophy', which sees *all* knowledge claims as social phenomena, and does not distinguish social and irrational sources of error from rational and detached knowledge (Bloor 1976; Knorr-Cetina 1981; Knorr-Cetina and Mulkay 1983; Latour 1987; Latour and Woolgar 1986; Lynch 1985; Pickering 1992). Apparent scientific truth and falsity are thus to be treated symmetrically.

This strong programme is supported empirically by many anthropological and historical studies of scientific practice (in addition to items just cited see also, for example, Latour 1988; Pinch 1986; Shapin and Schaffer 1985). Detailed elucidation of events like Pasteur's stand for a microbial theory of infection are shown conclusively to erode the distinction between socially sustained error and rationally sustained truth (in this case between Pasteur's truth and his opponents' theories of spontaneous generation). There are innumerable social contingencies in the development of knowledge, but, most importantly, this has been established regardless of the distinction between true or false theory.

Philosophical support for the strong programme comes in part from Quine's notion of the undetermination of theory (Quine 1981, 1990). With any theory *never* fully underwritten by data or 'rational' argument, other factors, some psychological, some sociological, some historical contingency, are involved in forming a conception of the world.

Thus it can be legitimately argued that recent sociologies of knowledge are effectively countering the traditional criticisms of relativism. Knowledge can be constructed without threatening the security of claims to truth (recent archaeological argument: McGuire and Shanks 1996; Lampeter Archaeology Workshop, forthcoming). Indeed it now seems that the onus is upon those who deny the social construction, as opposed to discovery, of knowledge to provide what they need to sustain their view of the generation of knowledge, and that is a transcendental origin of objectivity and rationality.

I have made this short detour into constructivist ideas to bring me to three conclusions. The first involves the creativity of our efforts to construct archaeological knowledge, and includes an exhortation to think laterally in those connections which sustain interpretation and understanding. The second is that there is an inherent and irreducible pluralism in our interpretations and narratives of the material past. The third is a temporal extension of the principle of symmetry introduced above: that archaeologists are in principle no different from those in the past whom they study, each constructing their own knowledges and lifeworlds.

Relational philosophy – summary points
Consider again Figure 1.1 and the question – what is this artifact?

Multiplicity   It has been argued that, conceived as an assemblage, the pot has dimensions (conventionally conceived as external to what the pot is) which provide the pot's particularity. Crucially, these relations between the pot and its dimensions are internal and are not to do with signification or being (the aryballos *represents*; the pot *is*). So I would supplement a conception of attributes upon a pot with association and displacement, understanding the aryballos in following lines of suggestion and affiliation (subsuming signification – a unity of signifier and signified) through design, form and decoration. An understanding of the singular or particular artifact, such as this aryballos, is not only to be found in a separation of the one and many (implied when the artifact, identified as one, is compared to many others, or placed in a class with others). The artifact, as assemblage, is a substantive multiplicity.

Singular works of art?   The paradox is therefore that the more singular and 'particular' the artifact, the more it is multiple. Is this not indeed the character of the work of 'art' – an over-worked cultural product, referencing so much more in what is conceived as, paradoxically, its singularity (Ovid (*Metamorphoses* 10.252): *ars adeo latet arte sua*, art so conceals its own art)?

Classification and the articulation of assemblages   Artifact classification, and associated procedures such as discrimination and ordination, usually involve an idea of similarity between artifacts as the object of analysis, with similarity established according to attributes upon an artifact. I suggest also an agglomerative and *synthetic* articulation of assemblages (Fig. 1.3). This is based not upon a sense of internal, but external difference, though I should write ~~external identity~~, according to the argument for internal relations of non-identity.

Non-identity   The *assemblage* of association and displacement is the *non-identity* of the aryballos (a supplementary dimension of identity 'i' subtracted from 'n'): Fig. 1.2.

The creativity of interpretation   Identity is *asserted*, not *discovered*.

Interest and discourse   Desire, interest and discourse are instrumental in initiating and constraining the dispersal of the aryballos.

Continuities of interpretation   The questions raised of what the aryballos is, its materiality, and relation to notions of pot, painter, style and social context are resolved in the persistence of *acts of interpretation*. The pot is the product of the interpretive act of potter, acting upon clay, interpretation of decoration by potter,

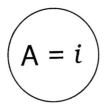

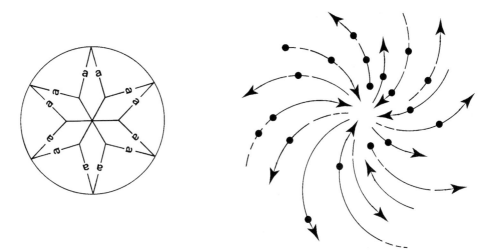

Figure 1.2 Conceptions of an artifact (signified by 'A'). Identity (i) may be asserted, or the n dimensions of association and affiliation followed in the artifact's *assemblage*, while its 'identity' is suspended/subtracted (−i).

Figure 1.3 Classification and identity. Classification may consist of asserting the self-contained identity of an artifact defined according to attributes (a), or it may also involve following an agglomerative and synthetic articulation of the artifact's *assemblage*.

trader and whoever placed such pots in graves, but then of the farmer (probably) who found the pot again, the person who bought it and sold it to a museum, and the scholars and others who have reinterpreted it then and since.

Past and present in symmetry   The primacy of interpretation: a concomitant argument is that style or culture are to be conceived as production, taking sources and resources (clay, creative insight, decorative sources, skill, interest, desire . . .) and making something of them. A homology is thus implied between potter and pot (or rather clay), and between pot and archaeologist. This is the *persistence* of acts of interpretation; it is a temporal *continuity*; there is no separation of original past and secondary present.

Time and life-cycle   The temporal continuity of cycles of interpretation is the *life-cycle* of the artifact, 'economic' cycles of production, exchange and consumption whose outcome is material culture.

Origins deferred   There is thus no signified origin (the past or dead potter or dead society), beyond or within the artifact.

Following tracks   Interpretation of an artifact now comes to consist of establishing associations (the dialogue I have mentioned), of building connections through the assemblage that is the artifact.

A relational method of an interpretive archaeology

How is relational thinking put into operation? Rather than begin with the question of what an artifact is, it is better to ask what it does, inquire of the social work of an artifact. This may be reworded as what it connects through its design, exchange and consumption. With the artifact understood as assemblage, the task is to establish the (internal) relationships which make an artifact what it is, and to make sense of them. There is nothing mysterious or new about this empirical method of following the tracks leading from a particular artifact.

The following are four kinds of connection and some methods appropriate to their investigation:

> empirical association (as in Clarke's concept of assemblage); things found together)
>> methods: inductive reasoning, statistical analysis (based upon data definition, collection and classification)
> logical links:
>> methods: structuralist readings, formal/mathematical analysis of patterning and design
> conceptual alignment, causal relationships, narrative employment:
>> methods: historical and social interpretation, semiotics, deductive reasoning
> creative elaboration:
>> methods: abduction (Peirce 1958: 89–164; Shanks 1996a: 39–41) rooted in exploration of metaphor.

This is heuristic and not a definitive listing; there are many cross connections. It is necessarily an eclectic collection – just as in conversation, many different strategies may be adopted in engaging with what the interpreting party finds interesting.

Concepts and bodies of theory play the important constitutive role of explaining, making sense or giving significance to different kinds of link or association. They may deal with anything relevant: for example, historical motivation, social practice, economics and manufacture. Some, concerning style, design and agency, have already been provided in this chapter. Others (including ideology, translation of interests, technology of power, sovereignty) will appear later when needed. The main point is that bodies of theory, tools for constructive thought, are essential.

Traditional qualities of scholarship are all appropriate and valuable in developing the links running through an artifact's assemblage: wide and deep reading; familiarity with 'the material'; historical interpretation and source criticism. Note should, however, be made of two vital moments (Shanks 1996a: 126–8). One is critique, which attends to interest, working on the (discursive) relationship between object and interpreter, past and present, asking questions of the purpose of interpretation and ideological motivation, issues of cultural politics. The other vital moment is creative interpretive choice, working against the strictures of discourse under the practical recognition that interpretation is about exploration and possibility in taking up the remains of the past to make something of them which enlightens, enriches, edifies. After all, a conversation which begins and ends with a rigid questionnaire may miss much of value.

Interpretation always deals with historical fragments. This feature is given added poignancy by the character of archaeological sources as ruin in the face of decay. But it is never any other way: there is never plenitude in understanding or explanation, in the sciences or humanities. Interpretation is always provisional. This does not mean that nothing of lasting value may be said or done. This is not a pessimistic stance but one of optimistic realism, that in the melancholy that is history we can take up the pieces and make something of them again. The call is simply to recognise our humility and reject the claims of total systems of thought to end history and know the place of everything. In constructing our interpretive journeys there is simply more or less material and time to work with.

I end this section with an aim of historical interpretation to create, in Walter Benjamin's phrase, dialectical images. The term acknowledges the roots in dialectical thought of what I have been proposing – the construction of archaeological assemblages (see also Shanks 1992b). Benjamin's great project, the *Passagenwerk* (1982, superbly annotated and read by Buck-Morss (1989)) was to be a collage of historical materials relating to Paris in nineteenth-century modernity, its shopping arcades emblematic of an emerging consumer capitalism. A work of *Geschichtsphilosophie*, the frictions of juxtaposition run structural, historical and anthropological vectors (such as historicity, myth and the modern, nature and industry, dreams and class conflict) through the intensely empirical and richly textured historical fragments.

The task of constructing archaeological assemblages is one of montage – the cutting and reassembling of quoted pieces, of fragments of meanings, images, things, quotations, borrowings. This process is proposed to be dialectical because of tensions and mediation on several grounds. Something is taken out of what may be considered to be its time and replaced in the coordinates of the interpreter's present, taken out of its 'original' context and placed in another, with the aim of constructing something new out of old. Such quotation mediates past and present. The paradox is that the past is revered (with micro-archaeological interest in detail, in the particular) in order to break with it and generate insight.

In so placing them in a new context, fragments once incidental and arbitrary may attain extraordinary significance. Transient archaeological ruin, broken out of the context of times past, may become emblematic, bringing alive the past by breaking with it, renewing it. The perfume jar, once perhaps a mere aspect of the quotidian, may, quoted in contexts it could never have known, unlock all manner of insight. This is a redemption or rescue of the past from the decayed and moribund, with its fragments turned into charged particles, electro-cultural elements of an archaeological assemblage.

Montage may be openly constructive, preserving the integrity of fragments imperfectly joined, highlighting the frictions between the pieces, but the joining also implies a continuity, perhaps expressed in a smoothed-over line of narrative, a whole picture revealed through the fragments brought together. Past and present, representational images and artificial constructions, wholes emerge through the parts.

The broken pieces of montage attest as much to absence as to a fluid and coherent story present through the construction and interpretation. Anticipating the presentation of the next chapters with their focus upon masculine sovereignty, the presence of certain classes and gender positions may be marked out, but through their conspicuous absence.

An objective passivity before the empirical remains, a necessary respect for their particularity, accompanies a creativity like dreamwork, seeking and forging links which know no necessary limits.

The assemblage of an aryballos

Let me anticipate the interpretation a little and show what I mean by drawing upon what has already been mentioned of the aryballos in Figure 1.1.

– miniaturism – fine ware, technically accomplished – animated bodies – illustrated violence – weaponry – animals and monsters – assertions of power – the geometric and floral – perfumes – exotic design – travels out to sanctuaries and colonies – offering to divinity – deposition with the dead . . .

Is this not a strange constellation? What is to be made of these associations? This is a task of interpretation. Immediate contrast may be made with the familiar stories of decorated pots, artistic genius, the (inexorable) evolution of style, impending Korinthian commercial success.

A productive map

For this aryballos in Figure 1.1 I begin, quite conventionally, with a life-cycle (broken in antiquity) (compare also Kopytoff 1986). Figure 1.4 is a summary diagram of the conceptual space suggested by an aryballos such as that in Boston, from production and technique through to consumption, expanding from the pot (circled point).

Figure 1.4 attempts to summarise 'design', a term which disperses into style, the technical, economic relations of production, class, ideology and social or subjective identity. Some of these may be treated relatively autonomously, such as technical matters and workshop organisation, but all come back to the pot, its tracings through production, style, distribution and consumption; energies, powers and desires. There is no hierarchy to these questions, no primacy of the economic or of artistic creativity over other aspects of design, and no pre-defined social context. And the description of an aryballos immediately implies a constellation of concepts (bodies of theory): style, value, ideology, class, creativity, identity, for example. As indicated, such concepts are like tools for constructing descriptions and stories of design.

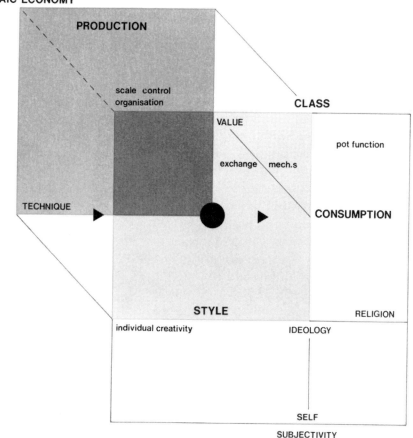

Figure 1.4 The life-cycle of an aryballos, a *general economy* from production to consumption. The pot itself (centred in the figure) is the product of technique which involves questions of the possibility of individual creative input into the design, which in turn begs the question of the control and organisation of production. Questions follow about how production was scaled according to perceived demand, questions of patronage and information flow, as well as more practical issues of workshop organisation and ownership. (It is assumed that it is meaningful to identify individual artist styles, but this assumption implies much about the whole ethos of material production and is to be carefully examined.) The style of the pot may be interrogated, from creativity of design through its iconography to its referencing of structures of social relationships – ideology. This latter involves considering the occurrence of particular designs (of violent figured scenes and decorative order) within their apparent location of consumption as accessories to death and worship. The use of miniature figured perfume jars and drinking accoutrement in ritual and religion suggests questions of the subjective identity of people who used such pots in this way; what does it mean to associate such style with religion and ritual? That the pots were exported to be consumed in such ways involves questions of value and the mechanisms which achieved the widespread dissemination of the pots. This is not a simple matter of abstract exchange values and mechanisms. The pots and their carriers engaged in the experience of travel. Referenced also are social distinctions such as class (the absence of merchant middle class?). The possible functions of jars as perfume containers (oil for body and dedication) and vessels accompanying drinking party reference lifestyle, as does the control and organisation of production (free artisans or functionaries for social elites looking for stylistic emblems of social status?).

The figure I present is a map through production, exchange, distribution and consumption: 'economic' categories which disperse beyond the boundaries of the economic. So this is a *general economy* of the aryballos. I draw this term especially from Georges Bataille (Bataille 1977; Derrida 1978; Habermas 1987; Richman 1982), a major source for the ideas of social power which inform the interpretation to follow. (Profitable comparison may also be made with Hebdige's presentation of the post-war scooter (in Hebdige 1988), shifting through design, production and consumption.) The aryballos is to be conceived as 'total social fact'.

Mapping narratives: interpretive beginnings

Considering this aryballos in Boston has led me to raise the questions of style and design, and to digress into questions of the conception of an artifact, an archaeological ontology. Concepts of assemblage and general economy describe the artifact as a substantive multiplicity, an assemblage of internal relations through production to consumption. The starting point is an interpretive choice, depending on strategy and interest. The task I have set myself is to provide and plot pathways, lines of association and dispersion.

Craft production in the early city state: some historical and material contexts

Fine accomplishment, and risk (with an aside on the skeuomorph)
Let me continue with the aryballos of Figure 1.1. It is an accomplished piece. Recognisably fine is the ceramic fabric, Korinthian in its smooth, consistent and regular colour and texture. Slips, applied by brush, were turned to contrasting dark by a clever, careful, and necessarily practised manipulation of kiln and firing environment (Noble 1988; Winter 1978; further references in Oleson 1986: 300–15). Clay body and slip also required very precise preparation. The techniques used to produce Korinthian pottery are those commonly employed to produce fine ware in Greece generally in the first millennium BC, from protogeometric pottery style to red figure and beyond. The potters of Korinth were staying with a wider and old tradition of fine ware manufacture.

The appearance is highly regulated; the workmanship is of the sort where achievement seems to correspond closely with the idea (of its design): lines are fine, precise and regularly spaced, and there appears to be control over shape and height too. There is a sense of 'prototype' or concept of 'right shape' behind the easily recognisable aryballos (and other shapes too). This term has been used most usefully by Miller (1985a: 9, 44, 166–7; see also Boast 1990). It is based upon anthropological studies of categorisation (Mervis and Rosch, 1981; Rosch, 1976, 1978) and is related to the concepts type and token. The strong sense of prototype makes possible studies such as those of Neeft (1987) which concentrate on one pot shape. Emphasised is a clear and explicit sense of correctness as well as tradition (though the shape of the aryballos is new to Korinth in the seventh century). As with geometric Korinthian of the previous centuries, the pots of the late eighth century and after were decorated on a banding wheel (a turntable), and probably often with a multiple brush (Boardman 1960). All this affords a good degree of certainty that the desired result could be achieved: regulated linearity. Geometric is the product of a *workmanship of certainty* (Pye 1980: 4–5, 24 and *passim*, and on workmanship generally).

There is a change which comes at the end of the eighth century. The figured aryballos here was drawn upon free-hand and then the surface was scratched or incised. It displays immense control. But whereas the painter of geometric decoration (which continues to be produced alongside figurative, when it is known as sub-geometric or linear) must have been quite certain of achieving the desired appearance, the precision and regulated accomplishment of figured scenes such as

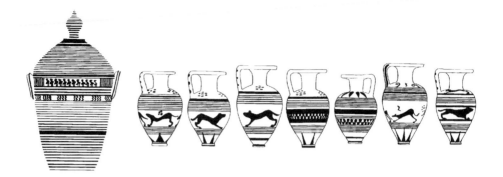

Figure 2.1 Geometric workmanship of certainty. A pyxis from Messavouno Cemetery, Thera, and typical later 'subgeometric' aryballoi.

these were achieved at *risk* of the painter's hand or brush slipping, and they depended largely on the painter's individual care, judgement and dexterity (as opposed to the traditional and shared technology of banding wheel and multiple brush). Pye (1980: 5) illustrates the contrast with the example of printing versus writing with pen.

I propose that such risk on the part of the potter is a significant reason for the development of figured Korinthian pottery. The figures are painted free-hand with silhouette and outlined features. A mistake in painting could be corrected perhaps – the oxide slip wiped off. But the incision through the applied slip into the body of the pot was a scar that could not easily be removed. Incision marks decision, finality, and risk of spoiling the work's regulated surface and decoration. It also heightens the appearance of regulation, with its ability to render very fine detail.

Whether the idea of incision came from metal working, as has often been mentioned (for example Cook 1972: 48), is irrelevant. Cook has added (*ibid.*) that an origin in metal working 'would account for the unnecessary incising of outlines in earlier black-figure work'. Such an observation supports my contention here that incision displays risk; and the more incision, the more risk.

Relationships between potting and metal working are central to an argument developed over a decade by Michael Vickers and then with David Gill (Vickers and Gill 1994) that Attic, and perhaps more generally archaic and classical Greek, ceramics were copies of metal vessels – skeuomorphs. Korinthian kotylai were often pared down to eggshell thickness – imitating metal plate? Applied to seventh-century Korinth, such arguments for the primacy of imitation of metal would undermine or exclude the interpretations I offer here. Let me now counter the view that skeuomorphism is an adequate explanation of archaic and classical Greek ceramic forms.

I first argue that one of the main features of all design is skeuomorphism. Far from being unusual, it is ubiquitous. Ideas are taken by designers and makers from all sorts of sources and applied or translated into another medium. It is of interest to note possible sources for design (metal forms, natural forms, anthropomorphic forms etc.), but it is of greater note, I suggest, to consider the reason why such borrowings are made. Here Vickers and Gill propose that Attic ceramics *emulated* precious metal vessels, that they were cheap substitutes for high status items.

The process of emulation is potentially a powerful social explanation, as so ably indicated by Miller for example (1982) as well as Vickers and Gill. But there still remains the question of why certain designs were used and not others, and for ceramics to be explained by reference to metal forms still leaves the question of interpreting and explaining the design of metal vessels themselves. Reference may be made to the inherent properties of a material (for example metal being suited to plate and riveting), but what of iconography, for example, and what when the medium is such a plastic one as clay (so amenable to many processes of forming and making)?

So the argument does not go far enough, even if Korinthian ceramics were in emulation of metal vessels and nothing more. There is still a need to encounter the imagery, the distribution and the use of *ceramics*. I would also argue that the concepts of skeuomorph and emulation do not take us far into understanding design, making and workmanship. The idea of incision may have come from metalworking, but the interesting question is in what circumstances did it *make sense* to incise clay. There are many ways to make a vessel look as if it were metal, and in this regard incising the surface is not very convincing.

Two master ceramicists, Yang Quinfang and Zhou Dingfang, from Yixing, China, made a rare visit to the west in 1995; I was lucky enough to witness their working practices (also Wain 1995a). The design of the teapots they make is some five centuries old. Traditional designs explicitly copy metal forms (Wain 1995b). One of the potters actually uses archaeological bronze age pieces as inspiration and is known for his teapots inlaid with silver.

Skeuomorphism is fully accepted: radically new designs copy leather, basket, wood and bamboo forms. In making a teapot techniques are used which superficially relate to metal working: beating clay and luting slabs. But it is *superficial* resemblance because they are *not* the same techniques. These master craftworkers spend long apprenticeships acquiring the skills necessary for working *clay*. Beating clay is not the same as beating metal; luting is not welding or soldering. The tools and associated skills are entirely different from metal working and have different traditions. Most notable is the considerable effort in the preparation of and constant attention to the raw material, the *zisha* clay. Metal as a source of a design idea, emulation as a social urge or force may help understanding, but there is much more to the practical knowledges of clay-working, the *chaînes opératoires* (Lemonnier 1976; Pelegrin, Karlin, and Bodu 1988), the apprenticeships and learning, the workmanships, the raw materials, the aesthetic systems.

After this digression into design theory, let me return to Korinthian perfume jars. This aryballos appears in two-tone upon the pale ground; there are two dark slips. Such polychromy occurs infrequently, but regularly, with more elaborate designs; its use is a mark of Johansen's *style magnifique* (Johansen 1923: 98f). Payne proposed its origin in 'free painting', that these designs were copies of wall-paintings (Payne 1931: 8, n. 1, 95–7; discussion by Amyx 1983: esp. 37–41); he relates this to the complex scenes depicted. But slip on slip was used for many plain linear aryballoi (for quick reference see Neeft 1987). I suggest instead that polychromy was another mark of technical mastery; adding a secondary colour of slip complicates an already difficult process. I am not aware of any study which has investigated the technical difficulty, or otherwise, of producing colour upon colour, slip upon slip, in the black figure process (Farnsworth and Simmons (1963) do not deal with the issue). But it is something else which risks spoiling the vase (pers. comm., Michael Casson).

Korinthian potters opened space in the Geometric linear field for figured designs, such as on this aryballos, which are intricate and complex. But a great increase in time and labour expenditure is perhaps not involved; the key factor would seem to be risk. Estimates of labour investment are difficult to make. Studio potter Michael Casson (Ross-on-Wye) reckons a contemporary craft potter could throw perhaps 200 aryballoi in a day. His experience and recollection of the hand throwers in the Stoke factories of the 1940s and afterwards lead him to think that they could throw far more. Much of the decoration, like the pot shapes, is repetitive. The areas of freehand and incised figured work are set off in linear friezes by border lines and areas of repeat geometric and floral devices. These all require much less skill, dexterity and risk, and could be undertaken by someone of less experience than the frieze painter, an apprentice perhaps. The less precise and regulated handles of many aryballoi, and their application to a more accomplished thrown body also indicates a subdivision of production into throwing by someone of more skill, and the application of handles by someone of less skill. Painters who have acquired the skills necessary for figured painting in miniature are needed, as are new fine brushes (Casson considers this the decisive factor), but the designs within the small linear bands opened on the pots, with their predominantly 'confident' line (few breaks, hesitation, signs of holding back), were probably quick to produce. Many indeed are 'hasty' and 'free'. The workmanship of risked hand and brush is new, but occurs within a frame (literally) of dependable technological and technical practice and knowledge.

This is mainly a miniature style: most figured friezes are only a few millimetres in height, most aryballoi less than eighty millimetres. Held in the palm of the hand, or between finger and thumb, the designs upon this aryballos are at the threshold of visibility. The figured scenes particularly invite scrutiny and recognition of the accomplishment of precision and regulation, and so by contrast the new mode of painting. This, I propose, is the significance of miniaturism. It defines a personal space within primary reach (of the human arm), close-up.

A sample of 2,000 Korinthian pots

I will be making reference to a sample of nearly 2,000 well-published and complete pots conventionally classed as protokorinthian. This sample comprises all complete pots known to me (1,951 items as of 1991) with figured decoration, and those which have geometric or linear decoration (conventionally termed 'sub-geometric' proto-korinthian) from the main sites of discovery. The sample is drawn in part from the lists of Amyx (1988), Benson (1953 and 1989), Dunbabin and Robertson (1953), Johansen (1923), Neeft (1987 and 1991), Payne (1931 and 1933). Beginning with a decision to include no fragmentary material, each reference to a complete vessel was followed to trace an illustration and description. Also consulted were all the main excavation reports, museum collections reported in *Corpus Vasorum Antiquorum*, and minor studies, for stray figured pots and for complete linear or sub-geometric vessels, although aryballoi are covered adequately by Neeft (1987).

Differential publication means that the sample is probably somewhat biased towards figured wares and aryballoi (percentages of different types of pots are therefore meaningless), but I attempted to include as full a range as possible of design types in the sample. Given the art historical significance, there is good reason to believe that figured protokorinthian will elicit publication, and that a heavy reliance on published material will not be inappropriate. First hand encounter with many protokorinthian pots is impractical for all but a very few scholars, given their dispersion around the art museums of the world – a factor of perceived art historical value. Nevertheless, the sample, descriptions and illustrations of many pots were checked in visits to the major collections in the Museum of Fine Arts, Boston, the British Museum, London, the National Museum, Athens, Korinth, the Museo Nationale Paolo D'Orsi, Syracuse, the Museo Nationale, Naples, and the Louvre, Paris. So attempts were made to ensure that the sample was as 'representative' as possible, though, as is usually the case with archaeological sources, the sample is in no way a random representation of some 'real' population. The sample is the result of an encounter with a discourse and its constitution of an object – protokorinthian.

Nothing is assumed about the meaning of this designation 'protokorinthian', only that such pots were probably made in Korinth. An argument will be presented later for the abandonment of the term.

Fine-grained classification is not necessary for the sorts of interpretation presented here. Accordingly, and to avoid controversy, a coarse relative chronology was adopted – earlier and later. Some further justification of this chronology is, however, offered here.

The sample begins with the emergence of protokorinthian style (Neeft 1987: 17–19). This includes the appearance of aryballoi. There are stylistic changes to other pot shapes (see, for example, Coldstream 1968: Chapter 3; Neeft 1975, on the *kotyle*). I have not included pots classed as transitional (to ripe Korinthian) on pragmatic grounds, that publication is not as detailed or complete. Nor have I included the aryballoi with pointed base, scale decoration and the like, dated later by Payne (1931, catalogue nos. 478, 478A, 479, 479A, 802A, 643–5), in spite of Neeft's comments (Neeft 1987: 275 and Chapter 5). On the other hand, unwilling to accept a fine-grained relative chronology based on stylistic criteria but mindful also of the ambiguities of classification, I have allowed some geometric and transitional pots (as conventionally classified) to slip into the sample.

I found difficulty in accepting the conventional chronological divisions – early, middle 1 and 2, late – into which protokorinthian is normally split. Relative chronology is, of course, based on the observed stratigraphic sequence of shape and decoration. But the number of good stratigraphic contexts containing a lot of varied protokorinthian is surprisingly small. The big Italian cemeteries, including Pithekoussai, are of only limited use, offering some synchronic groupings and correlations (see Neeft's review: 1987: esp. 301f). The stratigraphies of the sanctuaries Aetos on Ithaka (Benton 1953: 255–60; Heurtley 1948) and Perachora (Payne 1940) were mixed and only offer coarse chronological conclusions, the case with most sanctuaries. Even the so-called Potters' Quarter at Korinth (Stillwell 1948) was not particularly well excavated (Williams 1982: 15–18) and cannot be trusted (Charles K. Williams, pers. comm.); it is also lacking in figured vessels. Hence most of the relative chronological sequence has come to depend on stylistic and typological interpretation of distinctive figured pots. This is open to the charge of circularity (recognised as a general problem by Neeft (1987: 301)). Stylistic typological analysis also often makes an assumption of linear development. Morris (1987: 17, 163f) has heavily, and I believe rightly, criticised some assumptions behind style and early Hellenic chronology on the grounds that they do not consider social aspects of use (particularly emulation – inter-class rivalry). Even accepting a sequence to figured decoration, most of the linear sub-geometric pots are very difficult to place with any accuracy. This is not to deny that there are recognisable changes in the design of these pots with time, but diagnostic features are so often few or lacking (Neeft 1987: 315).

Consider Neeft's major study of sub-geometric aryballoi (1987) and his assessment of chronology, a defining aim of his book. He assumes that a uniform linear development is natural, and that exceptions are 'deviations' (*ibid.*: 260). There are however stratigraphical co-occurrences of typologically more and less developed aryballoi – conical and globular (*ibid.*: 305f; Johansen 1923: 17). And he summarises, 'dating within the ovoid period on stylistic grounds (that is, on a supposed development of decoration) is generally impossible because there is no single, rectilinear development for the period as a whole' (Neeft 1987: 315). I take this apparent methodological contradiction to mean that a general temporal trend of shape is discernible (Johansen's globular to ovoid), but then chronological supposition becomes difficult. But this seems to presume an independence of shape and decoration: Johansen's sequence of *shape* is accepted as a starting point, while *decoration* of ovoid aryballoi does not conform with it. As indicated, the evidence of grave groups is not at all conclusive. Given this, these inconsistencies, the difficulty of assessing a presentation which makes no use of quantified or statistical description, and a conception of style in accordance with those I have criticised above (descriptive attribute and independent force), I am unwilling to accept any of Neeft's fine-grained chronology.

It is for these difficulties also then that a minimalist distinction has been adopted between *earlier* and *later*. This is *approximately* equivalent to conventional early and middle 1, followed by middle 2 and late: globular and conical aryballoi succeeded by ovoid and pointed or piriform. I still consider there to be a great deal of overlap.

It seems reasonable to accept the approximate association of the foundation of some early Greek colonies in Italy and the style protokorinthian. Hence, following standard absolute chronologies, the pots were made between approximately 720 and 640 BC or later (Amyx 1988 II: Chapter 3; Neeft 1987: 363f). Again, though, a precise absolute chronology is not crucial to my argument.

The aryballos in a workshop

An area out by the west wall of the old city of Korinth was excavated in the 1940s. From the quantity of broken pottery it was thought to be the pottery production area

of Korinth, and has been named the Kerameikos or Potters' Quarter, on analogy
with Athens (Stillwell 1948). One of the earlier main buildings, from towards the end
of the seventh century, the South Long Building, was interpreted by Stillwell (1948:
15) as a stoa, a row of shops or booths in which pottery was sold. Roebuck too (1972:
121–2) has this building as part of a potters' agora away from the main agora of the
early city. There are no remains of kilns; Stillwell claimed they would be temporary
structures (1948: 17). Presumed water channels were found dating from the production of late Geometric pottery; one later is more elaborate, replacing those which are
earlier and less regular (*ibid.*: 11–12). There is nothing to connect these channels
with pottery production, but for Salmon

> There can be little doubt that they were connected with it . . . [they] are too
> large in scale to have been built to serve a single establishment. The
> numerous early channels were perhaps the result of competitive enterprise by
> individual workshops; but by the mid seventh century they combined to
> provide themselves with a common superior service.
> (Salmon 1984: 96).

He considers the Potters' Quarter an economic foundation and a

> direct result of the rapidly increasing popularity of Korinthian ware . . . the
> development of the quarter was a conscious attempt by an enterprising potter
> – either accompanied or soon followed by others – to exploit an expanding
> market by producing large quantities of fine wares with simple geometric
> decoration.
> (*ibid.*: 97).

However Williams doubts (1982: 17–18) that this South Long Building was a single
unit, as claimed by Stillwell (1948: 15, followed by Salmon 1984: 101–2). For
Williams, this and the later North Long Building are better interpreted as part of 'city
blocks' of housing. He interprets the Potters' Quarter as a relatively self-contained
and well-populated residential area with its own cult-sites and cemeteries, in an early
'city' which appeared not centralised, but as a collection of villages, like the area of
Archaia Korinthos today (Williams 1981: 412f, 1982: 18). Roebuck too (1972)
envisages a village-based early city.

The site of the 'Potters' Quarter' seems to be a compromise between the demands
for raw materials and access to farmland (in this 'city' of farmer villages) (Arafat and
Morgan 1989: 315). Whitbread (1986: 391–2) has doubted the viability for pottery
manufacture of clay in the gorge next to the Potters' Quarter (*contra* Stillwell 1948:
3). He contends (Whitbread 1986, Chapter 6.6 and 6.7) that suitable sources are in
the area of the Anaploga well (*ibid.*: 383–4) and further north near the later tile
works, with the best clays being associated with lignite deposits (*ibid.*: 392–3, 398–9).
I would however argue that the identification of clay sources is very difficult, those at
Korinth have not been identified with certainty, and no sharp association with
manufacture can be surmised. My experience of studio ceramics at Cardiff and

Carmarthen Colleges of Art in Wales indicates that raw material is a very flexible concept. It frequently depends not upon the character of a clay deposit, but on the willingness to invest labour and energy in the preparation of a clay body of desired characteristics. Consider this in the context of the variable and, for potting, difficult characteristics of Korinthian clay deposits (Farnsworth, Perlman, and Asaro 1977: 459–61; Farnsworth 1970). Whitbread does suggest clay processing based upon several types of clay (1986: 375–6). It is enough to say that there are sufficient supplies of clay at hand in the area of Korinth, that transportation of clay from distant sources was unnecessary (Arafat and Morgan 1989: 315), but the careful processing of raw material was essential.

The deposits of the so-called Potters' Quarter produced only a fraction of the range of known Korinthian wares (Benson 1984; Stillwell and Benson 1984). There was a dump of workshop debris from the seventh century BC in the Anaploga Well, to the south of the Potters' Quarter towards Akrokorinthos (Amyx and Lawrence 1975). Note might also be made of the discards from a later potter's workshop found at Vrysoula (Pemberton 1970: esp. 269). There is the later tile works too, to the north of the city (discussed by Salmon 1984: 122). It seems likely that there were several or more places where pots were made in the archaic city (see Jones 1986: 175–89 for a general summary of traces of pottery production). The range of wares produced in the Potters' Quarter, from fine clay fabrics to terracotta figurines and tiles, indicates that a variety of skills were to be found there. On the other hand, the absence of some classes of wares (particularly figured: Stillwell and Benson 1984: 10–11; see also Amyx and Lawrence 1975: 6–11), and the lack of any candidates for a production site of earlier (late geometric) Thapsos ware (references see pp. 65–6) indicates that different types of pot may indeed have had their specialists.

Estimates of the scale of production of ancient ceramics, based upon what has been found of the output, are notoriously difficult to make. The most reliable attempt remains that of Cook (1959). He estimated the rate of survival of Attic Panathenaic amphorae, a pottery form produced in fixed and known numbers for prizes in the games, as one quarter of 1 per cent (*ibid.*: 120). Cook's figure of total Panatheaic amphorae upon which he based his fraction of those remaining has been raised by Johnston (1987), but not enough to cause a significant alteration. Cook accordingly suggested 500 workers were involved in the whole Attic pottery industry of the fifth century, and half that in Korinth at its height of production.

Salmon (1984: 102–3) stresses that the Potters' Quarter specialised in mass production. He also cites the apparently extraordinary numbers of Korinthian vases (most later than the period of my study) found in the Greek colony of Megara Hyblaia – perhaps 30–40,000 complete vases found in the period to 575 BC (Vallet and Villard 1964), these of course representing only a fraction, and perhaps less than $\frac{1}{500}$. I might also add here the high relative numbers recovered so far from Pithekoussai, yet only a fraction (1,300 graves, constituting no more than 10 per cent) of the ancient cemetery has been explored (Ridgway 1992b: 46). Although the number of sites in the western Mediterranean with Korinthian imports is considerable

Figure 2.2 The so-called Potters' Quarter, old Korinth; the cutting for perhaps an angle tower in an archaic defensive wall is in the foreground; Akrokorinthos in the background.

(Fig. 4.1), Salmon concludes that 'pottery production was an almost insignificant sector of the Korinthian economy even though many Greeks used the ware' (Salmon 1984: 101); he is here largely following Cook's figures for people involved in the industry. Snodgrass (1980a: 127f) also notes the quantities of ancient Greek ceramics recovered, and again plays down the importance of fine ware production, arguing that the archaic economy was dominated by only a few activities: agriculture, warfare and religion (*ibid.*: 129–31).

Stylistic attribution of individual pots and fragments to artistic hands, with its associated style histories, assumes a workshop structure of masters and apprentices, necessary for the learning and transmission of skills and styles. The logic of this position has been criticised elsewhere (Shanks 1996a; see also Whitley 1997). Differences in painting and style can indeed be identified, but this is a pragmatic pursuit, one interested in discovering artistic ego and personality. Arafat and Morgan (1989: 323) have criticised assumptions made of specialisation in the production of Korinthian pottery: 'mass production is commonly identified on the basis of quality of output, and fine work is automatically equated with small workshops and mass production with "industrial areas" (Benson 1985)'. They relate this model to what may be termed *metanarratives* of the discipline – overarching conceptions (in narrative form) of the character of ancient Greek society and history (Shanks 1996a, for full definition and discussion). One metanarrative of classical art history requires individual hands and workshops producing art-works; the extensive distribution of Korinthian ceramics and associated ancient histories of Korinth as a trading power, with the supposed economic role of colonies, has led to market determinism and the terminologies of mass production and industry. This is particularly evident in Salmon's recent account (1984) of Korinthian pottery and its export. As indicated already, he has the Potters' Quarter as a foundation of an enterprising entrepreneur exploiting an expanding market. He also repeats the old story of the decline of Korinthian pottery: mass production led to a decline in quality, consumers recognised its complacent poorer quality, superior Attic wares were taken instead (*ibid.*, especially page 111f). Consider here also Coldstream's remark that 'the success of Korinthian commerce must owe something to the high artistic and technical qualities of Korinthian artifacts' (Coldstream 1977: 167). Market forces are often taken to account for everything, as, for example, according to the old economic model of Blakeway (1932–3; see also the standard accounts of Boardman 1980: 16f and *passim*; Dunbabin 1948: Chapters 8 and 9). I concur with Arafat and Morgan (1989: 323) when they criticise this imprecise and unreflective use of economic terms. I will return to general models of the ancient economy.

Arafat and Morgan (1989) have suggested another and more social approach to the question of the organisation of the production of Attic and Korinthian pottery. They distinguish four archaeologically visible factors which affect the level of personal investment in pottery production:

clay sources and their location;
the acquisition, practice and transmission of potting and painting skills;

necessary workshop equipment;
the spatial organisation of production.

Korinthian clay sources would have been quite close at hand, and those who produced pots could have quite practically extracted and prepared clay themselves. Fine figured decoration required, of course, considerable investment in the acquisition of necessary skills. The skills required for throwing in miniature are also quite considerable (Michael Casson pers. comm.). Arafat and Morgan remark that 'it is not surprising to find a number of cases of family involvement, especially in view of Plato's reference to potters teaching their sons (*Republic* 421)' (Arafat and Morgan 1989: 327); they suggest extended families as the basis of workshops. I would also stress here the experience necessary for regulating the black figure firing process, with its alternation of reduction and oxidising atmospheres at critical temperature points. Miniaturism, as I have written, makes skills more critical in producing accomplished pieces. Equipment, Arafat and Morgan claim, would not be an expensive outlay. But I consider that quality of wheel and brushes in particular would be crucial for miniature figured pieces, but not so much in terms of cost as *design*. Regarding the spatial organisation of pottery production, Arafat and Morgan contrast the scatter of facilities at Korinth with the concentrations in the city centre of Athens, perhaps representing a 'distinction between the household and the household cluster or village as the unit investing in such facilities' (Arafat and Morgan 1989: 328), *oikos* as contrasted with 'suburb'.

The demands of the agricultural cycle in Greece and slack periods in the spring and dry summer would suit a seasonal production of pottery; wet winter weather would make clay extraction more difficult, clay drying, and outdoor firing less predictable and controlled (Arafat and Morgan 1989: 328; citing Arnold 1985: Chapter 3). There is a related issue of whether demand for pottery would stand the permanent removal of a small but significant proportion of the population from agricultural production. Religious festivals, when there would be an increased demand for ceramic dedications, also came at gaps in the agricultural cycle (Morgan 1990: Chapter 2, referring to Arnold 1985: Chapter 6, p. 161, Fig. 6.6). Korinthian was exported widely; trading ventures may be considered most likely in the summer sailing season, again fitting with a seasonal production of pottery.

What are we looking at in this production of pottery in the early polis of Korinth? Two centuries of connoisseurship have paid great attention to fine figured wares, but what is the relationship of this interest to the significance of ceramic production in the seventh century BC? Snodgrass points out (1980a: 127) that the sample of recovered archaic Greek ceramics may be a reasonable one, equivalent to 70,000 voters in an opinion poll in modern Britain. It is feasible to estimate basic parameters of the original industry, and here I wish to consider further the relative scale and importance of the production of figured pots.

The sample upon which my study is based consists of 1,951 complete pots derived from the main publications. Many linear or plain pots do not receive full publication, and so could not be included; the numbers and proportions of these are not reliable for estimating the division of pottery manufacture. Complete pots (and indeed fragments) bearing painted friezes of varied figures, particularly incised, do elicit notice and publication; they are significant to art history, are collected and achieve good prices in the art market, they are chronological indices, signify trading links, and may have iconographic significance. They are heavily invested with meaning for conventional antiquarian and disciplinary interests. So the number which remain outside my sample is likely to be relatively small. Of 804 earlier pots, seventy-five bear figured decoration in a frieze or friezes (accounting for more than 25 per cent of the surface). There are 122 figured, out of 1,147, later pots; I have not counted simpler friezes containing only silhouette animals such as dogs (there are many of these). So, in total there are 197 figured pots, about one tenth of the sample.

My sample does not include fragmentary material. The works of connoisseurship and stylistic attribution do. Dunbabin and Robertson (1953), Amyx (1988) and Benson (1989) found it possible to attribute 241, 296, and 294 pieces respectively to protokorinthian hands or workshops. Even allowing for fragmentary material unattributed to hands or workshops, relatively few figured pots are known, probably under 500.

Cook's proportion of pots surviving is probably somewhat high as the Panathenaic amphorae were prizes, special and valued. So if the number for seventh-century Korinthian is scaled up by 1,000 (instead of Cook's 500), there were 6,250 figured pots produced a year. To shelve this average annual production would require about 320 metres of shelf, enough to cover the walls of a large workshop.

Estimates of labour investment are difficult, but I suggest instructive. I have already discussed workmanship and held that there was no major increase in labour investment over the previous geometric canon of linear decoration. Figured work was painted in a context of repetitive design (linear, floral, geometric; consider again Figures 1.1 and 3.1, in comparison with Figure 2.1). Figured pots would be quick to produce given a division of labour into skilled throwers and figure painters, less skilled finishers (handles definitely, perhaps necks), and painters of lines and simple decorative devices. There was a dependable technological framework, centuries old, of clay and slip preparation, kiln building, regulation and management. These did require considerable experience to achieve successful results, but only very fine brushes would have had to be invented for miniature work. I repeat Casson's estimate that a skilled thrower could produce more than 200 aryballoi in a day. Cup forms are quicker by far: thrown accurately in less than thirty seconds by factory piece-workers, specialised throwers in the 1940s; kotylai could be separately turned down to their egg-shell or 'metal-plate' thinness in a few moments more.

So the production of figured and sub-geometric wares can be divided into the following grades of task.

Low skill: clay extraction, clay preparation (according to formulae), weighing of clay for throwers (crucial), water supply, pot handling, kiln building, kiln stoking.

Medium skill: slip preparation, throwing simple forms, turning and surface finish-

ing, handle and neck attachment, equipment maintenance (wheels and brushes), simple turntable and repeat decoration.
High skill: throwing closed forms, miniature figure painting, kiln management.

This range would certainly suit household-based production and associated apprenticeship, particularly since the skills are mostly traditional (by the seventh century BC), specialised, but well-tried. Arafat and Morgan (1989: 317) conclude their discussion of the organisation of Attic workshops with a unit-size estimate of six members of an extended family. A workshop of six to eight people could easily turn out several hundred fine Korinthian aryballoi (mixed figured and sub-geometric) a week. The conclusion is unavoidable that the production of figured pots needed only a few workshops. The character of the fine ware meant that the workshops would have had a marked technological independence from the rest of society: traditional but specialised skills would require considerable investment of time to acquire and maintain. This would fit with production based upon a family or other kinship group. Transmission of knowledge would be from parents to offspring, as a peasant economy would have found a long permanent apprenticeship a costly use of labour; Gallant (1991) details the economic vulnerability of the Greek peasant economy. Black figure added a new but limited dimension with miniaturism and figure painting.

There is difficulty in gaining a reliable quantitative estimate of the remnant remaining of early archaic Korinthian pottery production, both figured *and sub-geometric*, and therefore an estimate of total production is impossible. Many seventh-century Korinthian pots which do not carry figured decoration are of simple surface design, mostly linear. With or without the use of multiple brushes production would have been very rapid. Consider again the modern production rates of hand-throwers given above: a workshop could produce several thousand geometrically decorated cups in a twelve-week season. Salmon (1984: 97, 111) does write that protokorinthian was designed for large-scale production, and this notion is found generally in discussions especially of the development of Korinthian from smaller to larger quantities and from earlier tentative artistic experiment to later application of easy decorative formulae (for example Cook 1972: 50). But there is nothing at all to stop the manufacture of standard and repetitive designs by small household-based production units. I repeat the criticism made by Arafat and Morgan (1989: 323) about unreflective economic interpretation. The consensus, as reported for example by Salmon (1984), is that there is no need to envisage large-scale factories; a small-scale cottage industry could quite easily accommodate the production of both figured and sub-geometric styles. Full-time, year-round production again seems unnecessary.

In summary:

The notions of industrial districts in the early polis of Korinth and commercial mass production should be put to one side.

The new figured and incised wares required the specialised skills of only a few workshops. These need only have been small units, and they would have had a technological independence from the rest of society.

Producing figured designs was an interplay of tradition and innovation in terms of technique (workmanships of certainty and risk), technology (new brushes), and design (the geometric and figuration, reintroduction and development of new pot forms such as aryballoi, this latter point elaborated below).

A new workmanship of risk was an experiment of only a few workshops.

Elaborate figured designs were never more than marginal to the bulk of production of Korinthian pottery.

Production need only have been on a seasonal basis, related to, or compatible with religious festivals and sailing season.

The character of production is compatible with the range of skills acquired in a small family-based workshop.

The workshops were spread round an early city of loosely connected farmer villages.

Different workshops probably had their own specialities.

Pots and figured subjects

An aryballos has led discussion to the organisation of ceramic workshops in archaic Korinth. To what extent is the aryballos in Figure 1.1 'typical'? What were they producing? This section will present some general characteristics of the wares produced in Korinth at the beginning of the seventh century BC.

Up to the last decades of the eighth century Korinthian potters had produced a range of wares characterised by geometric ornament with very little figured design. Within a generation new pot forms, as well as old, carried a much wider range of designs, including figures, representations of animals and people.

The vessel forms are dominated by the miniature form of the aryballos. Other shapes are listed here.

Closed vessel forms: perfume and oil jars, jugs and containers for liquids.
The aryballos, alabastron, lekythos, oinochoe, olpe, amphoriskos, hydriskos, spherical vase and ring vase.
Open shapes: bowls and the like for mixing wine and serving food and drink.
The krater, *dinos* or *lebes* and stand, plate and *kalathos*.
Cups: the different names relate to the handles and body shape.
The *skyphos*, *kotyle*, *kyathos* and *kantharos* (the latter two terms sometimes used interchangeably).
Lidded forms: squat and tall boxes.
The pyxis.

An indication of how common they are in the sample is given in Table 2.1 (the figures are for broad guidance and do not carry any statistical weight, as indicated above).

The pots were painted in slip with decoration arranged mostly in horizontal friezes. In the descriptions and interpretations that follow the frieze is taken as a basic organising unit of surface design. Some contain figures, others geometric ornament; others are composed of lines of different weight and sometimes colour. There are 1,676 friezes upon 804 earlier pots and 4,470 upon 1,147 later pots in the sample

Table 2.1. *Korinthian pot forms*

	earlier	later
aryballoi	674	975
other closed forms	52	59
open vessels	3	33
cups	43	42
lidded 'box' forms	32	38
total pots	804	1147
sum total		1951

Table 2.2. *Types of frieze painted upon Korinthian pots*

	earlier	later	total
geometric friezes	1148	2145	3293
linear friezes/surfaces	329	397	726
figured friezes	199	1928	2127
components of figured friezes			
people alone	2	9	
people and animals	21	49	
animals	151	987	
dogs	25	883	
total	199	1928	

(totals: 6,146 friezes painted on 1,951 vessels). Table 2.2 shows the relative proportions of different kinds of frieze: most are geometric or floral in character, but the number containing animals and people rises markedly.

How is this range of ceramic and painted design to be understood? There is a clear sense of decorative order (regular design principles giving a sense of distinctive style). The vessel forms do form a complete range of table ware, but not in the proportions in which they occur in sanctuaries and cemeteries; ceramic production cannot easily and entirely be explained in functional terms of the provision of vessels for the table. Nevertheless many vessel forms are designed to accompany dining and drinking. Figured painting is dominated by bodily forms, animal and human; there are few other features other than floral and abstract ornament. Some scenes are of hunting and violence, races and contests, wild and undomesticated creatures and monsters. Some have been interpreted as illustrations of myth (consider immediately the aryballoi illustrated in this chapter). References to rural everyday life are almost entirely absent. Influence is clear of elite eastern iconography (the beasts and fights, rich floral forms, most obviously).

Table 2.3 records initial reactions to viewing the scenes painted in friezes upon the pots in the sample. War, banqueting, drinking, hunting, contest: these are conventional 'aristocratic' pursuits. It does not take much sensitivity to notice that archaic and classical Greek style, indeed culture, was dominated by what may be termed aristocratic interest. The supposition may be prompted that the pots are part of an

Table 2.3. *The subject matter of figured friezes: a record of initial reactions*

	earlier	later	totals
battle	4	12	16
violence or aggression	8	2	10
man or men and animals	6	6	12
hunt		12	12
animals fighting (usually lion attacking another animal)	7	6	13
lion attacking man	2	1	3
procession or race	2	7	9
beauty contest and judgement		1	1
parataxis or juxtaposition	36	15	51
figure scene of uncertain subject	6	3	9

aristocratic style, interest or ideology. More specifically it may be wondered if these pots served the symposion? Awareness of critiques of ceramic value (that fine wares were expensive items for social elites) may elicit an alternative, but related, supposition: that Korinthian potters began producing cheap wares attending to interests of lower classes in emulating their social betters (Vickers and Gill 1994). I have already dealt with the idea that black and red figure ceramics were skeuomorphs of plate vessels. I can also remark here that the suppositions of emulation are premature. For what of other aspects of design? What exactly was the character of 'aristocracy' and its ideologies? How did the potters respond to 'aristocratic' interest? Was there some system of commissioning? How do ideological forms operate? What of the details of the consumption of style. These are just a few questions begged.

Eighth- and seventh-century Korinth: political histories

οἱ δ᾽ ἀπὸ Ἡρακλέους Βακχίδαι πλείους ὄντες διακοσίων κατέσχον τὴν ἀρχήν, καὶ κοινῇ μὲν προειστήκεσαν τῆς πόλεως ἅπαντες, . . . ἐξ αὐτῶν δὲ ἕνα κατ᾽ ἐνιαυτὸν ἡροῦντο πρύτανιν, ὅς τὴν τοῦ βασιλέως εἶχε τάξιν

The Bakchiadai, descendants of Herakles, were more than 200 in number and held authority; all of them ruled the city in common . . . they chose each year one of their number to be *prytanis* and exercise the functions of the king. Diodorus 7.9.6

ἦν ὀλιγαρχίη, καὶ οὗτοι Βακχιάδαι καλεόμενοι ἔνεμον τὴν πόλιν, ἐδίδοσαν δὲ καὶ ἤγοντο ἐξ ἀλλήλων

It was an oligarchy who called themselves the Bakchiadai. They ran the city, and married only among themselves. Herodotos 5.92b1

Diodorus (7.9.3) and Pausanias (2.4.4) record the transition from a monarchy in Korinth to an aristocratic oligarchy, the Bakchiadai. The name asserts a claim to a common ancestry; Herodotos remarks upon their endogamy: they defined themselves through birth and descent. Andrewes has doubted that there were major differences between the character of the hereditary monarchy and the appointed magistracy of *prytanis*: 'the political machinery of the monarchy was not much changed by the Bakchiadai . . . their annual magistracy was not so different from a king that the continuity of the system was broken' (Andrewes 1956: 48).

> καὶ οἱ Βακχιάδαι τυραννήσαντες πλούσιοι καὶ πολλοὶ καὶ γένος λαμπροί . . . καὶ τὸ ἐμπόριον ἀδεῶς ἐκαρπώσαντο
> Wealthy, and numerous and of lustrous (*lampros*) birth, the Bakchiadai ruled as tyrants and gathered the fruit of the market (*emporion*) without stint.
> Strabo (378)

Whether or not Strabo is rationalising later Korinthian commercial success and providing an origin, it is clear that the spread of Korinthian artifacts occurred under this Bakchiad rule, as did colonisation. Syracuse and Kerkyra were both founded by members of the Bakchiadai (discussed by Salmon 1984: 65). There is also the story of Demaratos the Bakchiad who traded with Etruria, moved there with craftsmen after exile by the tyranny, and even came to father a king of Rome (Dionysios of Halikarnassos *Roman Antiquities* 3.46.3–5; Blakeway 1935; recent discussion and review in relation to Pithekoussai: Ridgway 1992a).

> ἐν δὲ πεσεῖται
> ἀδράσι μουνάρχοισι, δικαιώσει δὲ Κόρινθον
> he will come crashing down on these men who rule as kings and will bring justice to Korinth (*dikaiosei*)
> Herodotos 5.92

In about 655 BC the oligarchy fell to the tyranny of Kypselos. Herodotos (5.92) gives an anecdotal account of his parentage, on the fringes of the oligarchy (also Pausanias 2.4.4 and 5.18.7–8). He tells of his infancy when oracles from Apollo of Delphi (one of which is partly quoted here, others below) predicted his tyranny setting Korinth to rights (*dikaiosei*). Nikolaos of Damascus (*Die Fragmente der griechischen Historiker* 90 F 57), following fourth-century BC Ephoros, claims that Kypselos was *polemarch* in his earlier years and popular for, among other things, his treatment of fines. The revolution seems to have involved violence (Nikolaos, and Herodotos, discussed by Salmon 1984, especially page 190) as the Bakchiad *basileus* was murdered. The popularity of Kypselos seems to be indicated by the fact that he did not need a bodyguard.

Once in power, Kypselos exiled the Bakchiadai, confiscated and perhaps redistributed their property, brought back from exile and restored enemies of the old oligarchy. This is Nikolaos' account, but the restoration of exiles may be an anachronistic view from the fourth century, when tyrants did just these things (Salmon 1984: 195). Herodotos too records (5.92) the exile of Korinthians and property confiscations. Will (1955: 477–81) argues for a redistribution of land to landless supporters of the tyrant, but with little evidence. There is evidence (for example Pseudo-Aristotle *Economics* 1346a) of Kypselos taxing for the purpose of dedication at the sanctuary at Olympia, perhaps a colossal statue (Strabo 353 and 378). Details, as ever, are obscure (discussed by Salmon 1984: 196), but other early tyrants are known to have exploited a connection with divinities and their sanctuaries (see the standard histories of Andrewes 1956; Forrest 1966).

The tyrants' court, at least under the successor to Kypselos, Periander, was a centre of patronage. Herodotos (1.23–4) has the Lesbian poet Arion of Methymna, inventor of the poetic dithyramb, at Korinth. He is mentioned also by Pindar (*Olympian* 13.16f), who claims temple sculpture a Korinthian invention, along with horse bits. Pliny remarks that painting was invented in Korinth or Sikyon (*Natural History* 35.5). Eastern links, a feature of several tyrants' interest, are indicated by Phrygian and Lydian offerings in Kypselos' treasury at Delphi (Herodotos 1.14), and by the naming of Periander's brother Gordias (Aristotle *Politics* 1315b); Periander's short-lived successor and nephew was called Psammetichos, indicating the Egyptian connection (Pharaoh Psamtik). Colonies were founded. On the whole, Nikolaos concludes:

> Κύψελος δὲ Κόρινθον πράως ἦρχεν οὔτε δορυφόρους ἔχων οὔτ' ἀποθύμιος ὢν Κορινθίοις
>
> Kypselos ruled Korinth mildly, maintaining no bodyguard and enjoying the good will of the Korinthians.

Little can be said with any certainty regarding possible constitutional changes made by the tyranny. I have already quoted Diodoros who writes of 200 Bakchiadai, perhaps ruling in council (Salmon 1984: 56). Nikolaos has a council of eighty after the tyranny (Will 1955: 609–15) and assumes eight tribes, attributed to times before the tyranny by Roebuck (1972: 115–16; see also Schaeffer 1957: 1,222). Salmon finds arguments to locate the major constitutional restructuring in the times of the tyranny: tyranny was mainly a reaction against the aristocratic past, he claims, and it was during the tyranny that the need for new arrangements was greatest (Salmon 1984: 206–7).

The coup in Korinth seems to have been as much to do with opposition to the Bakchiad oligarchy, as with support for a charismatic leader. For Nikolaos (*FGH* 90 F 57.4), the Bakchiadai were generally 'insolent (*hubristai*) and violent (*biaioi*)', ignoring the *demos*. Strabo (378) describes them as tyrants themselves. The murdered *basileus* Patrokleides was 'lawless (*paranomos*) and oppressive (*epachthes*)' (Nikolaos). Herodotos relates the oracle which mentions in particular the exclusivity of the rulers (they monopolised power like monarchs), and that an application of *dike* was required, administration of justice and perhaps punishment (see also below on *dike* and the discourse of tyranny). Aristotle (*Politics* 1265b) records an early lawgiver in Korinth (presumably before the tyranny), Pheidon, who was concerned with the regulation of land tenure and citizenship. Whatever the details, the occurrence of a legislator implies a problem to do with land and property rights which needed resolution. Salmon, however, doubts (1984: 63–5, 194) that this led to discontent which was exploited by Kypselos. Andrewes (1956: 44–5) has discontent with the foreign policy of the Bakchiadai as a contributory factor. Salmon mentions also population pressure, which he, and others, consider as lying behind the foundation of the western colonies: 'The Korinthia may have been suffering from population pressure once more; if the Bakchiadai were unwilling to found further colonies that may have been a serious complaint' (Salmon 1984: 194). But Salmon sides with Forrest's analysis (Forrest 1966: Chapter 4) that, in the absence of formulated political discourse and organisation, the revolution and tyranny were to do with an accumulation of particular grievances centring on the arbitrary rule and application of power by the Bakchiadai.

It is not necessary for me to enter further the discussion surrounding the fragmentary written sources which recount the revolution and tyranny (on which: Andrewes 1956, Chapter 4; Berve 1967: 14–19, 521–5; Drews 1972; Forrest 1966: Chapter 4; Jeffery 1976: Chapter 10; Mossé 1969: Chapter 3.2; Murray 1993: Chapter 9; Oost 1972; Pleket 1969; Salmon 1984: Chapters 3, 15; Will 1955: Chapters 4, 5, 6). There are severe problems of anachronism or assimilation to contemporary understanding and practice: all accounts are centuries after the event: see for example Salmon's discussion (1984: 189–90) of Nikolaos and Aristotle and their view of the support for Kypselos – anachronistic in locating it within a 'democratic' power base, opposed to the oligarchic Bakchiadai. There are problems too of historical discrimination: Murray (1993: 147–50) makes a good case for the accounts of Herodotos and Nikolaos being more to do with mythography than history (see also pp. 59–61 on the discourse of tyranny). I also note that some accounts of modern ancient historians seem unsophisticated or anachronistic in their conceptions of the political motors of seventh-century history. For Andrewes (1956: 49), tyranny was simply the result of hatred of the aristocratic Bakchiadai, and his attempts to assess the conditions of social change are very limited. For Jeffery (1976: 146–7), tyranny was the result of the failure of the policies, home, foreign and economic, of the Bakchiad 'government'. I contrast the account of Forrest (1966) which embeds the political changes of the tyrannies in processes of social and conceptual modernisation and rationalisation.

So there are considerable problems with writing a political history of early Korinth which relies on written sources, 'sources' which anyway come long after the events themselves. The more sophisticated ancient histories raise vital questions of the social and political stresses which may have resulted in the things we read; but these so often remain questions and speculation. Critique is essential. I have, however, no need to stress the *details* of any particular account, details so hazy and uncertain. On the basis of conventional ancient historical discussion it is surely reasonable to make the following summary, but general, points.

An oligarchy was replaced by the rule of a tyrant in the middle of the seventh century.

Major constitutional differences (other than hereditary succession to kingship) between an earlier monarchy and the oligarchy of the Bakchiadai are difficult to establish.

The Bakchiadai were defined, the oligarchy established through descent.

They may have had an interest in trade and exchange.

Opposition to the oligarchy seems to have centred upon their arbitrary and exclusive power, and perhaps property rights and land.

Kypselos may have been related by birth to the Bakchiadai.

Kypselos was on the fringes of the oligarchy and may have held (military) office.

Kypselos drew on popular support.

Major constitutional changes made by the tyranny are difficult to establish.

There are no references to anything other than a narrow oligarchic council, and attendant magistracies, with power in Korinth.

The tyrants' court was a centre of patronage of religion and the arts and crafts: statuary, architecture, painting, poetry.

Eastern connections are apparent.

What was the significance of the tyranny? For Salmon (1984: 205), 'the structure of government was shattered by Kypselos' revolution' (also Andrewes 1956: 48–9). Revolution is a word not infrequently used to describe the coup of Kypselos (Andrewes 1956; Forrest 1966; Salmon 1984, for example). Indeed, it would seem that the monopoly of power of the Bakchiadai was broken. But the change was not a shift from narrow and aristocratic rule to a popular power of the people or *demos*, though Herodotos (3.82), Aristotle (*Politics* 1310b), Plato (*Republic* 8.565c-d), and Nikolaos (already noted), have tyrants beginning their careers as champions of the *demos*. I stress again that Korinth was never ruled by anything other than an oligarchy or tyrant who emerged from the aristocratic oligarchy. Andrewes (1956: 24, 48) goes as far as suggesting that Kypselos may have regarded himself as a new heir to the old monarchy (also Oost 1972: 21–8). However, an aristocracy or oligarchy may define itself in various ways, and this point has been central in discussions of the social and political conflicts of the seventh century and after in Greece. The questions concern the character and composition of the social groups in conflict, and the reasons for their conflict, which in Korinth produced tyranny.

I will deal with the social and cultural character of aristocracy in a later section, but let me preface that discussion with some points from ancient histories of the Korinthian Bakchiadai. The definition of the Bakchiad aristocracy through birth and descent has been noted. The resultant exclusivity may have been resented by other families, or by wealthy, and therefore influential, outsiders, with less claim to noble descent (though this can easily be asserted). A possible conflict is between ascribed and achieved status and power. This conflict between birth and wealth, between the leisure of an aristocracy and trades and crafts, between landed and commercial wealth, is a recurrent and important theme of early poetry. It is markedly present in the work of Solon, Alkaios, and particularly Theognis. In a well-noted comment, Thukydides points to an economic factor at play in the emergence of tyrannies:

> δυνατωτέρας δὲ γιγνομένης τῆς Ἑλλάδος καὶ τῶν χρημάτων τὴν κτῆσιν ἔτι
> μᾶλλον ἢ πρότερον ποιουμένης τὰ πολλὰ τυραννίδες ἐν ταῖς πόλεσι καθίσταντο
> as Greece became more powerful as the acquisition of goods grew for the
> most part much greater than before, tyrannies were established in many cities
> Thukydides 1.13

Figure 2.3 Hoplites upon a Korinthian aryballos, found at Gela and now in Syracuse Museum.

Ure made much of the economic factor, arguing a change in forms of economic capital and the emergence of commercial wealth exploited by tyrants, all 'first class business men' (Ure 1922: 30).

The emergence of discontented wealth is also often associated by historians with a military factor: the social changes of the seventh century have been related to *hoplitai*, the (new?) heavy armed infantry of the polis. Salmon (1977, 1984: 191–3) has argued that the strength behind the upheavals was provided by hoplites, and Kypselos was successful because he enjoyed their support. As Murray puts it:

> When therefore Aristotle says that 'in the old days, tyrannies arose when the same man was popular leader and general' (*Politics* 1305a), the natural inference is that the tyrants should be seen as the leaders of the hoplite class against the aristocracy: their success in overthrowing the traditional state would then lie in their being able to call on a new group of supporters, more powerful than the band of warriors which the aristocracy could muster – the hoplite class as a whole, that is the people (*demos*) under arms.
> (Murray 1993: 142)

Nikolaos does claim that Kypselos was *polemarch*, and some military functions may be surmised, though he does not mention any. However, evidence for the military factor is largely circumstantial and dependent upon extrapolation from Aristotle's analysis (*Politics* 1297b) of the connection between the military and the state, as I discussed above. The older extrapolation from the few fragmentary details known of Pheidon of Argos, a monarch who went beyond custom and became a tyrant, perhaps through his military success (Andrewes 1956: 39–42) cannot easily be supported (Kelly 1976: Chapter 7).

Kypselos must have had support, obviously from outside the Bakchiadai, and a class analysis appears attractive: the 'class' interests of hoplites, a group enriched by commercial wealth, or of the *demos* may have led them to back Kypselos. However I repeat the point that Korinthians never had anything other than a small oligarchic council. There were demands then for removal of the exclusive Bakchiadai who thought themselves monarchs (*mounarchontes,* Herodotos, quoted above), but the demands *for power* cannot have come from anything but a minority of Korinthians, otherwise there would not have been satisfaction with the narrow constitution centred upon a council of only eighty (satisfaction attested by political stability; see also Pindar *Olympian* 13.6–8 on Korinthian *eunomia*, settled good order, quoted also below). Forrest explains with excellent clarity:

> We must always ask how far down through society the desire for political power had spread. At this date the answer is likely to be that it had not spread very far. Indeed, in class terms, it seems probable that it had not spread at all – the politically active in 650 were still the same kind of men as the *basileis* of 750; they may have been more numerous than the *basileis*; they may have stood for a different immediate policy for their state; they may have had different friends; they may have had different interests; but neither policy, friends nor interests were necessarily, in the case of Korinth even probably, of a fundamentally different kind. (Forrest 1966: 121)

Salmon (1984: 191–2, 1977: 99) also makes the point that the Korinthian constitution was never wide enough to satisfy the political demands of a hoplite phalanx. Tyranny at Korinth was not the emergence into politics of a hoplite 'class' (*contra* Murray 1993: 141f). Snodgrass remarks generally (1980a: 112) that tyranny only involved the aristocracy. Both Snodgrass (1965) and Cartledge (1977) hold that the hoplite reform was not an immediate threat to aristocratic interests.

The essential point is to separate 'class' or sectional interests and discontent from political power. A long digression on class and the ancient city state is not necessary, particularly given De Ste Croix's monumental elaboration (1981) of Marxian and Aristotelian analysis of the Greek city state. I am satisfied to accept basic divisions between *euporoi* or a propertied class (sometimes, as in early poetry, called the *agathoi* and synonyms), those without property, the *aporoi* (or *kakoi*, later called the *demos*), and dependent labour or slaves. Morris (1987) has used this class distinction in archaeology with analytical success. The existence of a commercially enriched class has been supposed, but arguments over its existence and importance are less important than the ultimate value accorded to *landed* wealth and to aristocratic values and life-style. To these I will return.

It is important here to signal the need to treat critically the terms applied to the archaic Greek class system. There is an argument to be made for careful qualification, providing historical context for the concept of aristocracy itself. It is not, of course, an historical or sociological constant. As with the concept of king, aristocracy finds one set of origins in definitions of medieval absolutist monarchy, with monotheistic religion providing legitimation for feudal hierarchy. Michael Mann's fine and synoptic account of the history of social power treats this phenomenon as an ideological invention of medieval Europe; this could be taken to place dark age and archaic Greece beyond comparison (Mann 1986: 245). Without state bureaucracies and the religious ideologies, archaic Greek aristocracy was more fluid, perhaps better described by ethnological terminologies 'chieftains' or 'big-men' (Starr 1986; Whitley 1991; further discussion below). Other appropriate comparisons are with germanic society (Hedeagger 1988). I retain the term to mark its distinctive genealogy, while promoting such arguments for awareness of historical difference.

The significance of tyranny at Korinth in these ancient histories was simply that it removed the principle of *hereditary* aristocratic dominance; but the exercise of power did not shift from the propertied class. Whether hoplites were involved or not, whether Kypselos enlisted the support of the *demos* or *aporoi*, the tyranny depended upon conflicts within the propertied class. This argument implies continuity as well as something of a radical break in the mid-seventh century, and it is to continuities of different kinds that I will turn later.

Tyranny, power and discourses of sovereignty

οὗτοι ποτ᾽ ἄνδρες ἐξεπόρθησαν, σὺ δὲ
νῦν εἶλες αἰχμῆι καὶ μέγ᾽ ἐξήρω κλέος·
κείνης ἄνασσε καὶ τυραννίην ἔχε·
this city . . .
men never sacked it, but you
took it now with your spear and together great glory is yours.
Rule over it and hold tyranny.
Archilochos West 23.18–20

In this iambic fragment Archilochos draws on notions of autocratic power to construct metaphors for amorous attachment – all-conquering femininity. Elsewhere (Archilochos West 19) the tyranny of Gyges is used as a metaphor for greed, which he, mercenary and poet, does not share. For Archilochos and his generation the power of tyranny was a recent political innovation, source of poetic idiom. McGlew (1993) has provided a most valuable account of its discourse.

McGlew questions the bifurcation found in ancient histories of tyranny (as outlined above) into a reality of determinations (such as individual political motivations, economic, social and class-based pressures) and ideology, a supposed reality of political change, separated from its representation in 'propaganda', legend and folklore – the majority of the sources. McGlew's position on the politics of tyranny is that 'a process of complicity, not simple ambition, transformed one citizen into a ruler and his fellows into his subjects' (McGlew 1993: 5). This is based on the premise, following Foucault (as, for example expressed in Foucault 1980; for archaeology Miller and Tilley 1984), that power is less *acquired*, being some sort of commodity, than *exercised*, being a function of social relationships. With power centred upon translation of interests effected through discourse, the sources (such as Delphic oracles, poetry directed against tyrants and the fable that grew up around them) are not to be decoded to reveal the 'truth' of social and economic causation, the political reality of the seventh and sixth centuries, but read as part of the relationships between political agencies of archaic Greece, the tyrant and his subjects.

In this remythologised history the tyrant appears as the progenitor of a political vocabulary of sovereignty.

Consider again the Delphic oracles reported by Herodotos to have been associated with the rise of Kypselos. In them the tyrant's persona is an agent of justice.

αἰετὸς ἐν πέτρῃσι κύει, τέξει δὲ λέοντα
καρτερὸν ὠμηστήν· πολλῶν δ'ὑπὸ γούατα λύσει.
ταῦτά νυν εὖ φράζεσθε, Κορίνθιοι, οἳ περὶ καλὴν
Πειρήνην οἰκεῖτε καὶ ὀφρυόεντα Κόρινθον.
an eagle is pregnant in the rocks and will
bring forth a lion, a mighty hunter of flesh,
who will weaken the knees of many.
Be warned of this, you Korinthians who live
around the fair Peirene and the heights of Akrokorinthos.
Herodotos 5.92

For the oracles, tyranny arises from injustice, and this belongs with the city and its leaders, not with the motivations and ambitions of the tyrant. So the oracle quoted here reminds the Korinthians of the coming of tyrant Kypselos, whose rule is likened to a lion exacting punishment on (unjust) Korinthians. The tyrant's persona as a reformer required a conspicuous display of freedom (*eleutheria*), hence the lion. McGlew notes (1993: 67 n. 32) many instances of this use of the lion as a political symbol, fearful and irresistable, sometimes image of divinely willed destruction.

Κύρνε, κύει πόλις ἥδε, δέδοικα δὲ μὴ τέκῃ ἄνδρα
εὐθυντῆρα κακῆς ὕβριος ἡμετέρης.
Kyrnos, this city is pregnant – and I fear it may
give birth to someone (*aner euthunter*) who will right our wicked ways (*hubris*).
Theognis 39–40

In Theognis and Solon too, there is a reciprocity between crime and punishment. And Kypselos killed Patrokleides, the last Bakchiad king (Nikolaos). There is relevant imagery found also in the discourse of the new state (McGlew 1993: 60 and n. 18). The aim of *dike*, justice, is associated with (political) leadership and solidarity, visualised as the ship of state in calm or stormy waters (Archilochos West 105; Alkaios West 6, 208, 249) steered by the just rudder (*dikaion pedalion*) (Pindar *Pythian* 1.86–7).

By claiming and being supported in an unprecedented and unique right to autocracy, the tyrant implicitly defined that rule as untransferable. This is the basis of resistance to tyranny. McGlew argues that there was a clear complicity between tyrant and subjects in recognising the coherence of the argument for tyranny – the tyrant was a popular leader. The corollary is that resistance aimed not to overthrow tyranny so much as to appropriate the *eleutheria* of the tyrant for the people. Just as the tyrant's divinely willed *eleutheria* involved the subjection of fellow citizens, so the appropriation of that same freedom by the citizenry involved subjugation of slaves. After tyranny there was no return to political innocence. The persona of agent of *dike* was adopted, the treasury and foreign interests assumed, *eleutheria* preserved – those aspects of sovereignty which made the tyrant lord both attractive and dangerous.

McGlew maintains that there was no convincing precedent for the extraordinary power exercised by the early tyrants, no political framework in which it may be located. Instead, and in its rhetoric and reception, tyranny emerged through the manipulation of contemporary conceptions of *dike* (which functioned in the earliest accounts of the polis as the most pressing concern of civic action). Hence the discourse of tyranny is pervaded by notions of *hubris* (divine necessity) and *dike* (justice), Hesiod's divinity punishing those bribe-devouring *basileis*, big-men (literally kings), practising *adikia* (injustices), selling their judgement to the highest bidder (*Works and Days* 36–9).

In this context of the forging of new political discourses, it is not surprising that the discourse of tyranny is clearly related to that of other figures of archaic Greek politics – the founder, lawgiver (Pheidon here at Korinth), and liberator or tyrannicide. All reference the two sides of justice and sovereignty. For example, accounts of the colonial founder, the wandering *oikistes*, have a similar narrative structure to that of tyranny. The *oikistes* escapes the stain of domestic crime or illegitimacy by leaving the mother city and travelling to the ends of the earth to assume tyrant-like powers in founding a new city. Myth, cult and fable around his achievements turn his death into the city's coming of age, his individual rule into a single remote and unrepeatable event. In recalling the founder in celebration and legend, the citizenry of the polis celebrated their autonomy from him and their possession of the sovereignty, now collective, that their founders held.

Korinth, the material environment: a continuity of change
Public architecture: masonry and roof tiles
By the middle of the sixth century, there was a monumental stone temple upon Temple Hill at Korinth, and another dedicated to Olympian Zeus, a project initiated by the tyrant Periandros. The construction of such public and religious buildings began in the early eighth century with the small temple dedicated to Hera Akraia at Perachora, just across the Korinthian Gulf from Korinth. By the seventh century this was perhaps replaced with another temple, and what may have been a cult dining-room was added (Salmon 1972: 161–5, 174–8; Tomlinson 1977: 197–202). Among other dedications found in the sanctuary, there are pieces of perhaps five models of temples – small porched buildings, with geometric decoration and thatched roof (Payne 1940: Pl. 9). We should note here with Snodgrass (1980a: 61–2) the early connection in temple and cult between the sacred buildings which resembled houses, and communal dining or feasting (further discussion in Chapter Five).

Williams (1986 esp. 12–14) proposes an early date for knowledge of Astarte, an eastern Aphrodite, infamous at Korinth in later times. He cites, as evidence for an early cult, a seventh-century figurine from Korinth (Davidson 1952: 29, Pl. 6, No. 85) and a plaque from Perachora (Payne 1940: 231–2, Pl. 102, No. 183). The plaque

Figure 2.4 Bellerophon. An aryballos in the Museum of Fine Arts, Boston (95.10).

shows what Payne claimed to be a bisexual Aphrodite; on the reverse is a painted Pegasos and a dog or lion.

The date is debated, but between 700 and 650 or shortly after much larger temples were built at Korinth itself, to Apollo (dedication debated by Fowler and Stillwell 1932: 115–16, 130–3; Morgan 1994: 138–9), and at the sanctuary of Poseidon at Isthmia (Broneer 1971; Robinson 1976; the *terminus post quem* is 690–650 BC, after Gebhard and Hemans 1992: 39).

These were ostentatious and innovatory designs, drawing on new specialised building construction skills. At Korinth the temple had squared masonry up to roof height (Robinson 1976: 225–8). Isthmia definitely had a colonnade. Both temples were provided with painted ceramic wall-decoration, that at Isthmia claimed to have closest parallels in the Chigi Olpe found in Etruria (Broneer 1971: 33–4, 41, Fig. 54 and Pls. 5a–c; Robinson 1976: 228–30 for Korinth). Both also had tiled roofs (for Isthmia: Broneer 1971: 40–53; Williams 1980: 346–7). Decorative architectural ceramics were being produced in Korinth from the middle or third quarter of the seventh century BC (Weinberg 1954: 118f).

Figure 2.5 The sanctuary of Hera at Perachora, across the gulf from Korinth (the remains of the archaic temple are at the end of the terrace).

Figure 2.6 Temple Hill, Old Korinth (this is the later archaic temple); Akrokorinthos in the background.

These Korinthian roof tiles and especially the architectural ceramics, identified by their fabric and design, were used in many other early temples (Payne 1931: Chapter 17; Robinson 1984). Korinthian influence or design has been speculated for temple C at Thermon and for Calydon (Salmon 1984: 121).

So Korinth was an important innovator in early temple design and building (general discussion: Cook 1970: 17–19; Salmon 1984: 120–1). Coulton (1977: 32–50) has argued for a strong Egyptian influence upon Korinthian temple building.

Building Korinth: springs and defensive walls, graves and wells
Amenities provided for Korinthians in the late eighth and seventh centuries include the so-called Sacred and perhaps Cyclopean Springs (Hill 1964; Williams and Fisher 1971: 3–5). There are clear remains of a metal workshop from the early seventh century (Williams and Fisher 1971: 5–10); a mould for spearheads from a nearby well gives a clue to some of the things made there. I have already discussed pottery specialisation: most workshops were away from the central area of habitation. The pottery from the metal workshop house and well was plain linear Protokorinthian (Williams and Fisher 1971: 26–30).

I have also already presented the consensus on the early appearance of the city state as a collection of villages (Roebuck 1972; Williams 1982), although the evidence (the distribution of graves and wells) is not substantial (little of old Korinth outside the Roman centre has been excavated). Salmon (1984: 75–80) has challenged the idea that the centre of the early city state was little more than a village. He traces expansion of the early central settlement from the distribution of graves and wells (*contra* Williams), expansion due to population rise. Noting in addition the evidence for craft specialisation and public amenities and temples, he concludes: 'our limited evidence strongly favours the conclusion that Korinth was already, in respect of amenities, population and economic activity, a true city by the time of the tyrants' (Salmon 1984: 80).

The early 'city' may have been provided with a defensive wall at the time of the tyrants. The late seventh-century South Long Building in the so-called Potters' Quarter took account of the course of a wall of substantial scale at the edge of the neighbouring ravine. This has been interpreted as part of a defensive circuit (Salmon 1984: 220); Williams has also noted (1982: 15–17) cuttings in the bedrock for perhaps an angle tower. A city wall which took in even just the centre, the 'Potters' Quarter' and Akrokorinthos would have been a massive undertaking, and for this reason it may be doubted that the wall was to guard the whole of the new city. Stillwell (1948: 14, 62) suggests that it was only for the local quarter, Winter (1971: 64) that it was to defend just the approach to Akrokorinthos. Given only the short stretch of wall at the 'Potters' Quarter', the question of a walled Korinth in the seventh century must remain open, though the implications are considerable.

The living and the dead

Clear evidence for radical change in the eighth century is the shift of burials from in and around house clusters to the north cemetery with its organised grave plots (Blegen, Palmer and Young 1964 Part 2: 13–20). This implies also a change in conception of living space. Morris (1987: esp. 185–6 for Korinth) has made much of this in his thesis of class change in the early polis. From 800 BC there was an increase in the number of grave goods deposited in graves sited among houses. By 775 extramural cemeteries were established and soon after, by 750, mortuary rite required few artifacts as offerings. There was instead a rise in votive offerings in sanctuaries, a general trend noted also on p. 175. Morris comments: 'Korinthian wealth was probably not waning in the eighth century, but a new symbolic system of large, poor, homogeneous 'citizen' cemeteries had been established' (1993: 33). His proposal is that fundamental class change, new social relationships within the polis community and the emergence of a citizenry, was accompanied by changes in relationships between the living and the dead, mortals and immortals, the community and its heroes (*ibid.*: 35). Conceptions of time are implicated, in changed references to the dead and those beyond mortal frame. This is the ideological field I will be exploring particularly in the next chapter.

Pottery, metalwork, export and dedication

I will be considering the export and consumption of Korinthian pottery in detail in later chapters, but, given the dominance of pottery in the archaeological record and therefore in the material remains from archaic Korinth, a few remarks are appropriate here.

Korinthian pottery of middle Geometric style was already finding its way to Delphi and other places in the early eighth century (Coldstream 1968: Chapter 3; Dehl 1984). By the turn of the century in 700 BC Korinthian pottery was to be found in many Greek and other sites, particularly cemeteries and sanctuaries. Pottery of late Geometric 'Thapsos' style has been considered a style produced for export, because so little has actually been found at Korinth (Coldstream 1968: 103); the identification as Korinthian (according to fabric and style) has even been doubted because of this lack of finds in the supposed place of production and because of claimed decorative differences to Korinthian late Geometric and protokorinthian (see for example the discussion by Boardman 1970: 496, 1973: 278–9; Bosana-Kourou 1983; Grimanis *et al.* 1980; Neeft 1981). The distribution of the stylistic variety of Korinthian pottery (much of which is missing from Korinth) has also been taken to indicate that the pottery was produced primarily for export (Morgan 1988: 336).

Morgan (1988: esp. 333–8) has related Korinthian manufactured goods to a need for metal supplies to service competitive display (weaponry, sanctuary goods and items related to aspects of aristocratic lifestyle such as the symposion). In this respect the sanctuary at Perachora symbolised Korinthian interest in the west (*ibid.*: 335).

Many Korinthian pots found their way to sanctuaries. This is true also of other items of specialised manufacture. There is a collection of ivory seals from Perachora, dating perhaps from 700 onwards (Stubbings 1962). They are carved with figured scenes which closely resemble those of figured Korinthian pottery (*ibid.*: 411). A distinctive style of Korinthian votive metalwork has been identified, consisting of birds, horses and human figurines, most probably designed as attachments for tripods (Bouzek 1967; Coldstream 1977: 175–7; Herrmann 1964: 17–71). Pins were made, found with simple jewellery in some Korinthian graves (Coldstream 1977: 175). Some pins, too large for ordinary use, were clearly for dedication or some other special use; such pins for dedication are known elsewhere (Snodgrass 1980a: 62–3).

Salmon (1984: 118–19) has rightly pointed out that the number of such pieces of metalwork is small, and that much of Korinthian metal production may well have been for more mundane items. Nevertheless, the things which are found in the sanctuaries of Perachora, Delphi, Aetos on Ithaka, and at Olympia are part of a general rise in the number of dedications to divinity. Snodgrass (1980a: 52–4) has stressed this change in practice, away from the placing of things in the grave, to items in sanctuaries, many of which have a distinctive *cosmopolitan* ambience, with dedications of many local styles and forms. Here I am anticipating discussion in Chapter Five.

At Isthmia Morgan (1994: 127–8) reports the finding, among other dedications, of eight tripods and weaponry (a *Kegelhelm*, Illyrian helmet and a spearhead). Remains at Perachora indicate a sanctuary among the richest in the Greek world at the time, but no such dedications have been found.

Among the variety of terracottas found in the Potters' Quarter (Stillwell 1952) is a series of pieces of model carts or chariots. Raepsaet (1988) stresses the diversity of function of such vehicles in his treatment which searches for what the models are representing: they could be used for religious processions as well as having agricultural uses. He makes no consideration of the motivation of modelling – I note that these models may well be related to military or heroic ethos, if not function.

Warfare and the Korinthian economy
The mould for spearheads found in that early metal workshop in Korinth (Williams and Fisher 1971: item 31) may be coincidental, but Korinth has been implicated in

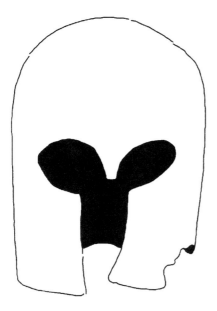

Figure 2.7 A Korinthian helmet. An early example from Olympia.

ὡς τότε ταρφειαὶ κόρυθες λαμπρὸν γανόωσαι
νηῶν ἐκφορέοντο καὶ ἀσπιδες ὀμφαλόεσσαι
θώρηκές τε κραταιγύαλοι και μείλινα δοῦρα.
αἴγλη δ'οὐρανὸν ἷκε, γέλασσε δὲ πᾶσα περὶ χθὼν
χαλκοῦ ὑπὸ στεροπῆς·

So now the helmets, thickly arrayed and dazzling bright, (*lampron*)
were brought out of the ships, the great bossed shields,
the hollowed corselets and the ash spears;
the brilliance swept to the heavens and all the earth around them
laughed under the glitter of bronze.
Iliad 19.359–63

the development of the new forms of weaponry and armour of the late eighth and seventh centuries. Herodotos (4.180) calls Korinthian the new bronze helmet, seen pictured upon many Korinthian pots, and it has been accepted as a Korinthian invention (Snodgrass 1964: 20–8). Beaten from a single sheet of bronze, such artifacts required considerable skill to produce.

The new figurative imagery upon seventh-century ceramics notably includes some illustrations of what appear to be hoplite battles (Salmon 1977), among many more images of warring males.

Sacred space

. . . τὰν ὀλβίαν Κόρινθον,' Ἰσθμίου
πρόθυρον Ποτειδᾶνος ἀγλαόκουρον·
ἐν τᾷ γὰρ Εὐνομία ναίει κασί-
γνηταί τε, βάθρον πολίων ἀσφαλές
Δίκα καὶ ὁμότροφος Εἰρήνα, τάμι' ἀνδράσι πλούτου
χρυσέαι παῖδες εὐβούλου Θέμιτος

> blessed Korinth
> doorway to Poseidon's Isthmus,
> brilliant (*aglaos*) in its young men.
> *Eunomia* (political order) dwells there
> and her sisters, *Dike* (justice) –
> safe footing for cities –
> and *Eirene* (peace) – with whom she grew –
> housekeeper of men's wealth,
> golden daughters of wise Themis.
> Pindar *Olympian* 13.4–8

In a most notable argument De Polignac (1984, 1994) has connected the establishment of sanctuaries to a dynamic of territorial sovereignty. Morris (1987: 189–92) also stresses profound eighth-century changes in boundaries between gods, men and the dead, with living space more sharply differentiated from the sacred spaces of the gods and dead – sanctuaries and cemeteries. Mention has been made of the shift in burial of Korinthian dead to formal designated areas. For De Polignac the rural sanctuaries in the *chora* of the polis were set up as focal points of mediation; these 'passages between two worlds' (De Polignac 1994: 8) indicate the importance of boundaries.

> ἐπεὶ οὔ πω Ἴλιος ἱρὴ
> ἐν πεδίῳ πεπόλιστο, πόλις μερόπων ἀνθρώπων
> since not yet had sacred Ilios been made a polis in the plain, a polis of mortal
> men
> *Iliad* 20.216–7

In an exploration of the archaic geographical imagination as found in Homer, Scully (1990) finds the conceptual space of the early polis a paradoxical one. Ephemeral polis within immortal frame, the new city represented an interplay of human and divine components, technology and the Olympian, the *oikos* (household) and the sacred space of the polis (*ibid.*: 61–4). Sanctuaries and shrines, so crucial to the structuring of city space and community for De Polignac, represent a divine presence and architectural force in a city of mortal men, though one defended by heroes, who are between men and gods (*ibid.*: 106–10).

Isthmia, through Pindar's doorway, is close to communication routes, land and sea, and lies on a dramatic narrowing of the isthmus. Akrokorinthos is clearly visible to the west across Korinth's *chora*. Sited in view across the bay on its rocky promontory, Perachora looks out west down the Korinthian gulf (is it true that on a clear day one may see the Ionian islands?). To the south, off the way to Argos, is another 'rural' sanctuary, Solygeia (Morgan 1994: 135–8; Verdelis 1962).

The sacred landscape, which is the polis, centres on frontiers, political borders between neighbouring states, but also boundaries between the sacred and profane (De Polignac 1984: 30), mortal and divinity, this world and that beyond. Axes are set out in the *chora* from *astu* to sanctuary, axes enacted in the sacred calendar with periodic processions and festivals (*ibid.*: 48–50, 54–6, 85–92). The soldier citizenry of the polis, the newly regulated or standardised *hoplitai*, would have figured prominently in these rites. Antonaccio (1994: 82, citing Connor 1988: 16–17) repeats the point that archaic warfare was not about territorial acquisition but civic representation, and was often focused upon borders, disputed or liminal territory suitable for a fight.

The sacred landscapes of the polis made use of the past with offerings at ancient tombs and with hero cults, material cultural expressions of an heroic ethos, of a concern for genealogical connection with land and ancestors. Were they justifications for divisions in the present? Much attention has focused recently on this aspect of the archaic state (Antonaccio 1993a, 1993b, 1994; Coldstream 1976, 1977: Chapter 14; Morris 1988; Snodgrass 1982, 1988; Whitley 1994a).

In all here is a nexus of landscape, cult, time, death, mediation and belonging or identity.

Morgan (1994) emphasises the continuities of activity at Isthmia as well as changes in the eighth century: there is evidence of offerings at an altar. Everything did not all suddenly start with the 'birth' of the polis. Continuities are also stressed and radical changes questioned by Sourvinou-Inwood, who nevertheless recognises that 'crystallisation' took place in the archaic period (Sourvinou-Inwood 1993: 9, 11) and that the mediation of sacred and non-sacred became a most significant feature of the design of the polis. She adds another aspect of cultic activity, one which she sees as paramount: 'what was fundamental in Greek sanctuaries, what defined a sanctuary in the Greek religious mentality, was that it was a sacred space centred around an altar, sometimes including another sacred focus such as a tree or stone, a spring or a cave' (*ibid.*: 11). The focus was the point and form of mediation between sacred and profane – sacrifice, consumption and the scent of burning meat.

Mobility and the polis – colonies
Disputes over land seem, from Aristotle's account (*Politics* 1265b 12–16), to have been the concern of archaic lawgiver Pheidon. Acquisition and partition of land was certainly a feature of colonisation. Korinthians set up colonies at Kerkyra in 734 BC and Syracuse in Sicily the year after. More followed. This primary feature of the early polis – mobility – will be a main feature of discussion in Chapter Four.

Material lifeworlds
Korinth in the late eighth and seventh centuries most probably still appeared as a collection of villages of peasant farmers. I have also noted that the production of fine pottery would not have required a large workforce and was not in contradiction with a fundamentally peasant economy, though specialisation and expertise were essential. The amounts of other specialised and fine products such as metal- and ivory-work were also not great, though, like pottery, they were growing.

However, Korinthians were innovators in religious architecture and building methods and materials, in new weaponry, and, above all for the archaeologist, in surface design and iconography – pottery, architectural ceramics (temple wall-panels), ivory- and metalwork (figurines). This specialised craft production was for a cultural nexus which bound together cult, war and death. Snodgrass (1980a: Chapter 2, esp. 62–4) has stressed the links in the archaic economy between metalwork and craft, religion and war: these are all aspects of the category of the 'economic', a category which, in fact, disperses, and cannot be held to have strong analytical importance. I would add to this cultural assemblage external connections, whether trade and travel, 'colonisation', export of dedications to sanctuaries and colonies, reference to oriental and 'exotic' motifs, or the mixture of Korinthian goods in a cosmopolitan ambience such as Perachora or Delphi. The Korinthians were supreme innovators in this field too, hence the claims for the long-vaunted 'economic success' of Korinthian pottery, but this is a field which cannot (*a fortiori*) be restricted to a category such as the economic.

New urban and political spaces and experiences involved figurative imagery, public areas and processions, with focal points of mediation, viewing and consumption. These ranged from the personal space of the miniature pottery, invitations to hold and look at goods in a new way, scrutinising scenes of bodies in action upon a jar of perfumed oil, to vistas from Perachora and Isthmia, to the sensations of citizenry ranked in heavy hoplite armour, bronze cuirass and horse-hair crest in the Greek summer sun. Springs were tapped in a formally designated and sacred city centre of designed ostentation of fine masonry, roof tiles and stucco. Graves no longer were laid between houses, but outside the city.

The mobility of goods and people finds analogy in the discourses of tyranny and colonisation: social mobility and redefinitions, reworkings of the metaphors and narratives of personal and collective sovereignty. I will turn to further reworkings in the next chapter.

Social histories: making anthropological sense of archaic aristocracy

Tyranny was predominantly to do with the old hereditary aristocracy and the propertied class of archaic Korinth. It involved a shift in interest and powers within this restricted section of society. Birth and a principle of hereditary succession are clearly implicated in the political struggles. However, the issue of kinship in the early Greek state is a complex and difficult one. The studies of Morris (1987) and Whitley (1987, 1991b) into burial in dark age and archaic Greece make much reference to the kinship basis of the burying groups, and they both investigated the possibilities and issues thoroughly. However, both also remained uncommitted on the precise nature of the social and kinship units (Morris 1987: esp. 87–93; Whitley 1991b: esp. 64–7), and with good reason. The relationship between mortuary practices, archaeological remains and kinship is very varied (Ucko 1969). The work of Bourriot (1976) has demolished the old certainty concerning the primary social unit of archaic Athens (the state about which most is known). It is no longer tenable to hold that the *genos*, originally conceived as a kinship group wider than the immediate or extended family, took any specific form. After also the work of Roussel (1976), the existence of a tribal and clan or lineage based early Athens or Greece can only be considered a mirage (Snodgrass 1980a: 25–6; see also Humphreys 1980).

Forrest (1966: esp. 48–50) provides a more flexible idea of pyramid-shaped units vertically dividing a peasant-based society with no formal constitution or state. At the head of each would have been an 'aristocrat' and his immediate *oikos* (see also Donlan 1985). Beyond would be other lesser households, relatives, retainers and slaves. The bonds were manifold: locality, kinship, ritual, as well as bonds of patronage and mutual help. The aristocrat may have originally provided defence and a security of wealth and resources accessible in hard times; those lower down provided service, recognition, surplus perhaps. The aristocrat needed the status afforded by followers; the peasant security. Gallant (1991: esp. Chapter 6) has provided a powerful argument, empirically well-founded, for the economic import-ance of such relationships in a peasant-based society. But the manifold nature of the links within these groups means they go well beyond the economic: they are simulta-neously economic, religious, political and more (aristocrats were also a legal system of arbitration, for example).

The flexibility of these groups means they are open to manipulation and change. The status of a group may vary according to its wealth and ability to fulfil ritual, military and economic functions; the political and other use of the rising wealth of a group may bring status and social dominance. There are no inherent constraints upon manipulation and change of existing groups, but descent and tradition could block outside *oikoi* from usurping position. This seems to have been the case at Korinth with the Bakchiadai. But the tyranny of Kypselos usurped birth and tradi-tion. I write usurped because birth and tradition were always options open for reference and manipulation in this system, both before and after tyranny.

De Ste Croix makes an appropriate contrast (1981: 278f) between the presenta-tions of the aristocracy in the poems of Hesiod and Theognis, a contrast of perhaps 100 years, between the eighth and seventh centuries. For Hesiod (*Works and Days*), political power was the exclusive preserve of a hereditary aristocracy, still in its days of security, though Hesiod has them as gift devouring and scorning justice (*dike*). The authors of the *Theognidea* express aristocratic sentiments, but they are on the defensive. Society was divided, between the good and bad, literally moral terms, the *agathoi* and *kakoi*, aristocracy and the rest. The reason was new wealth, supplanting birth. Hesiod (for example *Works and Days* 320) and Solon (for example West 13.9) both accept that there are ways of acquiring good 'god-given' (*theosdota*) wealth; but all new wealth is bad in Theognis. This was a state of affairs in which *philiai* (alliances and friendships) were breaking down and changing all the time, in contrast to the perception of old permanence. As Adkins put it: 'the writers of the Theognid corpus for the most part feel themselves unable to exercise any effective control over the economic, social and political development of their city' (Adkins 1972: 46–7). This was hardly a simple 'economic' matter of wealth.

What comes between Hesiod and Theognis; what made the difference? De Ste Croix gives the answer of the tyrants.

> Institutions suited to maintaining in power even a non-hereditary ruling class . . . did not exist . . . Even non-hereditary oligarchy, based entirely on

property ownership and not on right of birth, was something new and untried, lacking a traditional pattern which could be utilised without potentially dangerous experiment. Until the necessary institutions had been devised there was no real alternative to aristocracy but the dictatorship of a single individual and his family – partly according to the old pattern of Greek kingship, but now with a power which was not traditional but usurped. (De Ste Croix 1981: 281)

Here is reference to that renegotiation of sovereignty, already discussed. I suggest a modification of this general point of De Ste Croix. Here is a mixture of the traditional (monarchic power) and innovation (usurpation and new means of legitimation). With a principle of hereditary succession threatened, other means of legitimation were enhanced or sought; discourses were contested and redesigned. The evidence from Korinth suggests that this substantially involved the Bakchiadai, the hereditary aristocrats themselves.

The idea is a strong one that the organs of power centred upon the aristocratic *oikoi* and their retainers (Finley 1973: *passim*; Murray 1993: 84p5; Redfield 1975; 111, 123–7; Runciman 1982). It is possible to accept this primacy of the household form while also recognising, with Scully (1990: Chapter 7) the physical and conceptual space of the polis. These *oikoi* were flexible social forms which combined economic, religious, military, legal and household functions. I have also outlined a continuity of changes from the mid eighth century: an increasing interest in public religion and dedication; innovation and interest in the field of war; new physical and visual environments with the development of the settlement of Korinth, the sacred city, and the emergence of a representational iconography; travel (of goods and people); and colonisation. The Bakchiadai were clearly an innovating and hardly stagnant aristocracy. Their wealth would (in the absence of any institutional resources) have been the basis for many projects and ventures, this continuity of material change. Not least, as will be discussed below, they may well have provided ships for exchange and colonisation; only professional traders could have otherwise afforded to own them, and their existence, given a small amount of trading, is doubtful. The patronage of this hereditary aristocracy must have played a significant part.

Patronage, design and ideology?

How would such patronage work? From simple registering of the character and geographical spread of the painted scenes it is clear that the design of pottery is implicated in this cultural complex whose components include war and violence, death and divinity, and travel, as well as innovation in the field of craft specialisation. But how? This is also to raise the question of the ideological motivation of style. Were innovative Korinthians commissioning new designs in support of their political and social strategies? How were potting Korinthians responding to their political and social circumstances? This is one line of questioning which will be taken through the following chapters.

3

Early archaic Korinth: design and style

I continue with the aryballos of Figures 1.1 and now 3.1. The first half of this chapter consists of sources juxtaposed with comments and leading to an interpretation of the Boston aryballos in the context of visual lifeworlds of ideologies centred upon corporeal form. In the second half Korinthian ceramic style is considered more widely.

Part 1   An interpretive dialogue through a Korinthian aryballos
Men in a scene: structure and parataxis
Upon this aryballos two figures, armed and male, appear with a horse-man and an artifact with birds. Males are the dominant human figure form painted upon pots of this time. Of 360 human or part-human figures illustrated on the other pots only six are definitely female, apart from the sphinxes. Three are named goddesses upon the famous Chigi Olpe (Villa Giulia 22679; Amyx 1988: 32); the others are identified as female by the presence of breasts. One is a modelled figure applied to an oinochoe from Aetos (Robertson 1948: No. 1026,); the other two are dressed in long checked robes, and one of these carries weapons. The sphinxes, apart from three males with beards, have no sexual features.

I will propose that gender is a significant focus of imagery and its lifeworld. As the social aspect of relations between the sexes, gender refers to socially constructed notions of sexual difference, which may or may not make reference to biological difference. Above all gender is to be understood as a *relationship* between masculine, feminine and other sexual roles in society (Haraway 1991). An illustration of the pitfalls to be avoided in the interpretation of this Korinthian imagery is in order here. I have been strict in avoiding contemporary and ethnocentric recognition of sex. Thus I have not counted long robes and long hair as indicators, on their own, of female sex. Consider the usual interpretation of the scene upon an aryballos in the Louvre (CA 617; Amyx 1988: 23) – the 'rape' or 'abduction' of Helen (Johansen 1923: 143–4, after Blinkenberg 1898) (Fig. 3.2). A robed figure at the centre of the main frieze is considered to be Helen, because of robe, hair (?), and the desire to make sense via mythological attribution. The face of the figure has lost some coloured slip, but close examination reveals the same line of incision used upon the other male figures to indicate a beard. A bearded Helen may be acceptable, but I suggest that the figure should be accepted as male. Consider also the passage of Xenophanes (West 3, quoted on p. 143) which criticises the aristocracy of Kolophon

Figure 3.1 Aryballos Boston 95.12 (Fig. 1.1). Detail: main frieze.

for their rich robes, long hair and perfume. This all invalidates the mythological attribution; another sense to the scene will become clear as I pursue this interpretive dialogue.

This aryballos of Figures 1.1 and 3.1 is of earlier date. The variety of types of human figure decreases as three-quarters of all later figures are either fighting armoured soldiers (hoplites), riders, or sphinxes (these amounting to about one quarter upon earlier pots). There is discard and invention of new figure types too: there are only seventeen types of figure (out of forty-six in all) which are found in both earlier and later scenes.

Here the centaur is not so much fighting the swordsman as standing in antithesis: the postures mirror each other. In spite of all the discussion of mythical subject matter for bibliography see Amyx 1988: 23) it is not really feasible to describe the whole scene as a particular narrative, other than in the most general sense of an illustration of a conflict by a tripod with attendant birds of prey and a mobile naked swordsman. The geometric devices give some clues as to the structure of the scene. The antithetical pair of centaur and warrior is surrounded by ten of the fourteen ornaments. One hook on each side of the staff for the human elements opposed; a double hook for the double-bodied monster; his split marked by the lozenge bar between the front pair of legs. The other swordsman has a hook above, as does the artifact (of human origin?). The birds of prey have their spiralled swastikas. Hence connections are suggested between the human elements (hooks), in contrast to the antithesis of man and monster; the birds have a separate association.

Many scenes on earlier pots are as fluid and indeterminate in their references, antitheses, juxtapositions and sequences of figures, animals and other devices. The majority are *paratactic* sequences, that is without clear connection between the component elements of human figure, animal, floral or geometric devices. I do not define parataxis in an absolute way. The term is used here *comparatively* to mark scenes which have fewer syntactic or narrative links than others. To define parataxis as the absolute absence of syntax brings the problem of having to assert the thoughts and perceptions of contemporary potters and viewers now dead, to assert that they perceived no connection within scenes. Of course what appears as *absolute*

Figure 3.2 The mark of gender? A frieze from an aryballos in the Louvre (CA 617) claimed to show the abduction of Helen. The figured frieze upon an aryballos in Oxford (Ashmolean 505/G 146), said to be from Thebes; the long-haired figure in checked robe in the centre of the scene has been thought to be Athena.

parataxis to an archaeologist now, may have appeared as fully syntactic and narrative then.

Consider Figure 3.3. The parataxis poses questions. In contrast, more scenes involving people on later pots are immediately comprehensible or thematic, as a battle between soldiers, hunt, race or procession (Table 2.3, p. 52). Nearly three-quarters (forty-seven out of sixty-five) of my immediate reactions to the later figured friezes were of recognition of narrative or syntactic themes. There are also clear examples of illustration of myth (for example, Bellerophon and the Chimaira (Boston 95.10; Amyx 1988: 37; Fig. 2.4)).

There is a contrast, often invoked in interpretation, between non-sense and sense or meaning, between design simply decorative and design pregnant with (mythological) meaning. Much classical iconology has searched for mythological and other meanings behind figured representations, relegating imagery which does not carry such meaning to an order of the decorative. I will consider this distinction again below, but here comment that the indeterminate itself may also *mean*. Fluidity and indeterminacy may tie a scene to a collective assemblage (posing questions of reference and connection). Parataxis, as I have thus defined it here, prevents the

Figure 3.3 Parataxis and clues to an assemblage: an aryballos in the British Museum (1869.12–15.1). I propose that, in contrast to other more 'narrative' or thematic scenes (for example the battle scenes found upon various pots, Table 2.3), this is a scene marked by parataxis. The use of geometric and floral designs breaks any strong syntactic or narrative links between the juxtaposed elements. Left is the collocation or sequence of floral, bird, soldier, rider, bird, dog/lion, deer. Progression from human to the animal *via* the bird is suggested, as perhaps are bird–flower connections (the two birds occur with the two floral elements in the main frieze, as in the shoulder frieze).

picture from falling under a rule or relation of signification and a subject. Centaur and warrior: birds and artifact: nudity and swordsman. These can be recognised; but there is much more which need not simply signify a 'subject'. I will explore this idea.

Tripods and cauldrons, stands and bowls, through heads and flora
The object in front of the centaur and behind the swordsman is a stand, ceramic most probably, for a *lebes* or *dinos*, bowls for mixing wine, and appropriate to the (aristocratic) symposion, drinking party. Amyx (1988: 19, after Cook 1972: 48) thinks that a bowl is seated upon the stand and is pictured from above. Such artifacts have been found; there is a stand and *dinos* in my sample, from Aetos (Robertson 1948, Nos. 225, 804). A series in Attika have elaborate floral and bird attachments to the rim (Hampe 1960: Figs. 30–2, Pls. 6 and 7). A Kretan example with figured painting was found in the cemetery at Arkades (illustrated by Hampe 1969, Pls. 13, 14, 15) and there is one from Gortyn (*ibid*: Pl. 18). They are analogous to the bronze cauldrons and bowls set upon tripods or conical stands. These have a known lineage reaching back to Mycenaean times (Benton 1935; Coldstream 1977: 334p8, Hampe and Simon 1981: 111f; Herrmann 1966; Maass 1978, 1981; Rolley 1977; Schweitzer 1971: Chapter 7). The variety with conical stands were eastern-derived. They sometimes had griffon, siren, or animal attachments, often protomes, on the rims, or large annular handles (Bouzek 1967; Herrmann 1979; Muscarella 1992; also, for Italy, Strøm 1971: 154, 157). Many have been found dedicated in the sanctuaries of Olympia and Delphi, and also on Ithaka. An inscription upon an example from Delphi confirms they were prizes in the games (Rolley 1977: No. 267) – an aristocratic reference again.

Six earlier pots show tripods or bowl-stands; Table 3.1 lists all the occurrences, with associations. Apart from the swords, weaponry and armour of soldiers, and the bridles of horses (recall Pindar's reference to Korinthian horse bits: *Olympian* 13), these are the only artifacts depicted in the figured scenes of Korinthian pottery. They are thus marked out as special. Their dedication in sanctuaries and their award as prizes at the games also mark them out as special artifacts. The Greek and generic term for them is *agalmata* – artifacts with value fit for a hero or god, mediating mortality and divinity (Gernet 1981).

The seated birds upon this aryballos do not appear to be attachments to the *dinos*, but rather live birds of prey resting upon the artifact. Other pots do show bird or avian protome attachments. Of seven sorts of tripods or stands, five are associated in some way with birds (Table 3.1).

On a pyxis from the sanctuary of Artemis Orthia at Sparta (Johansen 1923, No. 19, Pl. 24.3; Fig. 3.4) an object in an animal scene appears to be a stand, but instead of pot and protomes there emerge two plant-like growths (see Robertson 1948: 48–9). Three of these stands are associated with 'exotic' (that is, eastern-derived) floral ornament. Free-standing in the friezes, the latter are very stylised (lotus, palmette and tree-like derivations) and contribute to paratactic sequences, that is, again, sequences of (juxtaposed) items which seem to have little syntactic or narrative connection (see Figure 3.6 for all free-standing floral designs in the sample). Of the

Table 3.1. *Tripods, stands, heads and the floral: some associations in a field of the special found in earlier friezes. Listed are nineteen scenes and the different elements they contain.*

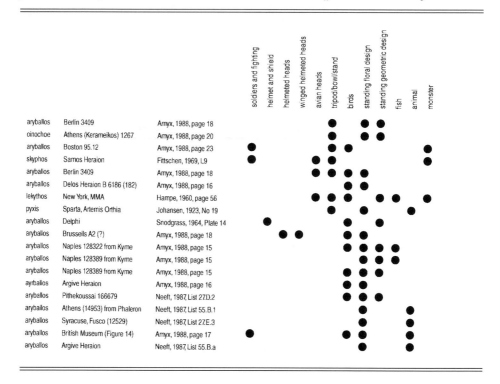

			soldiers and fighting	helmet and shield	helmeted heads	winged helmeted heads	avian heads	tripod/bowl/stand	birds	standing floral design	standing geometric design	fish	animal	monster
arybalos	Berlin 3409	Amyx, 1988, page 18						●		●	●			
oinochoe	Athens (Kerameikos) 1267	Amyx, 1988, page 20						●		●	●			
arybalos	Boston 95.12	Amyx, 1988, page 23	●					●	●				●	
skyphos	Samos Heraion	Fittschen, 1969, L9	●				●	●					●	
arybalos	Berlin 3409	Amyx, 1988, page 18	●					●	●	●				
arybalos	Delos Heraion B 6186 (182)	Amyx, 1988, page 16						●	●	●				
lekythos	New York, MMA	Hampe, 1960, page 56				●	●	●	●	●				●
pyxis	Sparta, Artemis Orthia	Johansen, 1923, No 19						●			●			
arybalos	Delphi	Snodgrass, 1964, Plate 14		●				●		●				
arybalos	Brussells A2 (?)	Amyx, 1988, page 18			●	●								
arybalos	Naples 128322 from Kyme	Amyx, 1988, page 15						●		●	●			
arybalos	Naples 128389 from Kyme	Amyx, 1988, page 15						●		●	●			
arybalos	Naples 128389 from Kyme	Amyx, 1988, page 15						●		●				
ayrballos	Argive Heraion	Amyx, 1988, page 16						●		●				
arybalos	Pithekoussai 166679	Neeft, 1987, List 27.D.2						●	●	●				
arybalos	Athens (14953) from Phaleron	Neeft, 1987, List 55.B.1								●		●		
arybalos	Syracuse, Fusco (12529)	Neeft, 1987, List 27.E.3								●			●	
arybalos	British Museum (Figure 14)	Amyx, 1988, page 17	●						●	●			●	
arybalos	Argive Heraion	Neeft, 1987, List 55.B.a								●			●	

eight examples of flora in the sample which do not occur on their own, five are associated with birds (Table 3.1).

Benton (1953: 331) makes the analogy between bird protome friezes and griffon or avian protomes upon cauldrons or bowls. Avian heads or protomes appear in line of repetition on six pots (like birds lined on many earlier and contemporary 'sub-geometric' vessels (Neeft 1975)). On the shoulder of another aryballos from Pithekoussai (Lacco Ameno 168268; Neeft 1987: 33.A.1) freely drawn designs look like bird protomes crossed with triangular stands (Fig. 3.4: compare with the protomes upon the two pots from Naples, also illustrated, and the tripod stands there and in Figure 3.5). The floral ornaments on an aryballos in the British Museum (1969.12–15.1; Fig. 3.3) again almost look like stands.

The similarity between protome, stand and (free-standing) floral is not simply a general impression. They have graphical schemata in common: (outlined) triangle (filled and crossed) and ('S') curve (turned out or in) (Figure 3.5 to be compared with Figure 3.6). The common schemata may be argued to be a function of force of visual habit, of graphical convention adapted to represent different things, and therefore implying nothing more than *formal* association. On this formal association of schemata Gombrich refers to the 'psychological fact that designers will rather modify an existing motif than invent one from scratch' (Gombrich 1979: 210). The

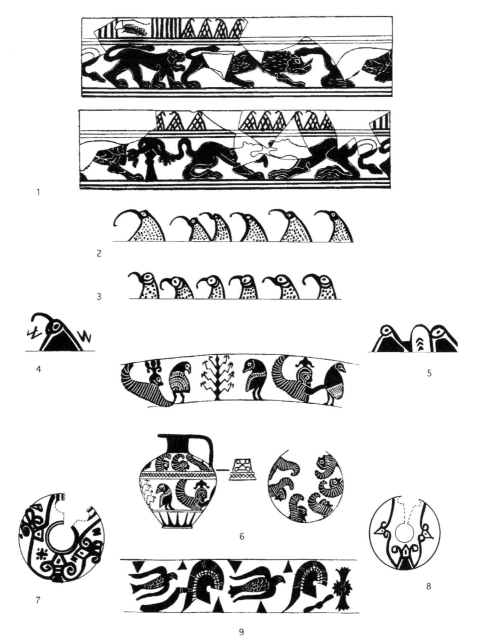

Figure 3.4 From conical stands through birds, heads and flora:
1 a pyxis from the Sanctuary of Artemis at Sparta;
2 a frieze upon an aryballos in Naples (128296), from the Kyme cemetery;
3 a frieze upon an aryballos in Munich (Antikenmuseum 6561), said to be from Italy;
4 design from an aryballos in Naples, from the Kyme cemetery;
5 design from an aryballos in Lacco Ameno (168268), from a grave at Pithekoussai (573.3);
6 an aryballos in Brussels (Cinquantenaire A2);
7 the shoulder of an aryballos in Lacco Ameno (167572), from a grave at Pithekoussai (359.4);
8 the shoulder of an aryballos in Lacco Ameno (168561), from a grave at Pithekoussai (654.3);
9 a frieze upon an aryballos in Delphi (6582), from a grave at the sanctuary.

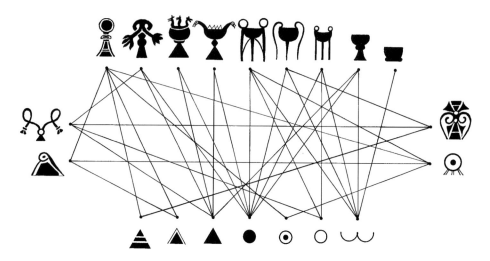

Figure 3.5 Tripods and cauldrons, stands, bowls and constituent graphical components or schemata. Here are shown the tripods and stands with cauldrons and bowls. Below are other designs which are graphically related. All are based upon inclined line and circle or curve: see also Figure 3.6.

similarity between these designs would accordingly be incidental, simply the way pot-painters learned how to draw. I hope to push the association and consider whether there is a semantic connection too.

An aryballos, probably earlier (Delphi 6582; Fig. 3.4), shows crested helmets and other objects which Snodgrass interprets as shields (Snodgrass 1964: Pl. 14). These are the only other artifacts detached from people on earlier Korinthian vessels in the sample. They too are associated with flying birds (of prey).

Helmets, heads, protomes. An aryballos in Brussels (A2; Amyx 1988: 18; Figure 3.4) provides another variation. On the shoulder is a line of winged male human protomes. Beneath is a scene of a tree-like floral flanked by three birds, two in contact with winged and helmeted protomes, crests growing from helmeted heads.

I argue that this all comprises a line or vector of connection or affiliation as follows – the tripod/stand *agalma*, special object, gift to the gods, prize in the games, convivial bowl from which may be taken wine for the (lord's) cup – bird heads (protome attachments) – birds – floral decoration – helmet heads growing crests and spread wings –. That these stands and weaponry are the only artifacts depicted, that the floral is adapted from eastern motifs (Johansen 1923: 115–28), that these are a radical break with geometric design (further details p. 160), that these are elaborated and manipulated with cauldrons and bowls growing avian heads, lotus palmette standing like tripods, that they are juxtaposed with animal creatures, people and birds marks them as different, extra-ordinary or special, I argue. That the graphical basis of tripods and free-standing floral designs is the same confirms this connection of things conceived special.

Compare also the experience, as in Geometric design (Figure 2.1), of an environment of ceramic surface which repels attention, providing only an accent of detail such as a bird (as upon the bird-cups of late Geometric and after, with a surface such

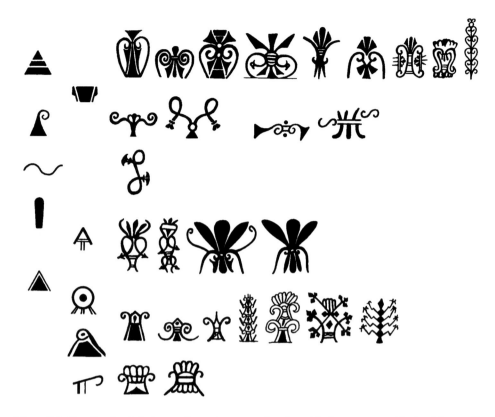

Figure 3.6 Standing floral designs and constituent or related graphical components. To the right are all the types of free-standing floral designs occurring in the sample. To the left are the geometric forms (frequently found) which are the basis of the floral: triangle (crossed, outlined and apex extended stem-like), 'S' curve and petal shape. Between is a column of rarely occurring composite forms which indicate the process of graphical composition of the floral to be elaboration of inclined line and circle or curve. The rows of floral designs are not meant as a definitive classification; there are many interconnections. The first group are developments from floral design with triangle petals and outside stems. The second row is of variations of stemmed triangles until the last on the right when the triangle is discarded. The third is of free-floating line-stems. The fourth group is of triple-petal and stemmed forms. There are then outlined triangle bases with dotted tops, stacked and stemmed. The bottom two designs are petalled bases with out-turned lines.

as this aryballos which invites scrutiny, poses questions. Earlier I claimed that the (graphical) fluidity and indeterminacy (of parataxis) tie a scene to a *collective* assemblage, posing questions of reference and connection. This is an order of the *affective* – assumption, movement, action upon, inclination, disposition. An ordinary world is not 'depicted'.

Gernet (1981) has drawn upon a seminal distinction made by Mauss (1954) between the *gift* and the *commodity*. The commodity is an artifact abstracted or alienated from its conditions of production such that it may signify something else which is external to it: money is of this order of commodities, of course. The gift, however, is inalienable; the artifact implicates its conditions of production and the people who made it; the artifact takes on the attributes of people. The gift is a *total social phenomenon*. Gernet contrasts the external value of a commodity, belonging with abstract exchangeability, with the intrinsic value of the symbolic artifact, at once the expression and guarantor of value. The inalienable artifact is *agalma*, charged with meaning, affective.

Gernet (1981: 145) proposes the distinction is appropriate to the shift to a monetary economy, with economic value eclipsing the older complex artifact. Mention may also be made here of Laum's older thesis (1924) of the sacred and cultic origins of currency – monetary forms emerging from being embedded in culture and social relations. Gernet outlines *agalmata* as religious, aristocratic and agonistic symbols, offerings, gifts and prizes, listing cups, tripods, cauldrons, weapons and horses. Media of aristocratic intercourse, these are never to be 'traded', but 'acquired' (as *ktemata*) through war, raiding, contest and hospitality – institutions of an archaic transfer of goods. *Agalmata* are aristocratic wealth, their possession implicating social power and authority, and may be, Gernet argues, associated with concepts of religious awe (*aidos*), *teras* and *pelor*, things extraordinary, mysterious, frightening, even monstrous.

The observed associations: these are not ordinary things, but a special assemblage of *agalmata*, weaponry, heads, birds, the floral and transformation, with connections beyond. Visual play or tropes; the risk of free-hand painting; and the variety and surprise of juxtaposed people, soldiers, animals, birds, the exotic: these are some creative elements of this earlier Korinthian design. They are no longer as apparent in later scenes. There are two later pots which carry depictions of tripod-stands and bowls/cauldrons: Taranto 4173 (Amyx 1988: 38; Fig. 3.19) and another aryballos from Syracuse, (*ibid.*: 44; Fig. 3.34). Both are in race scenes (presumably as prizes, symbols of contest). The only other artifact is a net in a hare hunt (depicted upon an aryballos from Nola and in the British Museum, 1856.12.26.199; Amyx 1988: 24). The character of the floral also changes, and it is to this that I now turn.

Flowers and garlands

I have mentioned how tripods and cauldrons, stands and mixing bowls, standing floral designs and bird protomes have a common graphical basis. The oblique line or inclination, the curve ('S', and tending to spiral or circle), and petal form are the basis of floral forms (and more). Operations performed upon these to generate different designs include combination, rotation, inversion and reflection: consider the different designs in Figures 3.5, 3.6, 3.9 to 3.12.

Korinthian Geometric design, as defined by Coldstream (Coldstream 1968: Chapter 3), used parallel linearity, 90°, 60° and 45° rotation (perpendiculars and diagonals, as in the meander, lozenge, cross forms, zig-zag and triangle). Snakes and wavy lines were not elaborated, and flow around a pot. 'Thapsos' graphics of the later eighth century (see also Neeft 1981: esp. Fig. 2.2) added particularly running spirals, but did not break with the linear and horizontal flow. Geometric angularity continues, but inclination (breaking with the tendency to parallel, perpendicular and 45° slope; asymptotic, tending to a limit or tangent), curve (freed from linear flow around a vessel), and petal form mark a character of the new graphics and the change from Geometric. This is illustrated and further explained in Figures 3.8 to 3.13.

Figure 3.7 A Korinthian cup from the sanctuary of Aphaia on Aegina.

Flowers are significant. Of 232 different designs (animals, people, monsters, artifacts, excluding simple lines or bands), half can be interpreted as floral or vegetal in some way (Figs. 3.5 to 3.12). Such floral or vegetal designs appear in 1,453 out of 3,293 friezes in the sample: 44 per cent of all friezes make some reference to the floral in this way. A floral theme dominates 8 per cent of all earlier, 14 per cent of later friezes (that is, these friezes consist entirely of floral elements). There are no floral antecedents in Korinthian Geometric design.

The aryballos itself may be painted as a flower. Petals are painted around the shoulder of earlier aryballoi, as are triangles. Viewed from above, this makes a flower of the aryballos, with the mouth as centre of a blossom (Fig. 3.14). There are 118 such petalled shoulders, 289 with triangles: 53 per cent of earlier pots are floral in this way. The proportion drops to 21 per cent of later pots. Many mouthplates of aryballoi are also decorated in floral fashion, with concentric petals and spikes. Plates are also decorated as flowers (from Perachora: Dunbabin *et al.* 1962: Nos. 738, 739, 741; from Aetos: Robertson 1948: Nos. 1062, 1065; Fig. 3.14).

The character of the floral changes in later designs. I have just mentioned the decline in the proportion of floral shoulders. I should also note though the marked rise in 'spiked' bases. With triangle points rising from the foot of a pot the whole aryballos becomes the blossom centre or fruit, the base forming the flower centre when the pot is viewed from below. Other major changes include a shift in preference from free-standing floral designs as major frieze elements to linked garlands and rosette forms in friezes and as minor ornament.

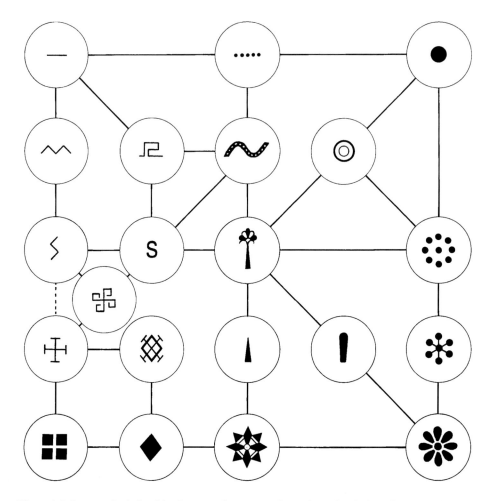

Figure 3.8 Suggested relationships between the groups of non-figurative designs. Here are shown the basic groups of non-figurative forms (indicated by a single representative) and how they may be linked via transformations and elaborations (such as deviation, division, repetition and addition). For example, the horizontal line (top left) may be altered according to 90° angularity into a zig-zag or meander, may be split into a line of dots. Separate dots may be combined into dot rosettes, and are associated with circle forms, in which they sometimes appear (top right and below). The dots of a rosette may be joined by lines; rosettes may be made with petal forms (moving to bottom right).

These vectors of graphical design are the subject of Figures 3.9–3.12 which contain all the non-figurative designs encountered upon Korinthian ceramics. The principle in constructing these figures is thus one of seriation – constructing series on the basis of minimum difference between adjacent forms. Figure 3.13 suggests a simple graphical logic to the design transformations. Forms which may be described as floral (to the right here in this Figure) can be derived from inclined line and curve or circle. Geometric forms (to the left) are based upon parallel linearity and 90°, 60° and 45° rotation.

Of course, other pathways through the geometric and floral may be found, but they would need to be related to another design analytic, another way of understanding Korinthian design.

I have already traced some links within the paratactic sequences of earlier friezes, from tripods through birds, flowers and heads. The basic graphical elements of oblique inclination, curve and petal are manipulated to form a variety of 'free-standing' designs (that is they appear used as people and animal creatures) (Fig. 3.6).

Figure 3.9 Circles, rosettes, stars and their variants, vectors towards the floral, cross and lozenge.

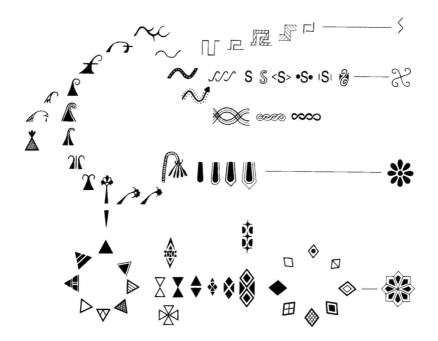

Figure 3.10 From lozenges and triangles to vegetal line and petals, vectors towards zig-zag, cross, rosettes and stars.

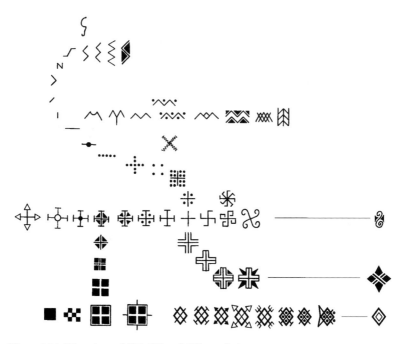

Figure 3.11 Linearity and 90°, 60° and 45° angularity.

Figure 3.12 Elaborated floral designs (garlands) of the later pots. Here are illustrated variations upon lotus and palmette, joined by lines or stems into 'garlands'. The graphical basis of all forms remains the curve and inclined line, combined in the petal form.

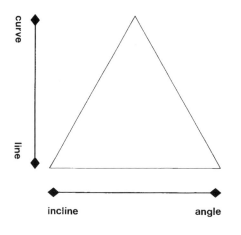

Figure 3.13 Analytic of the composition of the geometric and the floral. From the geometric to the floral, angularity (90°, 60° and 45°) deviates into inclination, and the line into the curve. The difference (between line/incline and curve/angle) is between the graph of an equation such as $x = y$ and the asymptotic curve generated by $x = 1/y$ as y increases and x approaches 0.

Figure 3.14 The aryballos as flower (smaller item in the figure) – aryballos 168021 in the museum in Lacco Ameno, from Pithekoussai grave 509, viewed from above. The plate as flower (larger item) – design from the surface of a plate found at Aetos.

The articulation of these floral designs is mainly through juxtaposition with other designs in the friezes (parataxis). In later friezes regular forms of petal and triangle (lotus and palmette) and wavy line (stem) are articulated and elaborated into floral garlands (Fig. 3.12; Johansen 1923: 115f for further descriptive analysis). Later floral decoration thus appears less generative of immediate association through paratactic juxtaposition. Garlanded floral decoration is rarely associated in the same frieze with animate or inanimate figures, though there is still the contrast between garlands and other friezes upon the same pot.

The dot rosette appears as a regular minor element in 259 later friezes (12 per cent of all friezes, 55 per cent of friezes with animals and people); dot rosette and dot flower variants account for 53 per cent of all minor or 'filling' ornament, a form of decoration which accounts for only 7 per cent of earlier design. I will return to this contrast between earlier and later design.

The association of aryballoi and floral decoration may seem a reasonable one, given aryballoi as probable perfume containers. This does not, however, explain the particulars of floral design: why should flowers transform into other things, why floral garlands and dot rosettes? And why the associations within a vocabulary of figurative design? I will need to consider these questions before returning to flowers and perfume.

Found on a third-century BC potsherd:

δεῦρύ μ᾽ ἐκ Κρήτας ἐπὶ τόνδε ναῦον
ἄγνον, ὄππαι τοι χάριεν μὲν ἄλσος
μαλίαν, βῶμοι δὲ τεθυμιάμε-
νοι λιβανώτωι,
ἐν δ᾽ ὕδωρ ψῦχρον κελάδει δι᾽ ὔσδων
μαλίνων, βρόδοισι δὲ παῖς ὁ χῶρος
ἐσκίαστ᾽, αἰθυσσομένων δὲ φύλλων
κῶμα κατέρρει,
ἐν δὲ λείμων ἱππόβοτος τέθαλεν
ἠρίνοισιν ἄνθεσιν, αἰ δ᾽ ἄηται
μέλλιχα πνέοισιν . . .
ἔνθα δὴ σὺ στέμματ᾽ ἔλοισα Κύπρι
χρυσίαισιν ἐν κυλίκεσσιν ἄβρως
ὀμμεμείχμενον θαλίαισι νέκταρ
οἰνοχόαισον

Come here to me from Crete to this holy shrine,
with its apple grove for your delight
and altars smoking with incense.
A cool stream sounds through the apple
boughs; the whole place is shaded
beneath roses; and from shimmering leaves
takes hold enchanted sleep.
Horses graze in the meadow with
spring flowers blossoming, the gentle breezes
blowing . . .
here Cypris, taking up the garlands, graciously (*habros*),
pour nectar for our wine into golden cups, nectar mingled with
our festivities
Sappho: Lobel and Page 2

Flowers and the vegetal appear infrequently in Homeric epic and early lyric metaphor and simile. Life is as the leaves of a tree (*Iliad* 6.146f); Mimnermos writes of the flowers of youth (West 1.4), a development of an Homeric formula – *hebes anthos* (for example *Iliad* 13.484; see also below on the soldier hero). The association is made also by Sappho (Lobel and Page 98). Solon has flowers of despair in social disorder (West 4.35). Flowers appear as a complement to amorous relationships (Archilochos, West 30 and 31; Alkman: 58; Sappho, Lobel and Page 96). In the *Iliad* (14.346f) the earth flowers as complement to the amorous fertility of Zeus and Hera in shimmering golden cloud. Sappho connects the Divine Muses, flowers and immortality, which are contrasted with death, loss and decay (Lobel and Page 55).

The fragments remaining of Sappho are the richest of early lyric in their references to the floral. Her poetic world is one of a refined aristocratic high-culture of religious cult-organisation, perhaps that of Aphrodite (Fränkel 1975: 175, 182, 187). Flowers and perfumes are part of the accoutrement of the girls of this environment. Associations are made between flowers, love lyric and perfume (Lobel and Page 94) and between flowers, adornment and divinity (Lobel and Page 81b). (See also Burnett 1983: Pts. 3.1, 3.2). Consider the imagery of the fragment quoted above (Lobel and Page 2). The association of divinity, erotic fertility, flowers, perfume, horses, divine food and wine drinking is one which will recur.

In two more fragments (Lobel and Page 105a and 105c) Sappho uses again the image of an apple orchard:

οἶον τὸ ψλυκύμαλον ἐρεύθεται ἄκρωι ἐπ᾽ ὕσδωι,
ἄκρον ἐπ᾽ ἀροτάτωι, λελάθοντο δὲ μαλοδρόπηες,
οὐ μὰν ἐκλελάθοντ᾽, ἀλλ᾽ οὐκ ἐδύαντ᾽ ἐπίκεσθαι.

οἶαν τὰν ὐάκινθον ἐν ὤρεσι ποίμενες ἄνδρες
πόσσι καταστείβοισι, χάμαι δέ τε πόρφυρον ἄνθος

Like the sweet apple turning red on the branch top, on the
top of the topmost branch, and the gatherers did not notice it,
rather, they did notice, but could not reach up to take it.

like the hyacinth in the hills which the shepherd people
step on, trampling into the ground the flower in its purple bloom
Sappho: Lobel and Page 105a and 105b
translation (Lattimore 1960: 42)

Here a contrast is made between the beauty of an exceptional individual and orchard workers below, analogous to a hyacinth trampled by shepherds in the hills. Sappho's (divine) world of flowers, perfumes and beauty is far removed from that of agricultural labour such as described by Hesiod.

Two scenes in the *Odyssey* confirm and extend this contrast. Sappho's pastoral evocation is close to the delights which Hermes finds on Ogygia, the island of nymph Kalypso (5.55f). Scented wood, flowered meadows, springs, vines, birds surround her cave (not a built structure). (Note too that birds are the only creatures, apart from horses, mentioned in the fragments of Sappho.) Natural (as opposed to man-made) beauty abounds. As divinity, Hermes eats and drinks fragrant ambrosia and nectar (5.93f), not the fruits of agriculture. The island is far from the home of Odysseus where await his legal wife, son and household. Kalypso's cave is a most startling description of floral idyll as her divine erotic charms keep Odysseus with her, though against his will, for seven years. According to Lilja (1972: 172–8) the erotic significance of flowers is generally clear in early Greek poetry.

Having left Ilion, Odysseus and his men came to the country of the Lotus-eaters (*Odyssey* 9.82f). Feeding on this strange and unique *anthinon eidar* (flowering food) (9.84), people do not want to return home. The contrast is drawn between the Lotus-eaters, and men, *siton edontes* (eaters of bread) (9.89), who know the way home (9.97).

Koch-Harnack (1989) has examined the contexts of lotus blossoms on Attic red and black figure vases. There are associations with lions and contests; the thunderbolt of Zeus appears in lotus form; their occurrence between animals and birds, in fights and erotic scenes suggests a multivalency centred upon might (*ibid.*: 62) and the erotic. An apotropaic function is also proposed (*ibid.*: 90).

So, in early Greek lyric poetry the following themes are associated with the floral: youth, perfume, beauty and the erotic, cult and divinity, power, wine, refinement and a world more than that of ordinary life, a contrast to labour and agriculture, bread and marriage.

The floral in Korinthian painting is a new deviation from a Geometric graphic into an expressive linearity of curve and inclination. There are associations too between flowers, birds and special objects.

Birds and lions, to sphinxes

Birds of prey appear upon this aryballos in Boston with a separate spiralled ornament and next to the *agalma*, stand and bowl. I have described the associations which run through birds, heads, floral ornament and artifacts upon earlier friezes. I turn now to ask more general questions of the birds.

Potters painted various kinds of bird. As well as flying and perched birds of prey (as on the Boston aryballos), there are short-legged birds with and without tails, cocks, water birds (long-legged, heron-like and crouching, curved-neck, swan-like) and owls, as well as protomes. The variety of types decreases between earlier and later; there are no herons or cocks in later friezes, and very few standing water birds, short-legged birds and protomes; most are swan-like water birds.

Birds are significant in this Korinthian imagery simply in terms of their numbers. Nearly half of all animate creatures on earlier friezes are birds. Of these, most (70 per cent) are water birds standing upright and repeated in rows, the linear fashion of Geometric, flowing around mainly drinking cups. Most other birds are next to floral or geometric designs; a few are next to people and artifacts, as I have already described. I have argued that reference is here made to an order which is out of the ordinary. Birds later come to crouch next to lions and sphinxes (people too); they are

Figure 3.15 Dogs hunting a bird. Design from an aryballos in Syracuse (13756) and from the Fusco cemetery, grave 378.

chased by dogs, while direct association and confrontation with other creatures is avoided.

When birds are chased by dogs in later scenes, they crouch quite static, in contrast to hares which run with the hounds; this suggests that perhaps the juxtaposition is valued above a more realistic depiction. With dogs and hares, birds are the only creatures to appear beneath racing horses. So birds go with dogs. Dogs, horses and birds are also the only candidates for domesticated animals in this imagery (see discussion p. 75). Dogs appear with hardly any other creature. They do not occur in association with people in earlier scenes and in only thirty-nine later hare hunts. Yet there are more than 2,400 dogs painted in the sample – nearly 60 per cent of all creatures; and dogs are the main domesticate. Birds do appear with people, and in this way they mediate between people and the dog, which does not belong with the men, domesticated though it may have been and however often it may have accompanied the hunter.

Birds occur mainly with lions and sphinxes (and people) in later friezes. What is to be made of this association? Of course sphinxes are composite bird, lion and person. But there is more.

Consider the devices painted upon hoplite shields (Table 3.2). If the designs upon the shields of painted hoplites are considered to indicate something of the soldier behind, then the bird, particularly the flying bird of prey, is the mirror of the hoplite infantryman. Table 3.2 also indicates that this *significatory* function of shields does not apply to earlier imagery. Birds go with the soldier. Of the different kinds of bird, birds of prey are also the type which appear with people in later scenes.

With birds, lions are an important creature simply in terms of the number that are painted. There are as many lions as people in earlier scenes, and they are the majority (apart from dogs) upon later pots. Yet there are few occasions when lions and people appear next to each other – only fourteen times in the whole pottery sample, out of 546 encounters between lions and other creatures. Lions and people do not go together in this way.

In the later imagery lions confront animals, appear with boars, bulls and goats, and are pictured with other lions. Of 257 lions, ninety-two are directly confronting another animal face-to-face. Of these, forty-three are boars and bulls, wild and violent animals, fitting opponents for lions. Boars and bulls also oppose each other. Lions are painted roaring, sometimes leaping and attacking; there are thirteen scenes of a lion attacking another animal or person. This order of violence and confrontation is one which connects with the violent and masculine world of the soldier depicted upon the pots.

Table 3.2. *Shield devices*

	earlier	later
bird of prey		22
bull's head	1	12
swan		5
lion's head		4
gorgon head		2
griffon head		2
cockerel		2
owl		1
cross and birds of prey		1
flying griffon		1
boar		1
boar's head		1
ram's head		1
hare		1
spiral		1
cross	1	
circles	1	
animal?	1	
floral	1	
Total	5	57

A link between lions and people is clear in the bodily form of the sphinx. And lions appear following sphinxes, rather than opposing them. The connection also occurs through a presence of birds, sphinxes and winged creatures in scenes with lions. It can be expressed like this: when, in a frieze which features lions, there is a human element present (soldier, person, or monstrous human), there is a 91 per cent chance that there will be a bird or winged creature next to the lion, or next but one (Tables 3.3 and 3.4). This association of lions, birds and people is not present at all in earlier scenes.

As I have written, many of the winged creatures next to lions are sphinxes, mixtures of lion, bird and human. They are the most numerous monster seen on later pots: eighty out of 116 monstrous creatures. Of these eighty, sixty-six are confronting another sphinx face-to-face. This direct confrontation often occurs over a geometric device or bird, hare or hoplite. So it might be said that the sphinxes are not so much confronting each other as focusing upon something between them. The intervening geometric element takes us back to the earlier association noted between birds and floral and geometric ornament; sphinxes are of an avian order. Indeed, just as sphinxes here do not interact with other creatures, so too most earlier birds appear only with other birds in rows. Sphinxes face over birds and hares. I have noted the association of birds, dogs and hares: is there something of the dog in the sphinx? Dogs too hardly interact with other animals.

Sphinxes confronting over something may be said to form a parenthesis. Scenes upon later pots involving lions often have a similar structure of opposition and parenthesis:

Table 3.3. *Birds and winged creatures*
near lions (in scenes with a human
element)

number of birds	occasions
0 bird	5
1 bird	16
2 birds	23
3 birds	10
4 birds	2

Table 3.4. *Birds and winged creatures*
next to lions (no human element present)

number of birds	occasions
0 birds	166
1 bird	9
2 birds	5
3 birds	0
4 birds	1

Figure 3.16 Confronting sphinxes from an olpe in Frankfurt (Museum für Vor- und Frühgeschichte *β*335).

This structure accounts for nearly half (42 per cent) of later scenes containing lions.

Birds and avian forms may be described as mediating and mixing various fields, themes or meanings: they may be both domestic and associated with wild animals; connected with floral and geometric forms (artifacts out of the ordinary); coming between people and domestic dogs; between people and lions (two orders of violent aggression). Sphinxes mix the lion, bird and person. If the similarity of lions and soldiers breeds contagion, birds overcome it. This may be summarised in Figure 3.18.

Table 3.5. *The structure of friezes containing lions*

Lion scene structure	occasions
→ ← LION A$_1$ LION	31
→ ← LION A$_1$ A$_2$ LION	3
→ ← ← ← LION A$_1$ LION BIRD/SPHINX/SIREN	10
→ ← → ← ← LION A$_1$ A$_2$ LION BIRD	3
→ ← LION A$_1$ BIRD/SPHINX LION	3
→ ← LION A$_1$ A$_2$ BIRD LION	1
→ ← → → ← ← LION A$_1$ SIREN LION LION A$_2$ BIRD LION	1

'A' indicates animal; arrows the direction faced by the creature.

Figure 3.17 A scene containing lions upon a conical oinochoe from Perachora in the National Museum, Athens.

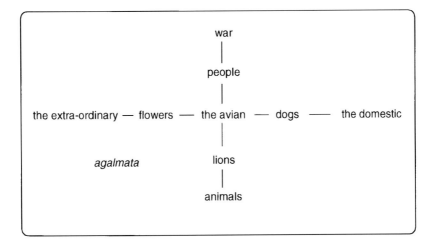

Figure 3.18 The space of the sphinx.

ὄρνιθες τίνες οἴδ᾽ Ὠκεάνω γᾶς ἀπὺ περράτων
ἦλθον πανέλοπες ποικιλόδερροι τανυσίπτεροὶ;

what are these birds that have come from Ocean's stream, from the ends of
the earth,
these wild duck, dappled necked, wide-winged?
Alkaios Lobel and Page 345

The general works of Thompson (1936) and Pollard (1977) make it clear that, for
the Greeks, there was a complex set of images and references surrounding the avian.
Birds variously were conceived as having magical powers and medicinal value; deities
took the form of birds, and human metamorphosis too was often into bird-form.
They were kept as pets, and given as gifts between lovers (Pollard 1977: 139–40). Of
course, birds were also the subject of divination. Even (pseudo-)Aristotle's treatment
of birds was predominantly mythographic (*Historia Animalium*: esp. book 10).

More particularly relevant to my inquiry, because concerned with near-contem-
porary texts and sources, are Schnapp-Gourbeillon's study of animals in Homer
(1981), and Vermeule's *Aspects of Death in Early Greek Art and Poetry* (1979). Birds in
Homer are not classed with animals, are not so much 'animals' as of another order,
'other', never integrated into the world of men (Schnapp-Gourbeillon 1981: 178,
190). The epiphanies of gods occur not as animals, but exclusively as birds. Their
otherness and association with divinity makes of birds a sign of the beyond. The
appearance of a bird is never without significance; their song and flight is sign of or
from divinity, requiring interpretation, the ambiguity and mystery a function of the
distance between men and the gods (*ibid.*: 178f).

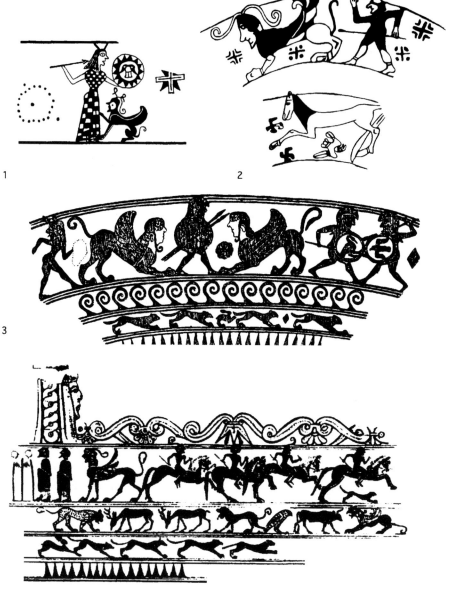

Figure 3.19 Sphinxes and people: four scenes. Sphinxes rarely interact with people upon Korinthian pots, but here are four examples:
1 a detail of a frieze upon a cup from Samos (see also Figure 3.27);
2 an aryballos in and from Syracuse, Fusco cemetery;
3 a cup (Perachora 673);
4 aryballos (Taranto 4173).
Associations are clearly and consistently with violence and soldiery, the hunting of lion, and with arbitration (of a horse race here; note also the judgement of the goddesses by Alexander upon the Chigi Olpe. Perachora 673 appears to be either a hunt or a herding of sphinxes, a taming of wild sphinxes – an ambiguity of the wild and the domestic? Upon the Chigi Olpe a double sphinx comes in the midst of a scene of male activities: hunting and arbitration or judgement, and the procession, display or racing of horses.

ὁ δέ θ᾽ αἵματι γαῖαν ἐρεύθων
πύθεται, οἰωνοὶ δὲ περὶ πλέες ἠὲ γύναικες

he rots away staining the earth with his blood
and there are more birds swarming around him than women.
Iliad 11.394–5

Dogs do hunt with men and are therefore, with the horse, associated with the heroic hunter (Schnapp-Gourbeillon 1981: 164); but for the most part dogs are below the level of the human, and to compare someone to a dog is an insult. Though domesticated, dogs eat dead heroes (*ibid.*: 168). Birds too eat the dead, cleansing carrion: 'on you the dogs and the vultures shall feed and foully rip you' (*Iliad* 22.335–6; the *Iliad* opens with such a scene, 1.4–5; see also 24.409f). This disequilibrium between domestication and feeding upon men places dogs, like birds, between order and disorder (Schnapp-Gourbeillon 1981: 168–9). Vermeule connects this cleansing function, eating, with burial and sacrifice. 'The gods oversee both sacrifice and burial, which are both acknowledgements of order and responsibility' (Vermeule 1979: 109). Burial and sacrifice are ways of avoiding pollution, as is the scavenging of dogs and birds. So in keeping order in this way, birds and dogs are allies of the gods.

οἱ δ᾽ ἐπὶ γαίῃ
κείατο, ψύπεσσιν πολὺ φίλτεροι ἢ ἀλόχοισιν.

they lay on the earth, much more beloved of vultures than those with whom they shared their beds.
Iliad 11.161–2

A further metaphor is of eating and sex. The dead hero in Homer is like a female 'loved' by attentive animals, dogs and birds (Vermeule 1979: 235, n. 24); and so too, when the city falls, will the hero's wife and children be in the same position. Birds and dogs go with eating, sex and death.

More generally it can be noted that culinary codes have been a favourite topic of structuralist analysis of ancient myth, interpreted as basic principles of cultural organisation (see for example Detienne 1977; Detienne and Vernant 1989; Mason 1987; Vidal-Naquet 1981b).

Vernant (1991b: 123–5) adds further connections to dogs, birds, eating, sex and death: barking, horses, snakes and the female Gorgo. Vermeule completes her assemblage with the sphinx: 'a waiting sphinx, a dog-bird or lion-bird of a kind, had been involved in such deaths since late Mycenaean times' (Vermeule 1979: 105). The sphinx was described as *kuon* (dog) (Sophokles, *Oidipous Tyrannos* 391; Aiskhylos fr 236 N2). In Hesiod the Sphinx's half-brother is Kerberos the dog (*Theogony* 311). Sphinxes do appear in late Mycenaean funerary scenes and were used as grave-markers in the sixth century (Vermeule 1979: 68–9). Less secure an association is the identification of the sphinx with *keres*, Homeric death daimones (in Aiskhylos the Sphinx is called *harpaxandra Ker*, (Ker, ravisher of men): *Seven against Thebes* 777).

From the end of the sixth century, sphinxes are shown carrying off young men (for example Boardman 1968: Chapter 7, esp. 68). As Vermeule picturesquely describes the sphinx: 'she combines the clawed body of a man-eater with the wings of a raptor and a face made for love, and clumsy man who prides himself on his intelligence is likely to end up eaten in her cave, a bordello full of bones, and a cavernous passage to other places' (Vermeule 1979: 171).

> λυσιμελεῖ τε πόσωι, τακεπώτερα
> δ' ὕπνω καὶ σανάτω ποτιδέρκεται·

and with limb-loosening desire she has a look
more dissolvant than sleep or death
Alkman Davies 3.61–2

Vernant (1991c) has elaborated upon this association in Greek literature of death and the female, an exchange between *eros* and *thanatos* which dates back beyond Hesiod, who had woman and death created together. 'In its fearful aspect, as a power of terror expressing the unspeakable and unthinkable – that which is radically 'other' – death is a feminine figure who takes on its horror' (*ibid*.: 95), as Gorgo or Ker. But death may also appear as beautiful woman, sweetly deceitful, as sphinx or siren or harpy, albeit with the claws of a wild beast. In this connection, and with reference also to floral pastoral idyll, I mention Vernant's observations (*ibid*.: 107) of the parallels between Kalypso's island and that of the Sirens. A flowering meadow encircles the island of the Sirens (*Odyssey* 12.158) who sing to seduce and destroy passers-by on rocky reefs. Kalypso too sings seductive songs in her pastoral idyll (*Odyssey* 1.56–7; 5.61), offering Odysseus escape from death (5.136, 209 and elsewhere), while he longs to die (1.59).

Faces, heads, and the look of the panther
Lions may not appear with people very often, but theirs is a similar aggressive environment. And simply in terms of numbers, lions are a significant character or design feature.

> δὴ τότε μιν τρὶς τόσσον ἕλεν μένος, ὥς τε λέοντα,

then the rage tripled took hold of him, as of a lion.
Iliad 5.136
(see also Tyrtaios West 13)

In terms of animal metaphor and simile, the lion is the most important creature of the *Iliad*. The animal incarnates, displays and signifies the qualities and values of the hero: *menos* and *alke* (Schnapp-Gourbeillon 1981: 40f). The lion is like the hero, indifferent, autonomous, provocative. Solitary hunter, the lion is opposed to domestic animals and those who tend them, shepherds and peasants. The lion consumes *krea*, the word used for meat obtained after sacrifice (*ibid*.: 56); this consumption implies the act of sacrifice (*ibid*.: 151). And it is the mark of prosperity and the hero to eat meat. So the lion enjoys the same food and the same pleasures of the hunt as the hero. The lion is both adversary and equal of the hero. As the hero is distinct from the mass of society, so the lion is opposed to domestic and other animals; as the hero is opposed to his enemy, so the lion is opposed to the society and world of the peasant (*ibid.*: 57). Schnapp-Gourbeillon describes the lion as 'sauvage socialisé' (*ibid.*: 63).

Heroes are not like the herd of ordinary people, they are part of a world beyond, or rather liminal characters, often in contact with divinity (*ibid.*: 197; see also Nagy 1979). So too, for Hesiod at least (*Theogony* 327–32), lions were creatures of myth; lions were no longer to be seen wandering the mountains of Greece. They were exotic creatures of eastern sculpture and painting (Payne (1931: 68f) identifies the schema behind the Korinthian lion as Hittite, later Assyrian).

Animals, as those upon the shoulder of the Boston aryballos with which I began, are drawn in profile, and so they run, step, graze or leap in lines which flow around the pots. Interruptions to the linear flow come with change of direction and with floral and geometric devices which provide punctuation. Both of these may attract attention, but the friezes keep to a world of their own: the animals and people follow or look at each other, or act upon one another, punctuated by lozenges and flowers.

However, the lion looks out from the friezes. The only animal drawn full-face is the lion. There are thirty-six big cats which look out from the friezes (an eighth of all lions and felines). They are conventionally called panthers: frontal felines are labelled *pardalis* on an Attic cup in Boston (61.103; Amyx 1988: 663 for discussion). Some frontal felines in this sample are spotted (for example a lekythos from Perachora; Amyx 1988: 30). The only other confrontation with a face is through the heads modelled upon the top of four aryballoi (Taranto 4173; *ibid.*: 38; the Macmillan aryballos in the British Museum, *ibid.*: 31; Berlin Pergamonmuseum 3773, *ibid.*: 32; Louvre CA 931, *ibid.*: 38), gorgon-heads painted upon a shield and below an aryballos handle (the Macmillan aryballos again), and a small female figure modelled upon the outside of an oinochoe (from Aetos; Robertson 1948: No. 1026). What is the significance of these faces?

The meeting of eyes is a recognition of the other, of their similarity (the gaze returned), and their difference (separation is the condition of a returned gaze). A panther looks at the viewer of an aryballos. It is different, not a person, but through the returned gaze, it is similar. So I argue that the look of the panther draws the viewer into the scene, effects an association or identification of the viewer and the frieze, by means of the panther. In however small a way, we too are like and different to the panther or lion and its animal world, like and unlike the analogous world of the hero. The gaze returned mirror-like is also a confirmation of the self of the viewer, a self defined in terms of the world looking back (Lacan 1977 on the 'mirror-phase'). And if we might wish to belong with that world, then the eyes are those of desire, another experience of the returned gaze.

As I have described, there are images of the violent world of the hoplite, particularly in some later friezes. The returned gaze of the opponent is an experience of close battle. I will later delve into the experience of soldiery and hoplite warfare, but here mention that phalanxes joined in combat involve a particular perception of individual and group. The hoplite has to be one of a formation phalanx, moving and fighting with fellow hoplites. Individual urges and actions of the hoplite are dominated and transformed by the needs of the phalanx to keep together and push forward; the individual becomes one of the group. Anonymous within helmet and armour, the hoplite in phalanx achieves human and direct contact with the enemy through the eyes; the moment of individual contact is that of the returned gaze of the enemy over the top of shields locked with fellow hoplites.

A late eighth-century grave in Argos, excavated in 1971, contained a bronze helmet with two extra eyes embossed on the forehead (Deilaki 1973: 97–9, Pl. 95e).

Korinthian potters painted the Korinthian helmet (Figure 2.7). A new invention for hoplite warfare (Snodgrass 1964: 20–8), it gave all-round protection at the expense of hearing and visibility, not so necessary in the phalanx as in open and one-to-one free combat. The Korinthian helmet focuses battle experience even more upon the gaze, eyes cut out from sheet metal, the only mark of the person. The only mark, that is, apart from shield devices and heroic actions performed. I have already marked an animal significance of shield devices; and actions performed return us to the world of the individual hero.

'Eyes meet, and the soldier is confronted with the seducer who has tempted him so long. The enemy surfaces as a momentary apparition of the soldier's own mirror image', Theweleit writes in his discussion of the psychology of the warrior male in inter-war Germany (1989: 195). The returned gaze is also erotic. Vermeule connects the world of violence and sexuality in Homer (1979: 101f; Vernant 1991c: 99f). Girard has also presented an analysis of violence and desire in Greek literature. Violence may be rooted in a rivalry based upon opponents sharing a desire for something (Girard 1977: 145). An association between sexuality and violence also exists through their respective dual characters and through notions of exchange and sacrifice. Violence is both terrifying and seductive (*ibid.*: 151). When purified through ritual, violence expends itself upon a victim whose death provokes no reprisals, no bloodfeud. It is as in the ritual violence of sacrifice, an exchange (of a slaughtered victim) to achieve order (between mortality and divinity). Such good violence is contained and ordered; distinctions between self and other, differences within and between social groups are established and maintained. This is generative violence, directed against an other who may be a scapegoat, a surrogate victim, expelled in a return to differentiated harmony. Bad impure violence is that which results from a crisis of distinctions, as in fraternal enmity; it is a sacrificial crisis, when purity is ignored or not possible (*ibid.*: 43, 51). The dangers of sexuality are incest and seduction which confuse the distinctions and order of (legal) sexual association, involving impurity and mixture. Marriage, in contrast, is a legal exchange of women which serves the reproduction of social order.

The lions facing us may well be panthers, as I wrote above. Detienne (1979: 38f) has noted that panthers were later thought to be animals which hunt with cunning and through their scent or perfume which attracts their prey. Deceit and seduction are related. Perfumes and spices are of the order of the gods, belonging with sacrifice and so heat. As aphrodisiacs, perfumes arouse and heat the seduced, their sexuality and excess threatening the order of marriage (*ibid.*: 60f, 127f).

Figure 3.20 Design from an aryballos found in Sellada cemetery, Thera (A419).

Here then is an assemblage which moves from faciality through panthers, violence, seduction, marriage, social order and disorder, and recognition of what the viewer may be and become. What, now, of those other faces, gorgon heads?

Grimacing, human yet inhuman, the gorgoneion is a mixture, revealing the alterity of human and animal. It was associated with marginal states such as death, sleep, exertion, drinking and music (Frontisi-Ducroux 1984). Vernant (1991b), following literary references, associates gorgoneia, martial themes, horses, the brilliant gaze, death, infernal sounds, worlds beyond; Gorgo was also, of course, female. Disquieting mixture and disorder, 'the face of Gorgo is the Other, your double. It is the Strange . . . both less and more than yourself . . . It represents in its grimace the terrifying horror of a radical otherness with which you yourself will be identified as you are turned to stone' (*ibid.*: 138).

With the gorgoneion, mask of death, Vernant (*ibid.*: 130–1) connects *Praxidikai*, goddesses who appear only as heads, and who guarantee oaths and execute vengeance by incarnating fright and the terrible.

Deleuze and Guattari (1988: 168f) have made an interesting distinction between the head and the face. The head, not necessarily a face, is connected to the body, is coded by the body in that it completes the organism. In contrast, a face is when a head ceases to be part of an organic body; the face 'removes the head from the stratum of the organism, human or animal, and connects it to other strata, such as signification and subjectification' (*ibid.*: 172). Faces, or rather the process of facialisation, do away with corporeal coordinates to replace them with a system of plane and holes – the face and expression. 'The face is not universal' (*ibid.*: 176), but depends on an *abstract* system or 'machine' of screen and holes, and which signifies, goes with the idea of a subject to and behind the face, and forms a different medium of expression. In contrast, the head belongs with the body, corporeality and animality. This contrast between animal head and abstract face makes it possible for Deleuze and Guattari to write 'the inhuman in the human: that is what the face is from the start' (*ibid.*: 171). The face provides an overarching layer of identity or expression, and in so doing makes reference beyond that which is the human or animal.

I noted an association which made reference to heads and helmets with *agalmata*, birds and flowers. Strangeness and the special were suggested as connotations.

Korshak (1987) has collected and examined examples of frontal faces in archaic Attic vase painting. The subjects who gaze out from the vases are satyrs, gorgons, komasts and symposiasts, fighters defeated or dying, athletes, centaurs. All are male, female examples only occur later. Masculinity is hereby related with sexuality and animality (the satyrs), death, the body and lifestyle, through faciality. Korshak associates satyrs, gorgons and symposiasts via masks (in drama), Dionysos as patron of drama and wine, and she makes a further association between masks and helmets. In summary, these all represent 'the coming together of opposites in frontality', that is occasions 'when governance of the self is relinquished and nature takes hold' (*ibid.*: 23–4). Vernant and Frontisi-Ducroux (1983) have also noted connections between masks, the gorgoneion, Dionysos, drink and states of 'otherness', adding also references to virgin huntress Artemis and the animal world.

In sum, these faces extend the assemblage I am following. The face and gaze met break the order of human and animal, mediating and pointing beyond to identity, death and desire, states of 'otherness'. Looking at the panther draws in animality, violence and warfare. And in hoplite warfare are associated the face, the helmet, the individual in the group, an armoured individual overcoded by the phalanx-group and the system of heavy armour.

Monsters: identity, integrity, violence, dismemberment

Monsters, such as the centaur upon this aryballos, are a distinctive, though, in terms of numbers, an infrequently encountered type of creature: there is slightly better than a one in twenty chance of encountering a monster in a pottery frieze.

Including sphinxes, there are the types of monster shown in Table 3.6.

Sphinxes, griffons, lion men, centaurs and variants: monsters are formed by the incongruous assembly of animal, bird and human body parts, heads and limbs or wings. Monsters are amalgams. I point out again the association and importance of the human, feline and avian in the constitution of monsters: even when sphinxes are excluded, almost all monsters make reference to the avian or to the feline. Centaurs are the exception.

Discussion of monsters in Korinthian painting will follow, but first let me remark that this is a very particular kind of monstrosity. Monsters, belonging to the realm of horror, may be defined by their form, actions, and position *vis-à-vis* human normality and understanding. With respect to their form, monsters may be exaggerations, distortions, amalgams, be formless or look normal. They may threaten, take action against people, be friendly or indifferent. Carrol (1990) has stressed particularly the narrative structures into which monsters are incorporated. Monsters may fit normality, be counterpart or analogy, belong in the gaps or at the edge, or be utterly other/unknown or unknowable. These Korinthian amalgams appear closely related to interstitial creatures (neither one thing nor another). Monster forms which do not appear include, for example, alter egos (looking the same), formless threats, exaggerations (giants) and freaky distortions.

In the mixing-up of different parts, the monsters deny difference. And on this basis the monsters are equivalent, many variations on sphinx, siren, griffon, centaur,

Figure 3.21 Soldiers, heads and the gaze: an olpe in Hamburg (1968.49) and an aryballos in Boston (95.11). The heads of the man and the lion upon the olpe are detached from bodies and are united in juxtaposition here through faciality, a field which I have described as separate from the body and to do with signification and ultimately identity. The lion's face is like the man's face (beard and mane are drawn in the same way); lion is as man. The scene upon this aryballos encapsulates so much of the cultural assemblage that is Korinthian ceramic imagery. Armoured integral hoplite faces monsters, the disjointed unities of lion and man and bird. The soldier's shield gives his identity as bird. The lion or panther behind is with him, backing him up (it does not roar at him), and, through the gaze, the viewer is with the hoplite. So the man is both with and against lion, while his eagle identity mediates. And it is armour, shield and violence which allow him to face and be at the same time a lion–man, or eagle–man. The mediating role of the bird is very prominent and clear. The avian, in its associations, forms and placing, is that which comes between and effects transition. Transitions are between human and animal violence (the hero has to be bird to become like the lion), and also, as in the presence of the monsters, between an armoured and protected interior identity, and a fluid and animal otherness which threatens, which may thus be described as contagious. Ultimately the avian communicates between that which can be controlled and held in and that which cannot. Through violence and the avian the soldier hero approaches another and strange realm.

Table 3.6. *Monsters*

with human features	Animal forms
male protome	winged horse
winged protome	griffon (eagle-lion)
winged male, clothed	griffon protome
lion headed male	griffon-bird (griffon head, bird body)
animal bodied male	goat-bird
lion with extra male human head	lion-bird (bird body)
bird with human head, sex indeterminate	winged lion
bird with male human head	chimaira (lion-goat-snake)
sphinx, sex indeterminate	
male sphinx	
double bodied sphinx	
horse-man (centaur)	
winged centaur	

chimaira; animal, bird and person. The mixture of different parts can be taken to deny the apparent stable differences between animal and human forms.

Empedokles, thinking and writing in the early fifth century, conceived the prehistory of bodily and organic form in three phases (Kirk, Raven and Schofield 1983: 302–5). At first animals and plants were in pieces, then the parts were joined anyhow, and only in the final phase emerged the whole and 'natural' forms of animals, birds and plants. Canetti (1962: 432–3) also works with such a mythical and primitive age of fluidity and transformation, as opposed to emergent fixity. Deleuze and Guattari (1988) propose a distinction between the molecular and the molar (comparable with Canetti's distinction between pack, and mass or crowd). The form of the *molecular* is multiplicity; it is constantly becoming something else through non-genetic or non-structural transformation, affinity, contagion and infection, flowing beyond boundaries. In contrast, the *molar* is a stability of identities and forms, and involves relations of conjugality and reproductive filiation. Korinthian monsters are of the molecular, forming a (heterogeneous) assemblage – lion, bird, person, monster. Monsters, in their Korinthian variety, are different from the animals which appear clearly speciated, posed and identifiable, painted in lines.

With these distinctions (pack and crowd; molecular and molar) Canetti and Deleuze and Guattari are concerned with relationships between the individual and the group, which includes the relationship between animal identity and species or pack. For Deleuze and Guattari, 'every animal is fundamentally a band, a pack' (1988: 239). By this they mean that animals may be classified according to characteristics extracted by natural history and science, but they remain more and something else; animality is an order which cannot be wholly subsumed beneath signifying labels.

Biers has noted that Korinthian plastic vases in the form of animals and monsters (Amyx 1988: 512p33; Ducat 1963; Payne 1931: 170–80) were made by combining and recombining wheelmade body parts, handmade accoutrements, moulded head and painted decoration. He uses Amyx's phrase of 'inventive hybridisation' (1988: 661) to describe this process of assembling ready made parts (Biers 1994: 509).

I have had cause already to refer to Girard's contention (1977: 51) that violence can result from a crisis of distinction (his context is that of late archaic and classical Greek literature). A disordered loss of difference is intimately related to violence, because order and peace depend on difference: equilibrium may lead to violence in an attempt to establish a preponderance of one over another, whether it is good over evil, the hero and his enemy, or a boundary between pure and impure. As Theweleit puts it, mentioning a German military saying that war will break out when men and women become so alike that you can hardly tell them apart: 'war accompanies the disappearance of the signifier' (Theweleit 1989: 51), a state of 'becoming-animal', according to the conception of animality just described.

Upon this aryballos of Figures 1.1 and 3.1 the clothed warrior opposes a centaur and its denial of integral human form, but the centaur is part human. Horses too are, with only ten exceptions (out of ninety-four), always shown bridled and ridden or harnessed to chariots, associated with men. The centaur has something of the swordsman: both hold the staff, and the brandished staffs or weapons mirror each other. There is an ambiguity or dialectical tension in the antithesis; I have remarked already that the surrounding ornament seems to confirm this dialectic of opposition and similarity. Behind the pair is a ceramic stand, *agalma*, prize, symbol of the *agon*. If equivalence and equilibrium can lead to violence (the mobile swordsman behind), then justice may appropriately be imbalance, winners and losers, the outcome of this conflict, the artifact standing to one side – prize for the winner?

Mediation and contest: the two later scenes which feature stands, *dinoi* and kraters (Taranto 4173; Amyx 1988: 38) and from the Athenaion, Syracuse (*ibid.*: 44) are both races. Horses on one and chariots on another race towards robed figures. Are these figures judges? On one a sphinx stands in attendance. Of the ten unarmed and long robed figures in the sample, six can be interpreted as being in a position of mediation. Of these, two on earlier pots hold what may be interpreted as wreaths. The 'abduction of Helen' (Louvre CA 617; *ibid.*: 23; Fig. 3.2), mentioned earlier, can thus be interpreted as two (racing?) riders and two swordsmen (rather than Castor, Pollux, Theseus and Perithoos) separated by an arbitrator or judge, hands upraised (the figure of 'Helen'). A similar argument may be made about the scene upon the aryballos in Oxford also illustrated in Figure 3.2.

Between monsters and people are protomes or severed heads without bodies. Play on the connection or separation of head and body is brought to maximum visibility in the aryballoi (later) which have modelled human and lion heads on aryballos bodies. Instead of monstrous bodies, the lion and people heads are attached to ceramic bodies. Some of the ceramic and metal dinoi and cauldron stands grow protomes too, of avian creatures (reference again to the assemblage of human, lion, bird, monster). Mention may be made again of plastic pots in the form of creatures.

An analogy or association is implied between pots and bodies. This is already familiar to us in the way parts of pots are described – foot, shoulder, mouth etc. And here these Korinthian pots are treated in the same way. Some Geometric pots are

Figure 3.22 An aryballos with sculpted lion head from Kameiros cemetery, Rhodes.

furnished with raised *mastoi* (breasts) (DuBois 1988: 47f), and plastic vases elsewhere suggest the vase as body:

> Aux mains des potiers, le vase est comme un corps qu'ils façonnent. Notre
> vocabulaire décrit métaphoriquement l'anatomie du vase, parlant de son col,
> de sa panse, de son épaule, de son pied, ou de sa lèvre. Du même en grec
> ancienne parle-t-on de la tête d'un vase, de son visage (*prosopon*), de ses
> oreilles pour les anses. Le vase a une bouche (*stoma*), un ventre (*gaster*),
> parfois un nombril (*omphalos*). Tel Prométhée, fabriquant les premiers
> hommes avec de la glaise, les potiers ont joué de ces métaphores.
> (Bron and Lissarague 1984: 8; see also Lissarague 1990: 56–7).

Hesiod (*Works and Days* 60f; *Theogony* 572) has Hephaistos, divine artisan, create
Pandora, the first woman, out of earth and water. And, like a pot, she is decorated
and filled with qualities given by the gods. Homer also implies (*Iliad* 7.99) that men
are formed of water and earth. DuBois (1988) has made much of Hesiod's account of
the creation of Pandora in her study of the metaphors surrounding woman in Greek
iconography and literature before Plato. She suggests a metaphorical series, woman–
earth–vase/container–body, in her argument that an archaic set of images of woman
as fertile, self-productive and self-sufficient was altered to become less of an ideological threat to masculinity (*ibid.*: 46f, 57f 132f). I am not so happy with the cultural
context of the Greek from earliest times to Plato adopted by DuBois: it is too wide.
And the analogy between pot and body seems to involve more than just the female –
here, for example, there are lions and avian forms. But whether the gendered

interpretation of DuBois is accepted or not, I think it can be accepted that there is an association or play upon the analogy between ceramic and bodily form. And reference is also made to productive activity and manufacture as transformation: earth transformed into (clay) body, oil and scented flora into perfume, fruit of the vine into wine for mixing bowl. I will return to this connection.

Violence, experiences of the soldier, the animal and the body
Violence and confrontation, perhaps arbitration through conflict, is a theme of the aryballos I have been considering. Violence and competition are a significant part of the imagery, as I have indicated. 155 out of 238 human figures (65 per cent) are armed or fighting. Most of the animals are characteristically aggressive and male: lions, boars, bulls, goats, rams. Animals are hunted (twelve scenes), lions roar and attack (58 per cent of lions roar; there are thirteen scenes of a lion attacking or pulling down another creature). Goats butt each other, and boars, bulls and goats stand in opposition to lions and each other. (See below on the apparent exceptions: birds, deer and dogs). Out of 184 human figures in thirty-two scenes upon twenty-seven later pots, 102 (55 per cent) are hoplites, heavily armed with helmet, shield, spear(s), and sometimes sword and body armour. All except one are fighting or dying.

Hoplite reform? The hoplite scenes have been examined to see if they show a change of warfare suspected at this time (some time in the first half of the seventh century) (for example, Salmon 1977). War is supposed to have become more open, with a shift from aristocratic heroes fighting singly, to formations of citizens of the new polis fighting together in phalanx. This change of fighting mode is also supposed by some to be related to a change in weaponry – the development of a hoplite package of heavy body armour, helmet, distinctive large two-handled shield and stabbing spear. The supposition stems from a passage in Aristotle about the replacement of cavalry by hoplites leading to a widening of the constitution (*Politics* 4.1297b: 16–29). This is backed by comparing Geometric battle scenes with those on later pots, contrasting battle scenes in Homer with those in later literature, and speculating on the use of weaponry found after 750.

Much of the literature has debated the character of the supposed hoplite reform, and its relation with the tyrannies and social changes of the seventh century (some discussion for Korinth appears in Chapter Two). After a brief review I will side with those students of ancient war who consider less the politics and tactics and more the experiences of soldiering.

Lorimer (1947) examined particularly the poetry of Archilochos and Tyrtaios for evidence of a change to massed phalanxes based on the new armour and shield. Snodgrass, after his work on early armour and weaponry (1964), argued for a gradual change to new tactics (1965), accepting a hoplite reform, but not that this had great political consequences. For Van Wees (1994: esp. 148) these military developments were the consequence rather than the cause of political change. In contrast, I have mentioned how Andrewes (1956) explicitly associated hoplites with the political changes of tyranny (tyrants representing the interests of a non-aristocratic hoplite 'class'), a position basically followed by Salmon (1977). He has considered the emergence of the hoplite phalanx as the catalyst for political revolution: 'it turned political revolutionaries, with deeply felt grievances but little opportunity to satisfy their demands, into actual revolutionaries by giving them new military strength. The introduction of massed tactics was the catalyst in an already explosive situation' (*ibid.*: 95). Cartledge too weighed the evidence for and against a sudden change to hoplite warfare in favour of the former on the grounds that the shield is suitable only for formation fighting and could not be used in another way, as implied by Snodgrass (Cartledge 1977: 20). Both Salmon and Cartledge suggest a context of discontent for the supposed military and political changes, but Cartledge, after Snodgrass, plays down the threat of hoplites to the aristocracy (*ibid.*: 23; Snodgrass 1965: 114). The weaponry required considerable wealth; hoplites were not a poor or a middle class, though they may have defused the assumed contradiction between *arete*, the values of aristocracy, and the more recent voices of *dike* in the polis (Cartledge 1977: 23; Morris 1987: 198).

In contrast, Detienne (1968) and Vernant (1962) have associated the emergence of hoplite warfare with the *mentalités* of the polis. For them, the hoplite phalanx and citizen body were the same; the hoplite phalanx was the emergence into warfare of the new order of the polis.

Bowden (1993) reads warfare in the *Iliad* and *Odyssey* as images of the hoplite warfare of the polis, and not an individualistic heroic duelling. Such a radically different line has been taken by Latacz (1977) and Pritchett (1985) and followed by Morris (1987: 196–201). They argue that there was no hoplite reform at all, and that there was no emergence of phalanx fighting; all early Greek warfare was fought by infantry formations. 'There is no evidence whatsoever to support the theory that there was a hoplite reform' (*ibid.*: 198); 'a technical progress in arms is not synony-mous with a new battle formation, and mass fighting cannot be invoked as constitut-ing a change in social relationships' (Pritchett 1985: 44). The main points are as follows. It is argued that Homer's accounts of battles are of infantry formations, with poetic attention focused upon the *promachoi*, the front rank of noblest and best-equipped soldiers. Ritualised duels, such as might be inferred in Homer, were possible and present in all ancient warfare, and are not inconsistent with formations of infantry. Chariots in Homer were either not part of the described battle, or were an effect introduced by Homer where horses would have been used by aristocrats moving to and around the battlefield (Greenhalgh 1973: 84–95 for depictions of mounted infantry). Ahlberg's conclusions about tactics (1971: 49–54), after her study of battle scenes upon late Geometric pots, are inconclusive. However, this argument against the existence of the reform overlooks and does not explain the important questions of the apparently different *motivations* for fighting before and after the proposed reform, and also the use of *uniform* equipment for soldiers from the seventh century.

There is confusion over this politics of warfare (Van Wees 1994 for a compro-mise), but some things are clear. There were undoubted changes in weaponry from 750 – armour, the helmet and significantly the two-handled *aspis* known as the hoplite shield. It seems a reasonable point that the design of shield and helmet are particularly suited to fighting in phalanx. The helmet would not allow easy hearing and visibility, important in some kinds of open fighting. The heavy shield held close to the body by virtue of centre strap and rim grip was not very manoeuvrable, more suited to pushing and static defence than deflecting varied blows and weapons; it also guarded unnecessary space to the left of the soldier, unless there was a fellow hoplite there. These remarks take me to another aspect of warfare.

Cultures of war in epic and lyric, and the *euklees thanatos* Ceramic imagery has already led to reflection upon eyes, helmets and the identity of the soldier in a phalanx formation. I suggest a redirection of interest from tactics and their relationship to weapon forms and class politics to archaic expressions of the *experiences* of fighting and associated lifestyles. Consider first epic and lyric portrayals of the cultures of war.

Warfare is a significant theme of Homeric epic, of course, and of much early lyric. But the evidence therein of a marked change from aristocratic duels to citizens in formation is ambiguous and inconclusive. Two passages of Homer (*Iliad* 13.128–34, also 16.215–7) describe massed clashes of heavy infantry, shields locked, spears stabbing. They are the basis of the striking evocation by Tyrtaios of confrontation with the enemy in what seems to be a hoplite fight (references to shield, spear, helmet and discipline):

καὶ πόδα πὰρ ποδὶ θεὶς καὶ ἐπ' ἀσπίδος ἀσπίδ' ἐρείσας,
ἐν δὲ λόφον τε λόφωι καὶ κυνέην κυνέηι
καὶ στέρνον στέρνωι πεπλημένος ἀνδρὶ μαχέσθω . . .

let him fight toe to toe and shield against shield hard-driven
crest against crest and helmet on helmet, chest against chest.
Tyrtaios West 11.31–3

Here the possible difference between heroic duel and infantry formation is not what matters.

The battles of Homer are dominated by the figure of the hero, and I have already had something to say about him; I will expand with an account of his conceptual world. The Homeric hero is a complex and subtle figure, and I have no wish or need to be controversial in interpretation, providing only further dimensions of the assemblage I am sketching with some synoptic remarks taken particularly from a reading of Homer with Adkins (1960, 1972), Fränkel (1975), Nagy (1979) and Vernant (1991a).

The subject of epic is the deeds of men and gods (*Odyssey* 1.338). In the *Iliad* the plain of Troy is no countryside or place, but a space or setting for the doings of men and gods. Physical features are lacking, except when needed as props, as are the seasons absent. There are no limits of time and space upon the action; nothing mechanical or casual happens; the focus is upon the unusual, and all seems suppressed except for persons, personal effects and personalised powers. The masses are in the background (for example, *Iliad* 17.370–5); the hero shines forth:

ἔνθ' αὖ Τυδεΐδῃ Διομήδεϊ Παλλὰς Ἀθήνη
δῶκε μένος καὶ θάρσος, ἵν' ἔκδηλος μετὰ πᾶσιν
Ἀργείοισι γένοιτο ἰδὲ κλέος ἐσθλὸν ἄροιτο·
δαῖέ οἱ ἐκ κόρυθός τε καὶ ἀσπίδος ἀκάματον πῦρ,
ἀστέρ' ὀπωρινῷ ἐναλίγκιον, ὅς τε μάλιστα
λαμπρὸν ταμφαίνῃσι λελουμένος Ὠκεανοῖο·

There to Tydeus' son Diomedes Pallas Athena
granted strength (*menos*) and daring (*tharsos*), that he might be conspicuous
among all the Argives and win the glory of valour (*kleos*).
She made weariless fire blaze from his shield and helmet
like that star of the waning summer who beyond all stars
rises bathed in the ocean stream to glitter in brilliance (*lampros*).
(*Iliad* 5.1–6, 136–8; see also, for example, 11.172f and 11.547f)

Here is romantic admiration of the awe-inspiring individual, the leader like a lion before sheep, champion apart from the others. The hero is an *agathos*, head of his autonomous household or *oikos*. Associated are *arete* (position, wealth, excellence and the privilege of leisure) and *time* (honour, compensation and wealth owing to position, and the possessions owned). A primary motivation of the *agathos* is to acquire and to hold onto *time*, or *philoi*, those things and persons, dear and cherished, upon which the *agathos* depended.

Γλαῦκε, τίη δὴ νῶϊ τετιμήμεσθα μάλιστα
ἕδρῃ τε κρέασίν τε ἰδὲ πλείοις δεπάεσσιν
ἐν Λυκίῃ, πάντες δὲ θεοὺς ὣς εἰσορόωσι,
καὶ τέμενος νεμόμεσθα μέγα Ξάνθοιο παρ' ὄχθας,
καλὸν φυταλιῆς καὶ ἀρούρης πυροφόροιο;
τῷ νῦν χρὴ Λυκίοισι μέτα πρώτοισιν ἐόντας
ἑστάμεν ἠδὲ μάχης καυστείρης ἀντιβολῆσαι,
ὄφρα τις ὧδ' εἴπῃ Λυκίων πύκα θωρηκτάων·
οὐ μὰν ἀκληεῖς Λυκίην κάτα κοιρανέουσιν
ἡμέτεροι βασιλῆες, ἔδουσί τε πίονα μῆλα
οἶνόν τῳ ἔξαιτον μελιηδέα· ἀλλ' ἄρα καὶ ἲς
ἐσθλή, ἐπεὶ Λυκίοισι μέτα πρώτοισι μάχονται·

Glaukos, why is it you and I are honoured before others with
pride of place, the choice meats and the filled wine-cups
of Lykia, and all men look upon us as if we were immortals? . . .
Therefore it is our duty in the forefront of the Lykians
to take our stand, and bear our part of the blazing of battle,
so that a man of the close-armoured Lykians may say of us:
'Indeed, these are no ignoble (*akleos*) men who are lords of Lykia,

these kings of ours . . . since indeed there is strength
of valour in them, since they fight in the forefront of the Lykians'
(*Iliad* 12.310–21)

The god-like *agathos* owed his position and its accoutrement to prowess in battle and this meant that success mattered – action not intention: good intentions matter not to the dead soldier. The compensation for the risk of the front line was *kudos*, success and its glory, the prestige and authority of the victor, and *kleos*, fame. This makes the culture of the hero a public one of shame and results, not inward intention and guilt. The Homeric conception of man is one where man and action are identical, and there are no hidden depths to the person; the hero is what others say of him. With no boundaries between feeling and corporeal existence and action, 'he does not confront an outside world with a different inner selfhood, but is interpenetrated by the whole, just as he on his part by his action and indeed by his suffering penetrates the whole event . . . Even what a man does to others is part of himself' (Fränkel 1975: 80, 85).

There is clearly an enjoyment of physical pleasures in the hero – food, wine, sex, sleep and festivity, even melancholy (*Iliad* 13.636–9; *Odyssey* 4.102–3). But in such an external selfhood the meaning of the act, indeed existence, lies in death and its confrontation. When fame and existence depend upon being talked about (and having deeds done sung in poetry), real death is silence, obscurity and amnesia. So the hero risks his life in the front ranks; 'life for him has no other horizon than death in combat . . . In a beautiful death, excellence no longer has to be measured indefinitely against others and keep proving itself in confrontation; it is realised at one stroke and forever in the exploit that puts an end to the life of the hero' (Vernant 1991d: 85). And the heroes in Homer do not have lingering deaths.

Vernant (1991a) establishes links between excellence achieved, a beautiful death and imperishable glory through the song which remembers and celebrates the death, in a sort of collective memory. The beautiful death is also an escape from the death associated with ageing. Old age, evil and death are contrasted by Mimnermos with love and pleasure, the 'flowers of youth' (West 1) (mentioned above in discussion of flowers see p. 89). Ageing only brings decay, a loss of the *kratos* or power that allows the hero to dominate an opponent, misery and an ignoble death. So at the moment of *euklees thanatos*, glorious death, the hero guarantees his immortal and heroic youth. The *hebes anthos*, flower of youth, is not so much a chronological age, but an attribute of the glorious death; the hero's youth, *hebe*, goes with his *aristeia*, and an heroic death is always youthful.

αἰσχρὸν γὰρ δὴ τοῦτο, μετὰ προμάχοισι πεσόντα
κεῖσθαι πρόσθε νέων ἄνδρα παλαιότερον,
ἤδη λευκὸν ἔχοντα κάρη πολιόν τε γένειον,
θυμὸν ἀποπνείοντ' ἄλκιμον ἐν κονίηι,
αἱματόεντ' αἰδοῖα φίλαις ἐν χερσὶν ἔχοντα –
αἰσχρὰ τά γ' ὀφθαλμοῖς καὶ νεμεσητὸν ἰδεῖν,

καὶ χρόα γυμνωθέντα· νέοισι δὲ πάντ᾽ ἐπέοικ᾽ εν,
ὄφρ᾽ ἐρατῆς ἥβης ἀγλαὸν ἄνθος ἔχηι,
ἀνδράσι μὲν θητὸς ἰδεῖν, ἐρατὸς δὲ γυναιξὶ
ζωὸς ἐών, καλὸς δ᾽ ἐν προμάχοισι πεσών.

it is disgraceful this, an older man falling
in the front line while the young hold back,
his head already white, grizzled beard,
gasping out his valiant breath in the dust,
his bloodied genitals in hand –
this is shameful (*aischra*) to the eyes, scandalous to see,
his skin stripped bare. But for the young man,
still in the lovely flower of youth (*hebes anthos*), it is all brilliant,
alive he draws men's eyes and women's hearts,
beautiful felled in the front line.
Tyrtaios West 10.21–30
(see also *Iliad* 22.71–6)

Here Tyrtaios and Homer both describe the awful and, for Tyrtaios, disgraceful (*aischra*) death of an old man; yet this would have been glorious and beautiful for a young man. There is an aesthetics to the death of the hero (Vernant 1991a; Loraux 1975, 1986; Dawson 1966, on the poem of Tyrtaios).

The beautiful death, as well as being contrasted with that of the old man, is marred by various things (Vernant 1991a: 67f). *Aikia* (disgrace) – dirt, disfigurement, dismemberment, the dogs, birds and fish, worms and rot which spoil the corpse, deprive it of its wholeness, integrity, beauty. These all threaten the proper securing of the beautiful death, the purifying funeral pyre which sends the *hebes anthos* off to eternity, retaining the corpse's unity and beauty, and the burial mound raised in his memory.

The lyric elegy of Kallinos and Tyrtaios moulds the old epic vocabulary and world with expression of the experiences of soldiery and with a new outlook of admonition, instruction and exhortation to fight as the heroes did of old. The call is for men to fight bravely. The emphasis on the glory and honour of war and death, in contrast to shame and the misery of disrespect, on the appearance of male performance in war in the light of opinion, is Homeric. But Tyrtaios (West 10, 11 and 12) and Kallinos (West 1) also are the first to articulate a new aspect to the ethic of *arete*: excellence lying in courage in the service of the country, city and whole community, an appeal absent from Homer (see Jaeger 1966; Murray 1993: 134–5; Greenhalgh 1972, on Homer and patriotism).

οὐ γὰρ ἀνὴρ ἀγαθὸς γίνεται ἐν πολέμωι
εἰ μὴ τετλαίη μὲν ὁρῶν φόνον αἱματόεντα,
καὶ δηίων ὀρέγοιτ᾽ ἐγγύθεν ἱστάμενος.
ἥδ᾽ ἀρετή, τόδ᾽ ἄεθλον ἐν ἀνθρώποισιν ἄριστον
κάλλιστόν τε φέρειν γίνεται ἀνδρὶ νέωι.

ξυνὸν δ᾽ ἐσθλὸν τοῦτο πόληΐ τε παντί τε δήμωι,
ὅστις ἀνὴρ διαβὰς ἐν προμάχοισι μένηι
νωλεμέως, αἰσχρῆς δὲ φυγῆς ἐπὶ πάγχυ λάθηται,
ψυχὴν καὶ θυμὸν τλήμονα παρθέμενος,
θαρσύνηι δ᾽ ἔπεσιν τὸν πλησίον ἄνδρα παρεστώς·
. . .
αὐτὸς δ᾽ ἐν προμάχοισι πεσὼν φίλον ὤλεσε θυμον,
ἄστύ τε καὶ λαοὺς καὶ πατέρ᾽ εὐκλεΐσας,
πολλὰ διὰ στέρνοιο καὶ ἀσπίδος ὀμφαλοέσσης
καὶ διὰ θώρηκος πρόσθεν ἐληλάμενος.
τὸν δ᾽ ὀλοφύρονται μὲν ὁμῶς νέοι ἠδὲ γέροντες,
ἀργαλέωι δὲ πόθωι πᾶσα κέκηδε πόλις

No man is of high standing in war
if he cannot stand the sight of bloodlet gore,
set blows at the enemy and stand close.
This is the highest good (*arete*), here is the noblest prize for men,
the finest for a young man to win.
And this is a common good for his city and all the people –
when a man plants his feet and stands in the front rank
relentlessly, all thought of shameful (*aischre*) flight altogether forgotten,
his spirit and bold heart laid on the line,
and with encouraging words stands by the man next to him . . .
And he loses his own dear life, falling in the front rank,
so bringing glory (*kleos*) to his city, his people and his father,
with many wounds in his chest, wounded through his bossed shield
and driven through his breastplate at the front as well.
Such a man is mourned alike by the young and the elders,
and all his city is troubled at the keen loss.
(Tyrtaios, West 12. 10–19 and 23–28)

In contrast, the lyric of Archilochos presents a frank realism before an ideal and exaggerated sense of epic honour. He is happy to throw away his shield to save his life – a usual sign of cowardice (dropping a heavy shield facilitates escape) (West 5); and the idea of posthumous glory is not in accordance with his experience:

οὔτις αἰδοῖος μετ᾽ ἀστῶν οὐδὲ περίφημος θανὼν
γίνεται· χάριν δὲ μᾶλλον τοῦ ζοοῦ διώκομεν
οἱ ζοοί, κάκιστα δ᾽ αἰει τῶι θανόντι γίνεται.

No one in this city, once he has died, is honoured and respected. Rather we living cultivate the favour of the living. It's the dead who always get the worst of things.
(West 133; see also West 11)

As Fränkel puts it: 'the fairy dream of epic is done with. For Archilochos' self-control is no longer a means of winning an imaginary final victory over all enemies; it could

Figure 3.23 A fight upon an aryballos from Perachora and in the National Museum, Athens.

only lend stability and power to resist and moderate excessive fluctuations of senti-
ment' (Fränkel 1975: 143). Archilochos was a mercenary, living and surviving
through fighting; this may account for him repeatedly asserting the reality of the
present and experience. Fighting was simply part of what Archilochos did.

Grand scenes of war: who is that man?
In contrast to the warriors here upon the Boston aryballos (Figure 3.1), hoplites are
anonymous within helmet, armour, and behind shield. The swordsman's dynamic
upon this aryballos is in his angled limbs. The hoplite's shield and spear are the focus
of his energy. Earlier scenes of conflict and battle, as well as scenes more generally,
pose more questions in the range of juxtapositions they present (Table 2.3), in the
range of situations of violence and aggression. Scenes of battle which contain hoplites
and no other pictorial elements occur only upon later pots; eight hoplites in earlier
and 108 in later scenes. These friezes focus upon violence and weaponry, particularly
shields, and upon the group: there are only nine friezes of hoplite fighting (the hoplite
appears in an average group therefore of twelve). Only the birds lined up in the old
Geometric manner, and bird protomes (human protomes on one pot: aryballos
Thera 419; Neeft 1987: 34.1), appear in groups with no other design element.

Only the hoplite shields mark difference, but one of bird and animal devices (Table
3.2). The hoplite looks like another and another. And they appear in groups, tangled
up in the fight – the hoplite battle is one of the few occasions when the pot painters
overlap figures (other times are the lion attacking or bringing down an animal, and
horse or chariot races: an association is here established). Consider also Payne's
observation of the contrast between Attic and Korinthian miniature painting (1933,
manuscript translation: 6). The Attic scene may focus interest upon a single point or
figure in a wide and otherwise empty field of vision: a star performer in an empty
stage (Payne refers to Beazley's discussion of the Phrynos cup in the British Museum: Beazley 1928: Pl. 1.1–2 and 4). In contrast, the Korinthian miniaturist fills the
scene with detail and complication, multiplying, not reducing the elements of the
design so that 'the surface seems almost to move before one's eyes, like an ant's nest

disturbed' (Payne 1933, manuscript translation: 6): all is mixed in the movement and unity of the whole.

In the tangle of fighting formation the armoured soldier's helmeted head has a closer pictorial connection to the head of his fellow hoplite than it does to his own torso or (greaved) calf: consider the depiction upon the Macmillan aryballos (Amyx 1988: 31; Fig. 3.24), with its line of helmets and crests, blazoned shields, and then legs below. I argue that this is a real and functional connection too. In the phalanx formation, bodies unite in the 'body of men' and their integration fears disruption and break-up. (Consider also the poem by Tyrtaios (West 11) quoted above, expressing the proximity of helmet and helmet, chest and chest, shield and shield, spear and spear.)

The hoplites appear anonymous. What identity does the hoplite have? And what identity in the group or phalanx, when helmet relates to helmet, and shield to shield, rather than to the soldier beneath and behind? In contrast to the rows of protomes and monsters of dismemberment and incongruous assembly, the physique of the heavy infantryman is held together and defended by the talismans of his identity – the weaponry. The hoplite's armour and shield hold him together, but he does face violence and risks death, risks bloody wounding, dismemberment and monstrous chaos. So the formation and the equipment forms new, centred bodies, and provides identity (on arms and the group in another scene of war upon a later Korinthian alabastron see Henderson 1994: 88).

What more of the identity of the soldier? Pamela Vaughn (1991) has drawn attention to the difficulty of identification after hoplite battle: facial injury across shield top was common, and bodies were bloated from being left after battle, cooked in cuirass, disfigured by the heat of Greek summer sun upon bronze armour.

Experiences of soldiering and techniques of the body

In short, anyone who paid attention to the poetry of Sparta . . . and examined the marching rhythms they used when going against the enemy to pipe accompaniment, would decide that Terpander and Pindar were quite right to associate valour with music. The former says of Sparta

> ἔνθ' αἰχμά τε νέων θάλλει καὶ Μοῦσα λίγεια
> καὶ Δίκα εὐρυάγυια, καλῶν ἐπιτάρροθος ἔργων.

> There the spear of young men blooms and flourishes and the clear-voiced Muse and Justice (*Dike*) who walks in the wide streets, that helper in fine deeds.
> Plutarch Lykourgos 21.4s; Terpander Bergk 6, Diehl 4 in Campbell 1982–93

The work of Victor Hanson and others (1990, 1991; after Keegan 1976), presenting a phenomenology of war, reminds us of the most simple fact, that archaic Greek warfare was based upon a particular conception of battle as direct and formal confrontation, face to face with long thrusting spears in a short decisive encounter, with risk of bloody wounding and death across the tops and below the rims of the

Figure 3.24 Soldiers together. A pyxis in the British Museum (1865.7–20.7). Three figures face an archer. Their identity has been suggested as a multi-bodied monstrous Geryon (Johansen, 1923, page 144, and others after him), facing archer Herakles. I suggest that there are three soldiers overlapped in formation, facing the representative of a different violence, the archer. The formation and hoplite equipment form a new centred body and provide an identity when risking death. The Macmillan aryballos in the British Museum (Amyx, 1988, page 31; photograph and permission courtesy of the British Museum).

round hoplite shield – the old man in Tyrtaios. War was not about drawn out, cowardly 'terrorism' or guerilla tactics at a distance. Risk was heightened and blood proliferated, at least in the front ranks. (Alternative experiences of war and battle are neatly summarised in Keegan 1993.) So what more was hoplite battle about? I have already discussed the aesthetics of heroic death. There was an aesthetics to the art of hoplite war.

There is the display of armour, crests and shields. Vernant (1982) has written of the ceremonial and ritualised character of early hoplite warfare (see also Connor 1988). War is not simply functional behaviour; but let me stay with experience and the body. The fighting formation moved rhythmically. Pipers accompanied phalanxes: this is known from illustration upon Korinthian pots (the Chigi Olpe, Villa Giulia 22679, Amyx 1988: 32) and an aryballos from Perachora (Figure 3.23). Henderson has commented (Henderson 1994: 109–10) on the splicing of war and dance in his reading of a Tyrrhenian neck amphora of the early–mid sixth century (see also Poursat 1968 and Spivey 1988).

The Korinthian helmet had particular effect upon the look and experience of its wearer. I have already discussed eyes and the gaze of the enemy. Consider also the body armour, again so evident in these illustrations. Muscled bronze torsos harden the hoplite against the spilling of blood and intestines, but follow the contours of the human body (however idealised). A widespread convention of Greek art is furthered when the hoplites appear naked apart from their armour and weapons. Other figures too are drawn naked. Why is this, if not because war and violence are a function of the *body* of these men, its aesthetic and politics?

Fighting in formation in this warfare required discipline, rhythmic movement, trained manipulation of weaponry – the cultivation of distinctive *techniques of the body*. This term is part of a realisation that the human form and its relationship with notions of the self is not, by virtue of its biology, a social constant (Foucault 1975, 1976; Martin, Gutman and Hutton 1988). Different social practices and ideologies constitute the body in different ways, and experiences of the body are a primary dimension of people's relationship with the social. Posture, dress, training, discipline, economies of pleasure and pain all help constitute distinctive experiential lifeworlds (meaning the social world as experienced and perceived) (for comparative source material: Crary and Kwinter 1992; Feher, Naddaff and Tazi 1989).

These techniques of the body and the bodily lifeworld of archaic violence are clear also in early lyric poetry. There is much reference to discipline and posture.

ὦ νέοι, ἀλλὰ μάχεσθε παρ' ἀλλήλοισι μένοντες

You, young men, keep together, hold the line.
Tyrtaios (West 1992) 10.15, translation (West 1993)

ἀλλ', Ἡρακλῆος γὰρ ἀνικήτου γένος ἐστέ,
θαρσεῖτ'· οὔπω Ζεὺς αὐχένα λοξὸν ἔχει·

make your hearts strong, for you are the race of the never-defeated Herakles; and Zeus does not stand with his neck held aslant.
Tyrtaios West 11.1–2

The hoplite stands upright and straight in the line. Contrast the death of a monster. Herakles shoots three-bodied Geryones in the head with an arrow:

ἐμίαινε δ'ἄρ' αἵματι πορφυρέωι
θώρακά τε καὶ βροτόεντα μέλεα
ἀπέκλινε δ' ἄρ' αὐχένα Γαρυόνας
ἐπικάρσιον, ὡς ὅκα μάκων
ἅτε καταισχύνοισ' ἀπαλλὸν δέμας
αἶψ' ἀπὸ φύλλα βαλοῖσα ν(

it stained with darkening blood
his cuirass and gory limbs.
Geryones bent his neck to one side
just as a poppy spoiling its delicate structure
suddenly lets drop its petals.
Steisichoros Davies S15ii.12–17

An image from Archilochos is another reference to neck, appearance and bearing:

. . . χαίτην ἀπ' ὤμων ἐγκυτὶ κεκαρμένος

. . . hair cut short, off the shoulder.
Archilochos West 217

Consider now early Greek sculpture: stone *kouroi* (and other figurines) (Richter 1970; Stewart 1990: 109–13, 122–6). These were dedications to divinities and are found associated with graves. The kouroi are all in stiff poses. Why? It is clear that they are the desired appearance of the ideal male. And they are naked. But there is no experiment with bodily form. This is not 'natural', not a function of 'normal artistic development'. I argue that this artistic conservatism (Snodgrass 1980a: 185) is a social requirement: contrast the radical experimentation of figures upon Korinthian pottery. There was no desire to sculpt *animated* naked males. They are made upright and hard, representing the valuation of a posture belonging with new and expressive techniques of the self and body. Simonides, has the *agathos*, the man of *arete* (virtue):

. . . χερσίν τε καὶ ποσὶ καὶ νόῳ
τετράγωνον ἄνευ ψόγου τετυμένον·

hand and foot alike, and in understanding cut foursquare, fashioned without flaw.
Page 542.1–3

Tetragonon (foursquare) is reference to *tetractys*, a Pythagorean term of excellence and justice, root of harmony and *arete* (Fränkel 1975: 276–7, 308). *Tetragonon* may also be connected to technique of manufacture. The method of sculpting kouroi is clear – separate views were sketched on the four faces of a block of stone prior to taking it down to the final form.

The relationship of kouroi to aristocratic ideologies has been well covered. Stewart associates kouroi, expensive artistic commissions, with the aristocracy and its ideals (Stewart 1986; Zinserling 1975). As grave-markers they are monuments to aristocratic virtue (*kalokagathia*) in the flower of youth (*hebes anthos*). Hurwitt puts it like this 'The kouros and kore forms were perpetuating symbols of the physical prowess, moral authority, goodness and beauty that aristocrats (naturally) considered innately aristocratic' (Hurwitt 1985: 198–9). What should be emphasised is the novelty of the *expression* of this ideal.

An aside here on another eastern, Egyptian, connection is appropriate. A few kouroi are to the same proportions as the Egyptian canon of proportions (Guralnick 1978; also Diodoros Siculus 1.98.5–9) The posture clearly owes something to Egyptian sculpture, even if the proportions do not match precisely (generally on this relationship: Hurwitt 1985: 190–9).

Further connections can be made between the anatomical detailing of kouroi and bronze armour (Kenfield 1973). Courbin noted a similar muscle schematic on the bronze cuirass found in the famous eighth-century warrior's grave at Argos as on an Argive statue signed by Polymedes at Delphi (Courbin 1957: 353, Fig. 36). Kunze's study of archaic greaves at Olympia (1991) shows clearly their artistic credentials; they are not simply functional items. The detailing of the knee joint is common to both greaves and kouroi (Snodgrass 1991).

Pots and bodies

Discipline, posture, aesthetics of war, hard and ordered physique involved working practices of sculpture and battle, and ideologies of *arete*. But what more have the pots to do with the body? The aryballoi, which carry the main elements of the figured decoration, were most probably containers for perfumed oil, anointment for the body. Most of the finds we have come from cemetery deposits (see Chapter 5), laid down with the body of the dead. And I have already mentioned the connection between ceramic form and the body, through transformation of earth and water. I have focused on the appearance of people in the figured paintings in an attempt to make sense of this scene upon an aryballos in a museum in Boston. But people are in a minority upon the pots. Let me return to more general impressions.

The scenes break down as shown in Figure 3.26.

The pie chart of Figure 3.26 covers a total of 1,219 figured friezes. There are a further 2,074 friezes decorated with flowers and geometric designs which all appear upon 1,225 pots; I have already pointed out the very frequent occurrence of the floral. Another 726 pots are decorated only with lines and one other type of ornament. In practical terms this means that there is only one chance in thirty-eight of coming across a scene containing a person. The general pictorial 'assemblage' is of ceramic surface linearly covered and ordered, with ornamental deviation from parallel, perpendicular and triangular angularity, and also animals around pots, animals which are not to do with agriculture and the domestic economy, so much as an other and wilder, even aggressive and violent field. These mingle and interact with other creatures, including people and monsters. The taciturn linearity of Korinthian

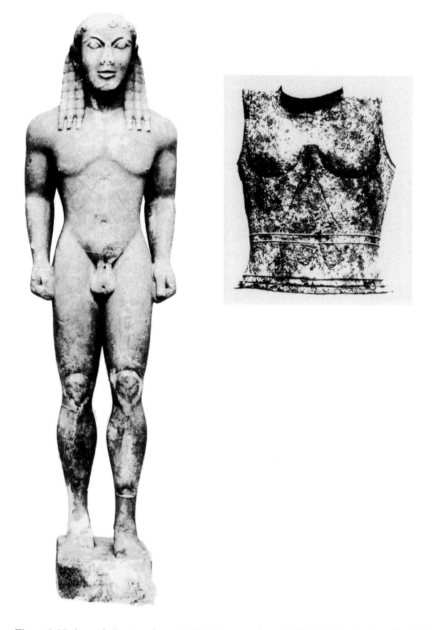

Figure 3.25 An archaic stone *kouros* in Delphi, one of a pair (Kleobis/Biton) signed by Polymedes of Argos, and a cuirass from a grave found at Argos. Note the similar rendering of the torso.

Geometric (Fig. 2.11) is opened into 'ornament' and the representation of the form of animate creatures. The animals are recognised through their bodily form, and the way this is conveyed in painting. I have already mentioned the play with body parts in creating monsters. 'Ornament', linear order, and the forms bodies take: there is nothing else, only a very few artifacts. So this Korinthian design is indeed in large part

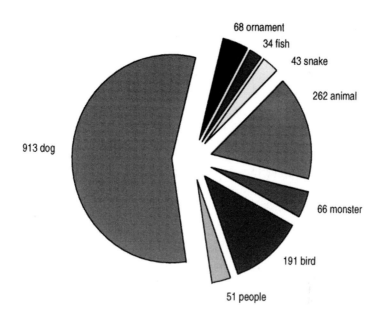

68 ornament
34 fish
43 snake
262 animal
913 dog
66 monster
191 bird
51 people

Figure 3.26 The different components of Korinthian figured friezes of the seventh century BC. Values refer to the number of friezes in which a particular figurative component occurs.

about bodily form. Here reference may be made to Schnapp's general remarks (1988) about the character of Greek art and its overriding concern with the body.

Animals such as those on the shoulder of this aryballos (Fig. 1.1) appear on the pots in great numbers and the soldier may conceive of himself as a lion, or one of the other wild creatures pictured on the pots (lions, boars, bulls, rams and stags comprise 90 per cent of animals shown on later pots). I have indicated already in considering the eyes of the panther that association between the animal and the person may occur through the viewer. There are thirty-eight friezes where people mix with animals. The juxtaposition of the two friezes upon this aryballos may suggest some analogy between animal and human worlds. There are, however, only nine cases of such a juxtaposition of a scene with men next to one with animals (dogs excluded, see p. 000). The main connection between worlds of people and animals is that both take bodily form.

Benson (1995) has argued that flowers act as metaphorical links in some figured scenes: 'the floral ornaments, in effect, function as would the word 'like' in a literary context' (*ibid.*: 163). His point is that major free-standing floral ornaments seem to occur in positions which point to connections between different elements of the designs upon the pot, basically mediating worlds of animals and men.

Creatures and men, *sauvages socialisés*

πάντα δὲ γιγνόμενος πειρήσεται, ὅσσ᾽ ἐπὶ γαῖαν
ἑρπετὰ γίγνονται καὶ ὕδωρ καὶ θεσπιδαὲς πῦρ·

> And he will make trial of you by becoming everything – all the creatures
> that move on the earth, taking the form of water and fire kindled by god.
> Odyssey 4.417–8

When held by the gods on Pharos, away in far-off Egypt, Menelaos discovered how he may escape home from Proteus, the ever-truthful Old Man of the Sea, who knows all the depths of the ocean (*Odyssey* 4.365f). But to get Proteos to speak to him, Menelaos had to be disguised as a seal and then hold onto the immortal and suffer his transformations through animality and matter:

> ἀλλ᾽ ἦ τοι πρώτιστα λέων γένετ᾽ ἠϋγένειος,
> αὐτὰρ ἔπειτα δράκων καὶ πάρδαλις ἠδὲ μέγας σῦς.
> γίγνετο δ᾽ ὑγρὸν ὕδωρ καὶ δένδρεον ὑψιπέτηλον.
>
> . . . First he turned into a great bearded lion,
> and then to a serpent, then to a leopard (*pardalis*), then to a great boar,
> and he turned into fluid water, to a tree with towering branches.
> *Odyssey* 4.456–8 Translation Lattimore

This experience of the 'form of all creatures that come forth and move on the earth' is one of fluidity and transformation as bodies change; it is a strange experience of the beyond, a divinity in Egypt. The transformation is also one that involves scent and divine perfume, for to resist the foul smell of the seal skins, Eidothea, divine daughter of Proteus, placed perfumed ambrosia, food of the gods, in each man's nostrils (*Odyssey* 4.441–446).

There is, *de facto*, the association of animal, human, avian and monstrous form made by Korinthian pot painters: it is their subject matter. However, animals and lions are of another order. Upon later pots there are scenes containing both animals and humans; however, lions, boars, bulls, goats and rams, those masculine and aggressive creatures, very rarely interact with humans. Those animal friezes which appear upon the same pots as friezes containing people are almost all domestic dogs. The dogs run and express a vital animal energy, but this is domesticated, without threat. So let it be said that animals are like, and unlike humans (the swordsman and centaur in dialectical tension upon this aryballos in Boston). Lions rage and fight like the hero, but animals are animated, complex, varied, changeable and unpredictable. This is especially true of those wild and dangerous animals which figure on the pots. Opposed to order and domestication, they are a threat to societal man of culture.

Considering the appearance of animal metaphor in Homer, Schnapp-Gourbeillon concludes (1981: 194f) that Homeric animals are not representatives of an all-powerful Nature, but are part of a cosmogony which contrasts human society with an other world of the gods. The contrast is between that which is under human control and that which is not, and animals come between. Animal analogy revolves around society: to be understandable, animals must be related to social behaviour. In discussing the animal fables of Archilochos, Fränkel argues (1975: 146) that animal natures need to be typed for simile to work. Animals *in themselves* are strange, nonsensical and irrational (*ibid.*: 200). So for a man to become an animal permits an encounter with that world beyond, of divinity (Menelaos as a seal suffering animality). To become an animal is to reject society, its norms and collectivity, and to become solitary, in intermediary spaces belonging to otherness.

The relationships I am exploring are thus as follows: between men and gods; animals as metaphorical reflections and strange wildness; between social behaviour and a world of savagery; heroic models and the monstrous; between epic and myth.

Bellerophon appears riding upon winged horse Pegasos and attacking the *chimaira* in a scene upon a Korinthian pot (Boston 95.10; Amyx 1988: 37; Fig. 2.4). The myth of the hero has cult associations with Korinth: among other things Pegasos was found drinking from Korinth's fountain of Peirene (Pindar *Olympian* 13.63–87). Homer describes the monster, lion-fronted and snake behind, a goat in the middle:

ἡ δ' ἄρ' ἔην θειον γένος, οὐδ' ἀνθρώπων

it was a thing of immortal make, not of the world of men.
Iliad 6.180

The creature belonged to the world of divinity.

I mentioned above (p. 104), in connection with monsters, the distinction made by Deleuze and Guattari between the molar and the molecular. The molecular is that which is not overlain by a dimension of signification: it is not possible to say that it *is* or *signifies* something, because the molecular is fluid and cannot be pinned down (except by a Menelaos who has become animal himself), because it is a multiplicity which is strange, always becoming something else. The molar is that which is stable, controlled and coded. So there are two ways to be like an animal. One is to imitate that animal entity which has been defined by its form, endowed with characteristics and assigned as a subject; to identify with it. The other way is to become an animal, to enter into a relationship with that other side of animality (which is part of us too, as human–animals), the realm of the molecular; it is to become savage (no orders of signs and definitions), so that it is difficult to say where animal ends and person begins; it is to encounter the monstrous, that which cannot be held still. Deleuze and Guattari (1988: 232f) thoroughly consider this distinction and give many examples of becoming animal. Some are familiar through popular literature and culture: Ahab encounters the monster Moby Dick with an irresistible desire to become whale, consummated in his death attached to the white whale's back.

Deleuze and Guattari (1988: 240–1) specify three types of animal: pets, those with personal and sentimental relationships with the human ('my' cat); then those animals with characteristics or attributes, species, classified, domesticated, tamed, understood animals. Finally there are demonic animals which go beyond singular definition, animals which are a multiplicity. The relationship with the distinctions made in Homer is, I think, clear.

The bodily form of animals and men is a subject of Korinthian drawing, but they are treated somewhat differently. There are thirty-five different types of person (from riders to robed figures), of which a good proportion are recognisable as hoplites (42 per cent); of the types remaining there is an average of four examples of each. There are 556 lions, boars, bulls, goats and rams drawn in twenty-one different poses: an average of twenty-seven cases of each animal pose. And the difference in the variability of people and animals is even greater than this indicates. Although many men are hoplites, and I have classified the rest into thirty-four categories, in fact hardly one figure is drawn like another – postures and activities differ. And whereas I have characterised the hoplite as anonymous within helmet and armour, and behind shield, they form varied battle scenes, with winners and losers, some chasing others fleeing over the dead. Other men are animated in various ways, hunting, racing, standing with others. So people are different from animals according to the way they are drawn, according to the things they do as well as the way they look. In contrast to people, six poses account for 502 animals (90 per cent of those species listed above): lions standing and roaring, 'panthers' facing, boars standing, bulls and goats 'grazing' (head more or less down). More than 2,400 dogs run around the pots. They may differ by number of legs shown and some are more carefully and skilfully drawn than others, but they are all remarkably similar.

Payne (1933 manuscript translation: 21f) made an elegant and sharp observation of the character of this Korinthian drawing of animals. They were drawn according to a system of principles (schemes of drawing or formulae) which embody a contrast between an *analytic* articulation of the structure or form of an animal, and a *synthetic* overlying curvilinear rhythm. Parts of an animal – head, haunches, legs, back, tail – are articulated, to a greater or lesser degree, under a characteristic contour curve. And indeed most animals have a distinct curved rhythm, even with the different abilities, interests and purposes of pot painters. So the animals do not appear in many poses, and they are very frequently overridden by the discipline of a particular graphic curve (Fig. 3.30). This does not apply to the men on the pots.

Nor were the painters obliged to draw their animals in this way. The drawing of people, indeed the whole emergence of this new style of decorating pots, breaking with the Geometric, shows that they were willing to take risks and experiment. The awkward angles of arms and outsize heads of the aryballos in Boston are distinct, different and individual. (This is one origin of the possibility of distinguishing different painters.) The painter was trying out ways of depicting people. The different poses and forms of monsters are further evidence of the willingness to elaborate and differentiate. And the painters could produce leaping goats, and accomplished scenes of lions leaping upon animals. But they hardly experimented with animal form; the wild animals are brought into a regulated code. This is particularly evident on later larger vessels. The animal friezes stylise and de-animate their animals, place them under a code, lined up in formal sequence. This is clear from Figure 3.27 which shows an olpe, technically classified as slightly later transitional protokorinthian.

Why is it that men do different things, interact and overlap in contest and aggression, or fight and die in armour? Why do animals appear in only a limited number of poses, stylised, with only formal indications of interaction (two animals facing)? I suggest that the answer to these two questions is the same. It is to do with how we may think of our bodies, animality, human and animal, and the animal within the human.

Figure 3.27 Stylised animals. Friezes from a later Korinthian oinochoe in the Louvre.

Lissarague (1988) has focused upon the figure of the satyr in later Attic iconography, a hybrid creature between men and animals. He reveals a clever play around anatomy, comportment, gesture and techniques of the body in various fields where men and animals come together – in sacrifice, the hunt and in the domestic sphere.

> En représentant les satyres, les peintures cherchent à explorer toutes les formes de comportements et de gestualités qui définissent l'homme et l'opposent à l'animal. Le satyre voit en lui même s'affaiblir, parfois s'abolir, la frontière entre humain et animal.
> (*ibid.*: 336)

This iconographic play is about boundaries between men and animals and their transgression.

This hybridity finds a different exploration in Korinthian iconography. Animals are brought to order in their stylisation upon Korinthian pots, I suggest, because their contagious otherness threatens. Violence and war are of an experience where the animal erupts into the human; Diomedes is as a lion in the fight. The soldier in the fight leaves order and security behind (the ceramic stand as arbitrated order, here on this aryballos in Figures 1.1 and 3.1) to risk the otherness of death (the otherness of the man–animal centaur). Violence, with its associated techniques of the body and material culture such as armour, allows the soldier to find identity with his bestial interior while avoiding being devoured by it. The animal interior threatens, so men upon the pots do not usually appear with the lions. And the lions are anyway de-animated, controlled through their stylisation.

I might say that the death risked through violence does not oppose life. The figures on the pots are animated precisely through violence. Carter (1972: 38–9) has argued that an interest in depicting narrative and action lay behind orientalising Greek borrowing of eastern design. Payne remarks on this Boston aryballos: 'movement is, as usual, the inspiration of the story' (1933 manuscript translation: 11). In all, death is opposed to the consciousness of life, and this is of culture, involving lifestyle (all the activity of the painted men), and is a negation of the animal.

War animates the dead within him. The fighting man is both hunter and hunted (scenes of animal hunts, animal attacks on people, soldiers fight among wild animals), finding the identity of his self in hunting and fighting the 'other'. That animal otherness is the opposite of its representation upon the pots: it is changeability and resistance to order and stylisation, qualities of unpredictability and deep powers

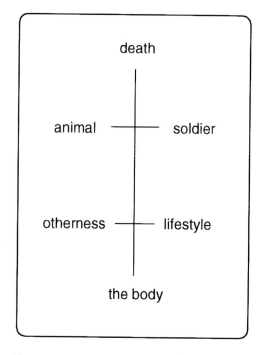

Figure 3.28 Death, otherness and lifestyle.

which lack definition. The animal interior of the soldier threatens to blow him apart or tear him to pieces – chaos of dismembered monster, and the dogs and birds which feed upon the corpse unattended by cultural propriety. His armour holds him together, and when one with the group, that threat is staunched; its integrity opposes the multiplicity and break-up that is the animal within.

Apart from the coursing hounds, the only other creature to appear in soldier lines is the bird: flocks of water birds, rows of heads. And the avian appears prominently upon the hoplite shields as talisman of identity. I have already shown how the bird seems to take a mediatory position, and forms an assemblage with the lion and the human. It would seem that somehow the bird allows the soldier to come to terms with that danger represented by the lion and the animal. At least the bird mediates.

War machines   In an interpretation of popular German military literature of the 1920s and after, Theweleit (1987, 1989) has provided fascinating insights into the psychology of a soldier 'society', the *Männerbund* of the *Freikorps*. With their militarism, male comradery and heroic youth, this militaristic grouping was part of the political and intellectual culture of the inter-war period, out of which indeed emerged fascism. I have already drawn on his work, and will now clarify and elaborate.

A major contention is that war is not only a restricted field of political authority and physical domination; war is a function of the body. The body is the site of the political ethos of militarism. Theweleit is concerned with the social psychology of male sovereignty and its world which elevates the experience of violence and war, hardship and discipline. The centrality of the body is apparent in techniques of the self which define and are practised by the soldier – bodily drills, group drills and regimes, countenance (those eyes and the helmet), keeping one's bearing and expression correct and upright, training, self-control.

A primary motivation is towards bodily and social unity. This will to wholeness arises because of the perceived threat of its opposite: those wild and disorderly powers which break down barriers, setting off floods and waves of lower and sordid elements; there is fear of dissolution, commingling with these base elements, fear of engulfment. For the member of the German *Freikorps* in the 1920s, this was the threat of engulfment by communism and bolshevism, the lower classes, and their women. This will to wholeness is a fear of the *molecular*, and is a will to power. It is a compulsion to put down that other which threatens his unity and integrity, to oppress those elements in the body of another, or the body in his own self, bringing to order. The relationship with bodies is one of violence and hierarchy, not commingling with the base and dirty, but establishing the preponderance of self over the other, of man over the animal (within).

So the soldier male's commitment to unity and the whole arises out of his own fear of splitting. 'Think in terms of the whole = don't forget that you are subordinate = don't forget that without us you would have no head, nothing above you. Think in terms of the whole = without us you would die = without us you would lack divinity (masculinity) and would be animals' (Theweleit 1989: 102). And the soldier is split if and when those 'lower', suppressed and animal elements demand independence.

Unity is the phalanx, those dangerous elements of the body damned and subdued by the machine-like physique of the soldier, his self displaced into armour and weaponry. Homer has *krateron menos*, the 'conquering energy' of the hero, put on like armour (*Iliad* 17.742–6; see also Vernant 1991a: 63 on the shining (*lampros*) armour of the hero). In Tyrtaios consider the imagery whereby the *arete* of the soldier hero is achieved through weaponry and death (West 12, quoted above, p. 113). Archilochos identifies the staples of life with his weaponry:

ἐν δορὶ μεν μοι μᾶζα μεμαγμένη, ἐν δορὶ δ' οἶνος
Ἰσμαρικός· πίνω δ' ἐν δορὶ κεκλιμένος
By spear is kneaded the bread I eat, by spear my Ismaric
wine is won, which I drink, leaning upon (*keklimenos*) my spear.
Archilochos West 2 Translation Lattimore

And *keklimenos* is the word which would be used to refer to reclining upon a dining couch in new eastern style.

Homer's conception of man is a complex mediation of the *molecular* and *molar* (introduced above). There are no words for the soul or indeed body of a living man, who was, as related above, a unity of energies, organs and actions (Fränkel 1975: 76f following Böhme 1929). It was only in death that *psyche*, soul, became separated from *soma*, corpse.

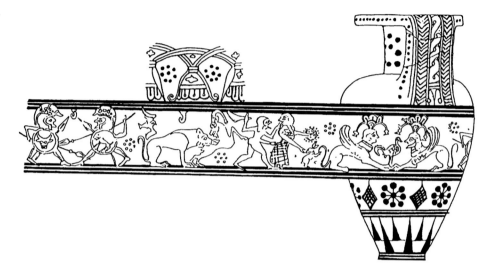

Figure 3.29 Warriors, women, monsters, birds and flowers: an aryballos in Brindisi. Fear of those threatening and dirty base elements leads to a stiffening: control, armour, hard bronze. And, of course, more: stiffening and hardness are supposed confirmation of manhood. Here a phallic and naked man (hard body bared) assaults with a weapon one of the few likely female figures. She is dressed in a checked flowing robe (soft), holds a wreath of flowers (?) and pats a hare. The hare touches a sphinx, one of a pair who sit on either side of a bird. One sphinx is bearded. Floral devices grow from their heads. So from the female extend the otherness of monstrosity, mix of animal lion, avian and human, the dubious sexuality of the sphinxes, the floral and the avian. The hare was later a gift between lovers (Schnapp 1984), hunted also by dogs. Behind the phallic man a lion jumps upon a goat, and two hoplites fight a duel. All elements of the assemblage I have been describing are here: armoured hoplite fight – drill (the hoplites mirror each other, as is proper) – violence and the animal – violent sexuality against the female – hard body, soft clothes – amorous gift – and an association of the floral, monstrosity, ambiguous sexuality, the avian.

> So long as the body is alive, it is seen as a system of organs and limbs animated by their individual impulses; it is a locus for the meeting, and occasional conflict, of impulses or competing forces. At death, when the body is deserted by these, it acquires its formal unity, and becomes *soma*.
> (Vernant 1991a: 62).

The fear of the hero is of *aikia*, disgrace done to the corpse, dirt and disgrace spoiling its wholeness, and preventing the death being beautiful. The images quoted above of the old man's death bring in another element: his death was disgraceful, because of his old age and because it was not masculine – the reference to the wound to the genitals (and to be eaten by dogs and birds (*ibid.*: 68). There is fear too of not receiving proper burial, which preserves the beautiful death, and provides, in the funeral mound raised, a mark which is stable and unchanging – *empedos* (meaning 'intact' or 'immutable') (*ibid.*: 69, citing *Iliad* 17.432–5). So unity is a protection from that death represented by dismemberment, splitting, decay, decomposition, being the food of birds and dogs. Unity is that which is preserved by the *kalos thanatos*, the beautiful death. Perpetual unity comes with the funeral pyre and the mound raised for all to see.

In questioning the application of modern concepts of war and violence to the ancient city state, Shipley (1993) has outlined the embeddedness of warfare, unquestioned by contemporary writers. There was no autonomous concept of war. In citing Garlan's argument for the 'omnipresence of war' (1989: 12–13) he comments that 'war was a fact of life: and though peace was different, it was not considered the norm, nor was war seen as an aberration' (*ibid.*: 18).

'People told us that the war was over. That made us laugh. We ourselves are the war. Its flame burns strongly in us. It envelops our whole being' (quoted in Theweleit 1987: x). Fear of that otherness is also fascination, and the struggle to retain hard control is a never-ending one. Battle and actually fighting is a supplement (in Derrida's sense too: Deleuze and Guattari 1988: 417). The warrior caste lives in permanent war. Why fight? For *kleos*, or for city, or for *dike*, justice? It does not really matter. The motivations are easily transferred.

μάχης δὲ τῆς σῆς, ὥστε διψέων πιεῖν

I would as soon fight with you as drink when I'm thirsty.
Archilochos West 125

War is just something that you do; it is even a necessity. Mercenaries appear almost with the beginning of the polis, it would seem, and in numbers. Herodotos (2.152) has 'brazen men' in Egypt in the seventh century (see, for example, the account by Murray (1993: 223f)). Of course, Archilochos was a mercenary. They travelled: there is, for example the famous graffiti scratched by some Greek mercenaries on the left leg of a colossal statue of Rameses II at Abu Simbel, 700 miles up the Nile. They were on an expedition in 591 BC (Austin and Vidal-Naquet 1977: 209). The mercenaries did not need the state. War does not need battles; it is more a war-machine.

Heads and bodies, helmets, armour, spears and stabbing; human, avian, animal and monstrous; torn, mixed, stylised. The major focus of Korinthian iconography comes to be bodily form; and the body, in my argument, is a primary site for the aesthetic ethos of violence and war. Animals are stylised under a graphic order. Linear, geometric and floral painting or decoration binds the 'body' of the pot in an aesthetic order (see the comments of DuBois on Geometric Attic pottery, 1988: 133–5). This, I argue, is emphasised also in the use of all available ceramic surface (bases may be decorated too, some with figures: consider a fine bridled horse-head on the conical lekythos from Aetos, Amyx 1988: 36). And emphasised also in miniaturism, where often complication is heightened in a display of painterly dexterity and risk such that the surface effect is one of textured movement, like an ant's nest disturbed, as Payne put it.

So these soldiers and violent battle scenes are not best understood as the depiction or reflection of a hoplite 'reform'. To consider them as somehow documentary source for a political and military history in this way gives little insight into the scenes. The term 'hoplite reform' is out of place here, though the issues raised of the interconnection of military, social and political change are pertinent. The pots are not about something else. I am instead trying to give an interpretation of the pots through their acts of making and painting. The potters were creating and responding to a demand, experimenting (less so later perhaps) for people who might want to use pots, to have a visual environment which made reference to those themes I have been following. This is a new *expressive* aesthetic.

Nagy (1979: esp. page 151–61; see also Vernant 1969) has interpreted Hesiod's myth of the five generations of humankind (*Works and Days* 109–201) as representing, in the men of gold, silver, bronze and the demi-gods (those generations preceding the present), the dual character of the heroic ancestor. Particularly interesting is the characterisation of the darker side of the heroic, the men of bronze: *chalkeion*, and made of ash (*ek melian*) (*Works and Days* 144–5) just as the warrior's spear. Hard and violent, they ate no grain (*Works and Days* 146–7) and died by their own hands. Nagy compares this violent and destructive masculinity with that of the warrior associations such as the *Männerbund*, and those figures of myth the Spartoi and Phlegyai who combine categories of mortality, immortality and the heroic fighter (see also Vian 1968).

Vernant (1991c: 100) draws attention to the description in the *Iliad* (22.373–4) of Hektor's dead body, stripped of armour. It was *malakoteros amphaphaasthai* (softer to handle) – *malakos* (soft or limp) refers to the feminine or the effeminate. Vernant relates the image to that series of terms, already discussed (see pp. 132–3), which associate combat to the death with the erotic embrace. In Homer *meignumi*, sexual union, also means joining in battle.

I will turn now to a consideration of gender and sexuality, long overdue.

Violence and sex, animals and the absence of woman

Of more than 4,104 animal and human figures in the sample only nine are drawn as being of female sex: six are women because named or according to physical characteristics; there are two lionesses, a dog-bitch and a sow. Some deer without antlers are of indeterminate sex and age; birds appear in different species, but again of indeterminate sex. There are also the sphinxes and bird people, again of indeterminate sex when not male.

Of the women, I have already introduced one, attacked by phallic male (Fig. 3.29). Three others are named as goddesses and are subject to the judgement of Alexander (upon the Chigi Olpe, Amyx 1988: 32). This scene is below the handle of the jug, the most inconspicuous position, and the myth represents female divinity beneath the gaze and subject to the human male. Another modelled female figure appears again beneath the handle of a jug, an angular oinochoe from Aetos (Robertson 1948: No. 1026). She is dressed in a checked and geometrically decorated robe, as is the whole pot decorated: it does not carry any figured scenes. So there are no associations to be made other than female and ceramic form; she is separate and bound to the pot surface by her form and decoration. A final woman is in checked robe and carries a shield and spear (Figs. 3.19 and 3.31). Thus the women are marginal, clothed in long robes, attacked or subject to men, while another stands armed.

Of the animals, the females identified by physical characteristics are treated as males in that I detect no distinction in their associations. Then there are those animals and creatures which may be female, or are of indeterminate sex. The deer are timid creatures, as are most of the birds, apart from the birds of prey. I have also marked out the birds as of a mediatory character, according to their associations. Later Attic iconography has them as gifts between lovers, like hares, the panther, wreaths and flowers and domestic animals (Schnapp 1984). The sphinxes and bird-people (sirens) are monsters.

So, the female takes these shapes: absent, marginal, goddesses, indeterminate, bodies beneath robes, timid, subject to man, armed, freak and associated with the avian.

There is no anatomical reference to sexual reproduction, other than breasts, the teats of those four animals and the phallic male. However, apart from creatures together in an animal line, a feature of the linear frieze, animals are frequently paired. Sphinxes mostly occur in balanced pairs (seventy-two of the eighty-eight); griffons and lions too. I have remarked upon this common feature of lions and sphinxes already (the link soldier–avian–lion). Of course soldiers are also arranged in fighting pairs. In the light of those connections observed earlier (the imagery in Homer associating death, violence and sex; the gaze of desire between soldier and lover), is it going too far to see an analogy between the pairing of violence and (absent) sexual pairing?

Apart from being violent, these pairings often involve an intervening element, such as a geometric device or bird, as with sphinxes. These are sometimes called heraldic pairs. So too upon this Boston aryballos. The intervening device distances and further stylises. Sexual union is hardly present here. If sexual reproduction involves pairing, it also involves joining and mixing. The monsters are, as I have argued, a principle of the mixture of different parts. Other mixing occurs in the only overlap of figures – hoplites in battle and the lions which leap upon animals and men – violence again.

A function of sexual union is reproduction. The only reference to reproduction is the fertility of repetition – the lines of birds, protomes, the soldiers and the coursing hounds. We return here to the principle of the group I discussed earlier (see p. 124). These are not groups propagated by sexual filiation; they are to do with affinity and proximity (the overlap). The scenes which show only animals might also be included in this category of repetition. They too operate through the simple principle of placing one animal next to another; they do not interact.

I might have said that stylisation of animals denies them a vital and, by implication, a sexual energy. But I do not think that this is the case. Some of the hounds do run around the pots with energy; some of the drawing is undoubtedly very vital. In citing Payne on analytic and synthetic principles behind the drawing of animals (see p. 127), I would claim that the dynamic comes from the quality of the line, a graphical schema. These tiny silhouette dogs are hardly 'naturalistic' in the sense of imitating or tracing the anatomical form and characteristics of a domestic dog or hunting hound. But some are 'realistic' in expressing the dog as it bounds along. This is that contrast I described above between being like a dog, and carefully depicting its appearance, and entering into a relationship with what the dog becomes, here as it

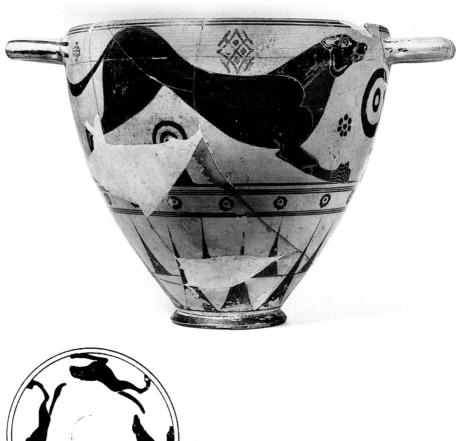

Figure 3.30 Dogs and energy: a kotyle in the British Museum (1860.4–4.18), and dogs from an aryballos in Syracuse (12529), from Fusco cemetery (grave 85). The energy of the curve prevents these animals from being a simple analytical articulation of body, legs and head.

runs. After all, the curved line so often encountered has nothing intrinsically to do with a dog, has no affiliation with it.

So, the figured scenes on pots such as this one represent a world of imagery which excludes or presents in a very particular way the possibility of the female, and while sexual reproduction is absent, there are references to the group and to an animal and vital energy.

καὶ πεσεῖν δρήστην ἐπ᾽ ἀσκόν, κἀπὶ γαστρὶ γαστέπα
προσβαλεῖν μηρούς τε μηροῖς

to fall to work upon the paunch, to hurl belly against belly,
thighs to thighs.
Archilochos West 119

But what then of sexuality? The soldier male is not celibate. Homer and Tyrtaios both give descriptions of the mingling of battle, man against man. Archilochos transfers the imagery to sex. Here is a symbolic exchange of *eros* and *thanatos*.

This exchange is very apparent in Sappho's lyrics. She uses the metaphor of love as war in a series of allusions to Homeric epic (Marry 1979; Rissman 1983), adapting narrative structures, epic imagery and Homeric language. This is particularly evident in fragments Lobel and Page 1, 16, 31, 105a and b. In one (Lobel and Page 16) Anactoria's gait and sparkle is likened to the splendour of Lydian troops – *lampros* (shining bright) is used by Homer for armour and heavenly bodies. The fragment Lobel and Page 31 is, according to Rissman, based upon the same lover-as-warrior system of metaphor as the encounter of Odysseus and Nausicaa in Book 6 of the Odyssey which it closely parallels. For Marry, this use of heroic language and imagery is ironic, a deliberate exposure of the code of Homeric chivalry. I will return to the contestation of ideologies, particularly in Chapter Six.

In his interpretive reading of the literature of the German *Freikorps*, Theweleit (1987, 1989) has challenged the idea that fascism and militarist authoritarianism are primarily to do with authority, that of the leader or commander, and with the desire for a leader. Also rejected is the explanation of the culture of military might as a terrorism to maintain authority. Nor is the military *Männerbund* about repressed homosexuality. It is clear that the soldier group and its wider culture are doing what they want to do, and find war, violence, repression, those techniques of the self already mentioned, fusion with the group of fellow soldiers, attractive and rewarding. In answer to the question of the energy which drives all this, the desire, Theweleit answers that it is to do with women.

Women, in the stories and literature that Theweleit has studied, are of three kinds. They are either absent; or are 'white nurses' – upper-class German women, chaste, bodiless, (dead); or are 'red women' – threatening, violent, deceiving enemies of the soldier male (Theweleit 1987). There is a profound hatred of women, their bodies and sexuality. Women are repudiated. But this is not a variation on Freud's oedipal triangle wherein is found the son's fear of heterosexual desire leading to punishment by the father, accompanied by repressed homosexual desire for father and authority. The repudiation of women is a fear of what they are taken to represent – holes, swamps, pits of muck that engulf and swallow, spitting, screaming, 'red' women in the tide of communism. Theweleit presents a long series of images and metaphors found in *Freikorps* literature involving waves, tides, effluent, emissions, floods of annihilation. This is a fear of fragmentation, no longer being self and one of the men, a commingling and fluidity, a fear of 'otherness'.

The threat is both internal and external. The soldier's own body is also a mass of blood and viscera, disorganised impulses and desires, an 'other', liquid and female body within. So the military male embraces that opposite which allows him to make sense of his identity: a hard metallised body and the soldier group. This militarism is thus an extreme case of sexism, the polarisation of gender.

And here too is the place of the animal. In being strange and bestial, of another order, the animal is feminine and monstrous. Both are multiple and fluid. But typed, tied to signifying order, the animal is tamed and can be integrated into the masculine. The only place and time when a man can risk the animal within him, that dangerous and contagious otherness within, *menos* or *furor*, is in war. Thus a key term in understanding the relationship of men and animals in this cultural order is that of the feminine.

Women may be needed for the simple physical reproduction of men. But the war-machine with its risk, violence and these structures of polarisation, with its awareness and control of 'molecular' forces within, is its own mode of reproduction of masculine identity. The productive force of that which is here gendered feminine is absorbed and channelled, in being a foil or opposite to that for which the masculine stands.

There is an implied correspondence between the feminine and bestiality, the animal within. For Deleuze and Guattari 'the man of war is inseparable from the Amazons' in a triad of soldier, animal, woman. 'The man of war, by virtue of his furor and celerity, was swept up in irresistible becomings-animals', that is, he risks that bestiality within. 'These are becomings that have as their necessary condition the becoming-woman of the warrior, or his alliance with the girl, his contagion with her' (Deleuze and Guattari 1988: 278); that is, the bestiality of war has affinity here with the feminine; so war brings forth the warrior-woman.

Hesiod's misogyny is well-known (*Theogony* 590f). The condemnation of feminine character by Semonides is notorious. In an interpretation of classical Greek marriage and sexuality DuBois (1979, 1984) has traced a metaphorical sequence from the animal to the female *via* centaurs (creatures doubly male) and amazons – mythical figures, 'masculine' and negating marriage. She makes a general summary comment: 'a response to women's imagined vulnerability, their killing-cure, is a return to the self-sufficiency of the Golden Age, a time before marriage, before women' (DuBois 1979: 46). Naerebout (1987) has sketched the separated fields of men and women in epic, the economic dependence of women upon men and the ideological buttressing of the dominance and subordination through ideas of honour and shame.

For Theweleit, the culture of the militaristic male is not, as in the familiar literary and movie genre, simply something innocent males (boys) go through in becoming adult (men). The cultural complex he uncovers reaches far beyond the lifeworld of the soldier, so that militarism is hardly an adequate label. And, of course, his subject includes the rise of the appeal of fascism, which can in no way wholly, or at times at all, be explained as a rite of passage. For some, at times many, war is a chosen experience, and a romanticisation of its supposed spiritual and character-building nature is to be avoided.

It is for these reasons that I have some difficulty in fully accepting Vidal-Naquet's interpretation (1981a, 1981c) of the *ephebeia* in archaic and classical Greece. He

Figure 3.31 Gender, ambiguity and violence: a cup from the Heraion, Samos. One of the very few women occurs upon this skyphos from the Samian Heraion. She is armed carrying a shield which may show a stylised floral device, and is attended by an importuning male sphinx with vegetal headdress. This coupling of violent and monstrous gender is detached from the rest of the frieze by geometric ornament. The female is here ambiguously violent and under appeal from masculinity turned monstrous. The male can risk the female only as monstrous bird–lion–person. Elsewhere are the animal, its violence, the special artifact and a creature doubly male, the centaur (a third set of genitalia are depicted upon one thigh). Here then, in this special world of *agalma*, animal and monster, the male risks violence. In a triad of soldier, animal and woman, which all belong with the war-machine, the bestiality of violence has affinity with the *molecular* and feminine. War brings forth the warrior-woman.

explains the institutions and characteristics of the young citizen male (*ephebe*) as a threshold to adulthood (*cf.* also Jeanmaire 1939). In contrast to the adult hoplite, married and ready to fight, armed, standing in phalanx, upon a plain of a summer's day, adolescent *ephebai* were associated, individual and naked, with wild mountain spaces, tricks and foraging of the winter night. Vidal-Naquet has the deception, disorder and irrationality of the *ephebeia* as the reversals often encountered in rites of passage, an identification strengthened by the association of *ephebai* with frontiers and marginal areas, like the transitional states of a rite of passage. But this contrast between pre-hoplite and hoplite also accords with the interpretation I have been following of the molar and molecular warrior, armour and phalanx as to feminine bestiality within, with all attendant problems of defining where one begins and the other ends. The later institution of the *ephebeia* could be explained as a ritual taming which, like armour and phalanx, brings masculine identity to order. Rather than relate these military and cultural institutions to a general anthropological category (rite of passage), they might better be seen as part of social strategies of power around a radical division of gender.

Masculinity and the domestic

Many of the painted animals are wild creatures. Dogs and horses are the main representatives of domestic animals upon the pots (more than 2,400 dogs and ten unaccompanied horses; more than ninety other horses are associated with riders and chariots). Dogs accompany the hunt, horses also war, and they race in the contests of those who can afford them. Horses are beyond the wealth of the small-holder. Nor, when unridden, do they interact with any other animal apart from people and a bird. I have already mentioned how birds and dogs are painted beneath racing horses, and dogs do not appear with men.

Dogs are frequently drawn in scenes chasing birds, which are another possible domesticate. Cockerels are certainly a domesticated species; they only appear with floral and geometric ornament, people and a monstrous winged human in earlier friezes, with a lion and a bull later. Most of the earlier birds are long-legged water birds, of the sort that appear on pots of Geometric style. Many of those that I have

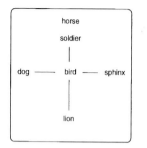

Figure 3.32 The space of the domestic animal.

classed as short-legged birds with short beak and tail could be taken for birds of prey; but the point stands that I made earlier – earlier birds hardly interact with anything other than people, other birds and ornamental designs such as flowers and rosettes. Most (63 per cent) of the later birds are those that I have described as swans, that is long-necked water birds. These are drawn seated or crouching, and might be tired earlier long-legged birds. They may be domesticated geese, in which case there is a switch of emphasis from wild to domesticated water birds from earlier to later friezes. These are the birds (more than eighty-four of them) which are chased by the dogs.

So, there is a distinct group of domesticated animals which, in their associations, are either kept separate, such as dogs, or confirm the themes outlined, horses, or act in a mediatory role, birds.

The domestic, the world of agriculture, the *oikos* (household), food and nutrition, sexual reproduction are conspicuously mediated and transformed, or missing, or detached from the world peopled by men. But these relationships cannot be reduced to a simple antinomy between culture and nature, or between domestication and the wild, for, as indicated, there are the following features of which account needs to be taken.

Wild animals are painted in great numbers, but in stylised 'tamed' poses.

Domesticated dogs do not appear in the same friezes with men, as might be expected.

The hoplite's shield shows him as bird, sometimes wild and sometimes domesticated, where the reference seems to be a link with the (wild) feline.

Birds are also the link between domesticated dogs and men.

There are monstrous mixed creatures, neither domesticated nor wild.

Earlier scenes make some play upon the connection and transformation between artifact, bird, head and flower.

All these scenes occur often amidst a flowering but stylised and overcoded 'nature'.

I have also argued the importance of gender relations: the feminine is a key term in understanding the relationships between creatures and men upon the pots.

A contrast used by Schnapp-Gourbeillon in her interpretation of animal simile in Homer was introduced earlier, (see p. 122) and is relevant again here: between controlled social terms and uncontrolled otherness or the divine. The soldier-hero oscillates between the two, controlling through the practices and characteristics of his male society, while having contact with bestiality and divinity in violence.

Vidal-Naquet, as just discussed, has contrasted the order of the phalanx composed of married and fighting citizens, with the marginal world of the *ephebe* which is more to do with deception, cunning and disorder. This is embodied in the contrast between spear and net. A prime example of the cunning warrior is Odysseus, described as *polymetis*, a man of many wiles, quick trickster (*Iliad* 3.205–24 for example). He too travelled out and around strange places at the edge, beyond human society, loved by divine nymphs, outwitting a witch who turned men to animals, Kirke, and a monster cyclops from a cosmogonic era before men.

Odysseus was *polymetis*, a man of *metis*. Detienne and Vernant (1978) have provided a detailed elaboration of the concept of *metis*, the intelligence of cunning. They distinguish between two orders of reality: that which is intelligible and is the object of propositional knowledge taking the form 'know that'; the other is sensible and is the object of multiple, unstable, oblique opinion. The contrast is between an order of being and one of becoming. *Metis* is a practical wisdom which oscillates between the two worlds; instead of contemplating unchanging essences it is involved in practical existence (Detienne and Vernant 1978: 44). Legitimate or physical power, *imperium* or *potestas*, may be asserted and used in achieving an outcome. *Metis* is a means of achieving what is desired by manipulating hostile forces which are too powerful to be controlled. Detienne and Vernant outline a semantic field of connections which runs through Greek literature. *Metis*: that which involves movement, multiplicity and ambiguity – metamorphosis and monstrosity – discovery of ways out, of that which is hidden – bonds, nets and traps – seizing the moment of opportunity – the world of the hunter, fisher, weaver, merchant. Further associations are with riddles, the oblique, curved and circular, rather than the direct and straight line. Some fascinating and pertinent details are that *metis* is the art of the charioteer in seizing the moment (Pindar *Isthmian* 2.22; Detienne and Vernant 1978: 16, 202f); that birds in navigating earth, water and air are of *metis* (*ibid.*: 217); as is the sphinx, whose questions are *poikila*, shifty and ambiguous words (Sophokles *Oidipous Tyrannos* 130; Detienne and Vernant 1978: 303–4). *Metis* is another aspect of that realm I am sketching as the molecular.

Violence and the state

Clastres (1977) provided a classic challenge to the evolutionary notion that the state (society with distinct and permanent organs of power) is somehow at a higher or later stage than segmentary societies. His thesis is that the state may be warded off or prevented from emerging by various social mechanisms. So a chief may have no institutional power base other than his prestige, being constantly in a position of having to account for his power. Clastres (1980a, 1980b) argues that war is one of the mechanisms that prevent the emergence of the state. The warrior chief has to display his prowess over and again, fighting in the front ranks, necessarily solitary in risking life for prestige, but ultimately a death beyond power. War also keeps groups segmented and dissociated in the violent and competitive lifestyles of its warrior leaders.

Deleuze and Guattari (1988: 12, 351f) reach further in setting the war-machine outside and against the state. They define four types of violence (*ibid.*: 447–8):

struggle – blow-by-blow personal violence;
crime – a violence of illegality, directed against rights, prohibitions and property;
state policing or lawful violence – incorporated or structural violence (which does not have to be physical); and
war – violence not overcoded by the state.

'The state has often been defined by a "monopoly of violence", but this leads back to another definition that describes the State as a "state of Law". State overcoding is precisely this structural violence that defines the law, "police" violence and not the violence of war' (*ibid.*: 448). The violence of war is not overcoded, but exists as a separable experience and culture.

In *A Thousand Plateaus* (1988) Deleuze and Guattari are often working with abstract and generic semantic fields, almost ideal types. Their contrast between the war-machine and the state is between multiplicity and the arborescent structures of the state; between *nomos* or custom, and law; between heterogeneity and the definition and reproduction of social forms and powers; between the pragmatics of the soldier risking death with the group, and the affiliated foundations of the 'state'. The state, in contrast with the war-machine, goes with notions of a republic of minds, a court of reason, public culture, man as legislator and subject, internal definition and differentiation. This allows them to write that the State is perpetual (*ibid.*: 360) as a potential vector of organisation and experience.

However, their universal philosophy of history does come to ground in the experiences of violence, warfare and animality I have been describing. It is better to think of warfare *and* the state, of a societal (state) taming of the violence of war, bringing war within its sphere. This involves the control of animal otherness through armour and the phalanx, the lifestyles of hero and mercenary, and animals overcoded and tamed, their otherness controlled. There are different forms of group appropriate to the war-machine and not the state, in particular, the warrior band, as opposed to legal and reproduced affiliations. There is a contrast of types of association: the (animal or molecular) affinity between soldiers is contrasted with the realm of affiliation of kinship and marriage.

So I argue that my interpretation of Korinthian can be extended to include gender through relationships between:

masculine	feminine
present	absent
war	the domestic
affinity	reproduction
warrior band	family

These themes are at the heart of the war-machine.

The lord, his enemies and sovereign identity

> The easiest way to get soldiers is to remove women from public life.
> (Theweleit 1987: 349)

In the separation of those things drawn from those not, and in the assemblage of forms and associations, a masculine sphere is distinguished from feminine. There are further directions suggested towards a contrast between the affinity of the male warrior band and the family reproductive unit. I therefore wish now to explore further the experiences which belong with this masculine culture, and as appear within this ceramic field.

I begin with the idea of risk of the self (in violence, war and confrontation with monstrosity, but I also make reminder of the workmanship of risk with which I started in Chapter Two).

Consider a reading of Hegel's dialectic between the master and slave (Hegel 1966: 229–40) (a philosophical anthropology, if you like). The identity of the lord or hero is established in the striving for recognition, and to improve himself over another through his qualities. In this men are opposed to each other and to any other. This, of course, tends to violence. It also means that risking life is a means to gain identity. To deny an attachment to mere life (the household, family, nutrition, reproduction), to a particular self, their life, is the attempt to reconstruct an identity for themself which is in-itself, separate, of another order, the heroic, the divine. This is the logic of the beautiful death, discussed previously (see pp. 111–12). A hierarchical order is implied between those who risk their life, accepting death, and lower people who are attached to mere life.

Because it is risked willingly, life is subordinated to the *lifestyle* of the fighting lord. This is what was meant earlier when I wrote that the death risked in violence does not oppose life. Death is opposed to the consciousness of life, and this is lifestyle, a negation of the animal, and of lower-culture. Lifestyle is the culture of risk and violence. But also it is style itself, which implies a *pure consumption* of goods, beyond the mundane, an expenditure serving no purpose other than style and culture. This is what I term an expressive aesthetic. Producing goods for the lord, a world of work: this is the existence of the lower class.

When death is the force of life (through violence and risk), death and the erotic are juxtaposed. The erotic is not reproductive, but is a world of pleasures and seductions opposed to legality and ordered marriage bonds. In desiring the risk of war, the lord assents to life to the point of death (see Scully 1990: 121, 124 on Achilles, mortality and death). This is an affirmation of the value of loss and excess. It is intimately related to the notion of the gift.

Gift-giving is a non-productive expenditure which breaks ties between the giver and the world of things (the work and production of the slave), and establishes instead a relation between persons, gift-giver and receiver. The social covenant created with those who receive the gift breaks a link with the lower culture of production. The goods destined for consumption by the lord are detached from the world of work (relations between people and things) and are instead of a lifestyle beyond. This is a sacred space of the hero confronting death and divinity.

The life of the lord is one of living pleasure (oiled with perfume, drinking from the cup), a pure consumption of goods produced by subordinate classes. Lifestyle: special gifts, wine, contest, perfume. The affirmation of expenditure means war becomes luxury and festival (nodding crests, shield devices, pipers). Violence is excess (the cost of the weaponry, horses, time and risk; a new and exotic visual order of style); the domestic (absent) is sufficiency. The risk is about limits and transgression: assenting to life to the point of death asks questions of the line between life and death. And the lifestyle and risk imply an aesthetic even unto the beautiful death. I have written too of a concern with the limits of the body, animal and human. Violence is also transgression of the law which is against murder because vengeance and blood feud result. But transgression asserts the identity of a self which refuses prohibition and survives, and this reward is accessible only to those of wealth who may fight the risk and display their sovereignty. This is not mere physical power, but a sacred space of risk and the aesthetic of lifestyle.

I have shifted from Hegel to Bataille and Mauss, ideas of the gift and interpretations of the economic 'irrationalities' of apparently purposeless excess and expenditure (Bataille 1977, 1985b; Mauss 1954). I have presented this elaboration of sovereignty to clarify some of the associations I have been sketching: the place of a symbolics of violence, war and display. Masculine sovereignty of this sort is an expressive dramaturgy, repudiating the everyday. I have also here tried to establish the roots of this cultural complex in a process which establishes the identity of a masculine self through the subordination of a lower culture and class. I have shown how this is identified with the feminine.

The relations with the painted imagery are clear. Ceramic design, I contend, is of this logic. I add that Korinthian potters broke sharply with Geometric design, and continued to *transgress* the Geometric canon, still represented in the pots decorated simply and linearly. I have described graphical schemata of parallel linearity and angularity which *deviate* into curve and inclination. Some figured pottery is a clear *excess* of surface detail in comparison with the Geometric, the point made by Payne. I argue that these are not contrivances or coincidences of verbal description.

Ceramic imagery and a cultural constitution of masculinity leads to the question of the possible structure of aristocratic social groups in archaic Greece. In Chapter Two an argument was presented for flexible aristocratic associations centred on the *oikos*. Some would characterise society at this time as a warrior chiefdom (Drews 1983; Ferguson 1991). The key point is an argument for a minimal or non-existent state and a lack of institutionalised structures of authority:

> Political power at this time was achieved, not inherited. In anthropological terms, *basileis* (kings) are 'big men', leaders whose position depends on their ability to attract and keep followers through personal talent, feasting, and gift giving.
> (Antonaccio 1993a: 64)

This clearly doubts an early date for hereditary legitimation of authority, though the importance to power of familial ties in early literatures can hardly be contested.

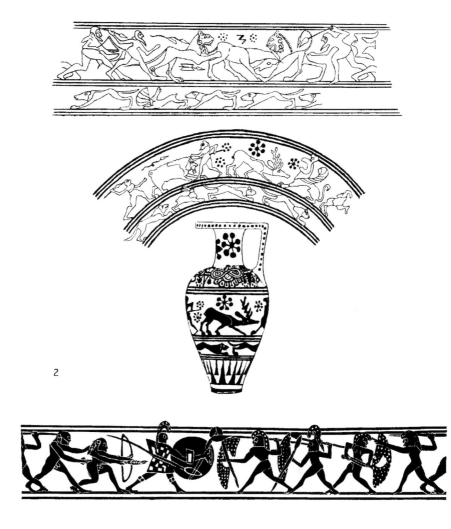

Figure 3.33 The hunt and the fight. Scenes from three aryballoi.
1 From Nola in the British Museum.
2 From Syracuse (13839; Fusco, grave 366).
3 From the cemetery at Lechaion (Korinth CP-2096).

The question of such social reconstruction, as with the issue of hoplite reform and its relation to political change, hinges on chronology: whether, for example, inherited authority was a recent invention or had long been a fundamental feature of dark age society; whether hoplite warfare was a cause or consequence of social revolution. The interpretation being developed here need only accept that ideologies of sovereignty were being contested.

The clear (but arguably superficial) similarities between competitive, prestige-based warrior chiefdoms and the sort of social relationships described and inferred in Homer has led to ethnographic analogy between parts of eighth- and ninth-century

Greece and the Waigal valley in contemporary Nuristan (Murray 1993: 73; Whitley 1991b: 192–3; after Jones 1974). Though no longer able to kill Muslims in warrior raids, the men of Nuristan nonetheless seek and achieve rank through competitive feasting, displays of wealth, and special objects of status, even tripods, bowls and cups. Van Wees (1994: 1, 8) compares Homeric warfare to battles in the big-men societies of the New Guinea highlands. Qviller (1981), again in analogy with Melanesian big-men societies, has provided a social model of competitive gift-exchange and consumption, coupled with population rise from 900, leading to social collapse (for difficulties and comment see Morgan 1990: 94–5, 191, 195f; Morris 1987: 203–4; Whitley 1991a). Big-men society may sometimes be connected to 'prestige-goods' economies. This latter concept has had tremendous influence in prehistoric and protohistoric archaeology (beginning with Frankenstein and Rowlands 1978 and Friedman and Rowlands 1978, both after the model of Friedman 1975; see Rowlands, Larsen and Kristiansen 1987 for further examples and bibliography). While what I have written so far about sovereignty and this conception of masculinity could certainly be related to the dynamics of prestige-goods economies and big-men societies, here I wish simply to refer to ideas about the contested character of early Greek aristocracy.

Donlan (1980) has presented the aristocratic ideal in early Greek literature as a defensive standard, that is an ethos and set of values responding to shifts (he calls them 'transvaluations') and challenges with cultural change. One was from an ideal of the warrior hero to a coded life-style (Donlan 1980: 52–63). There was a shift in attention to an aesthetics of lifestyle, those things considered proper:

> Dress, ornamentation, hair style, the cultivation of the skills of hunting and riding and athletics, playing a gentlemans' musical instrument, the ability to compose spontaneously at drinking parties, knowing when to be moderate in drink and speech and (equally important) when to carouse and speak intemperately, had all become, by the beginning of the sixth century BC, integral to the aristocratic pattern of behaviour.
> (*ibid.*: 62)

Dining and the *symposion* became a basic social experience at the heart of aristocratic power (Bremmer 1990; Murray 1982, 1983, 1990; Starr 1992: 134–5, 139–46), the argument goes. Lifestyle, centred upon the culture of a group of men expressing their identity through ritualised and high-cultural social events, became a fundamental feature of the working of aristocratic power. Donlan notes a shift though from the Homeric picture of heroic feasting, glorious acts of war, warrior graves, public funerals and posthumous cult, to a (masculine) world removed of private aristocratic luxury and entertainment, the generation of style and its emulation, and the exclusion of reproductive and civic womanhood.

ἔγω δὲ φίλημμ' ἀβροσύναν, τοῦτο καί μοι
τὸ λάμρον ἔρος τὠελίω καὶ τὸ κάλον λέλογχε.

> I love luxury (*habrosune*); and love has obtained for me
> this beauty and brilliance (*lampron*) of the sun.
> Sappho: Lobel and Page 58.25–6

Kurke (1991, 1992, 1993) has shown most persuasively how the new symbolic economies of praise and fame (*kleos* and *kudos*), earned in contest, and the poetics of luxurious living (*habrosune*) were far from unproblematic ideological solutions to the breakdown in the technologies of aristocratic power. In this general economy of the new state, civic usefulness opposed the glory of individual excess and transgression beyond (mortal) limits. Not everyone embraced eastern style and luxurious living as did Sappho:

> ἁβροσύνας δέ μαθόντες ἀνωφελέας παρὰ Λυδῶν,
> ὄφρα τυραννίης ἦσαν ἄνευ στυγερῆς,
> ἤιεσαν εἰς ἀγορὴν παναλουργεα φάρε' ἔχοντες,
> οὐ μείους ὥσπερ χείλιοι ὡς ἐπίπαν,
> αὐχαλέοι, χαίτησιν ἀγαλλόμεν εὐπρεπέεσσιν,
> ἀσκητοῖς ὀδμὴν χρίμασι δευόμενοι.

> Having learned useless luxuries (*habrosunai*) from the Lydians . . . they
> would go into the place of assembly wearing robes of all purple – a thousand
> of them, no less – boastful, glorying in their well-dressed long hair, drenched
> with the perfume of elaborate scents.
> Xenophanes West 3

Speed, the games and a band of men
Other experiences or events depicted in Korinthian iconography are races or processions, gathered in Table 3.7.

Robed figures frequently appear in these scenes; their identification as possible arbitrators or judges of contest seems clear. Mention should be made again of the stands, tripods and bowls – possible prizes. There are also, in three scenes, associations with winged monsters, and birds in another three – avian otherness, which I have found to play a role of mediation. The juxtaposition with soldier and lion hunt makes that connection with violence that I have explored. Many of the racing horses and chariots overlap, and I have identified overlap with the masculine affinity of the warrior band. Finally there is, in the judgement of Alexander upon the Chigi Olpe, an appropriate reference to divinity and the subordination of the feminine beneath masculine assessment. So here again is a variation upon the assemblage I have been outlining: contest and assessment can be added as part of this conceptual space of masculine sovereignty.

There is also clear depiction of the *speed* of the race in four of the scenes: the figures are stretched in dynamic running pose. The hounds and hares which race round 875 of the 1,219 figured friezes (72 per cent) are another and major reference to running and speed. I have commented on the poses which express well an (animal) vitality. Expressed in this way, speed and energy are to be added to the range of themes seen in the figured scenes. The races and hounds are an example too of groups' repeated

Table 3.7. *Races and horse processions*

vessel	reference	scene
Louvre CA617	Amyx 1988: 23	two riders: robed figure: two soldiers
Oxford 504	Johansen 1923: No. 1	two riders and winged centaur: robed figures and wreath:soldier: bird
Taranto 4173	Amyx 1988: 38	four riders: two robed figures: tripod: sphinx
Bonn 1669	Amyx 1988: 32	procession (?) three chariots: piper: four men
BM 1889.4–18.1	Amyx 1988: 31	seven riders: bird and man beneath
Berlin 3773	Amyx 1988: 32	five four-horse chariots: dog, hare and birds beneath
Johansen 1923 No. 54	Amyx 1988: 44	four four-horse chariots: tripod and bowls: robed figure
Villa Giulia 22679/97	Amyx 1988: 32	procession (?) four riders with extra horses: four-horse chariot with leader: sphinx: lion hunt: judgement of Alexander

Figure 3.34 Speed and the games. An aryballos from the Athenaion at Syracuse.

figures: there is reference to the group, of racing men, of dogs gathered for the hunt.

So this vector takes us further as follows: – groups gathered – the race – the hunt – speed – contest and prizes (tripods, and the hares and birds for the dogs).

The expression of speed takes me to another aspect of aristocratic lifestyle: the gatherings in inter-city sanctuaries for contest and glory sought, and for the display of speed and strength of athletic prowess, skills of horsemanship. I have made mention of the clever devious logic of *metis*, appropriate to the charioteer.

Pindar gives expression to the aristocratic ethos of lineage and glory won in victory at the games, albeit glory which accrues also to the home city of the victor. (See Kurke (1991) on the contradictions of this symbolic economy.)

The games were a cosmopolitan gathering of *agathoi*, a nexus of group, birth and identity (having the right to compete, belonging to the *agathoi*, representing the polis). The idea of group and belonging expressed here is that of selection, of the arbitrated order of winners and losers, an *agonistic* ethos of contest in the divine space of the sanctuary. This space, especially of the big sanctuaries of Olympia and Delphi, is beyond that of the poleis, often in conflict. In Chapter Two I referenced opinion (after De Polignac) about the marginal or interstitial place of sanctuaries (also Morgan 1990: 223f). Their relation with divinity and the 'other' world of the gods provides the edges, marginal spaces or other world according to which the identity of group or community is established. The (sacred) games help define a community of those who are able to take part. This is not a commingling of any and everyone, but an order arbitrated and beyond, in association with divinity. Kurke (1993) has described the emergence of the character of the hero-athlete, returning from the aristocratic games to civic canonisation in the late sixth and early fifth centuries, as another aristocratic bid for renewed talismanic authority in the polis of citizens, part of the development of a symbolic economy of *kudos*.

Davies (1981: 88–131) has made an analogous interpretation of the increase of chariot racing in the same period (later than that under study here) – an aristocracy looking for new ways to seize the political stage through deeds hailed heroic and through attendant charisma. The games sort out winners and losers. Part of aristocratic lifestyle beyond the city state, the games came to form a circuit of festival events, the *periodos* (Morgan 1990: 39, 212–23). The gatherings can be associated with the aristocratic institution of *xenia*, ritualised friendship (Herman 1987; Morgan 1990: 20, 218–20) – a class association without the state.

Snodgrass (1980a: 57) and Morgan (1990: esp. 203–5, 217) both stress that patronage of the early sanctuaries was not so much a state as an individual matter. The sanctuaries were a focus of inter-state aristocratic 'community'. I do not wish to push the analogy too far, but can make reference here to Theweleit's elucidation (1989: esp. 77f) of nation and the warrior male of the *Freikorps*. At the centre of the warrior male's conception of nationality are sex and character; nationality is of the body. The nation is the soldier male. For these groups of soldiers, 'the nation has nothing to do with questions of national borders, forms of government, or so-called nationality. The concept refers to a quite specific form of male community. . . . The nation is a community of soldiers' (Theweleit 1989: 79–81). Theweleit relates the nation group to ideas of unity and the identity of the soldier self. The soldier's unity is established through techniques of the self and the armouring of a hard body against the threat of splitting, disruption, the intestinal disorder within. The threat is overcome through a domination of those baser elements which are identified also with the lower-cultured mass and disorder of the feminine. The constructed, machinised whole which is the man's body is never sufficient unto itself: 'it always requires larger external totalities, compressed formations of existing reality within which *he* can remain dominant' (*ibid.*: 103). So the unity of the nation group is within the masculine self, as the battle for the nation resembles men's own battle to become men. 'The army, high-culture, race, nation: all of these appear to function as a second, tightly armoured body enveloping his own body armour. They are extensions of himself' (*ibid.*: 84). Unity is opposed to a simple equality of members, or the commingling of mass, is a state in which higher and lower elements are combined in violence to form a structure of domination, fusing baser, inferior and internal elements with those above. It is rooted in a series of relationships, further dimensions of this discourse of masculine sovereignty:

armour	internal and intestinal disorder
unity	decomposition
soldier formation	mass
nation	equality
intensity of will	effeminacy
victory	emptiness of anonymity
life-style	death
masculinity	femininity.

Unity is achieved through the relationship, the domination of one over the other, masculinity over femininity.

Theweleit also notes that the nation has a capacity for reproduction: the nation grows. But this is not the reproduction of heterosexuality; warrior procreation excludes femininity. The joining of masculinity and masculinity is a fertility which is productive of the future. He makes further connections between masculine procreation and fertilisation, war and creativity, in discussing Jünger: although birth has become related to the masculine and detached from the feminine, it still requires a body – the body of the earth, Mother Earth. Nation, of course, makes reference to Fatherland, the earth and land. Jünger:

> Something is in the process of becoming, something bound to the elemental, a level of life that is deeper and closer to chaos; not yet law, but containing new laws within itself. What is being born is the essence of nationalism, a new relation to the elemental, to Mother Earth, whose soil has been blasted away in the rekindled fires of material battles and fertilised by streams of blood. (quoted by Theweleit (1989: 88))

A striking image; an apposite comparison may be made, I suggest, between this asexual becoming of blood and earth and Hesiod's cosmogony before the creation of woman, Pandora. Consider also the Spartoi – warriors springing from the teeth of the dragon of Ares, sown in the earth (Vian 1968: 59f).

In a book which considers constitutions of subjectivity and personage and social conceptions of the body in ancient Greece, Halperin (1990) has explored what may be termed this erotic field of association and connection. He has argued that friendship, as articulated for example in Homer's account of Achilles and Patroklos, was part of the colonisation of a larger share of public discourse, of cultural space, for the play of male subjectivity (*ibid.*: 85). Male fellowship was established beyond society: 'friendship helps to structure – and, possibly, to privatise – the social space; it takes shape in the world that lies beyond the horizon of the domestic sphere, and it requires for its expression a military or political staging-ground' (*ibid.*: 77).

In widening the discussion to include observations already made, it can be claimed that fertility and productivity lie not in female reproductive sexuality and the world of work but in the warrior band and in action, in violence, styles of living, expression.

It has already been noted that the human bodily form is animated through violent action in the imagery of not just this Korinthian pottery, but also Attic Geometric (Carter 1972). Animate energy in Korinthian painting is that of violence, the clash of opponents, and the speed of racing figures, horses, chariots, dogs and birds. Here, upon the Boston aryballos with which I began, the paired and opposing figures of man and centaur are backed by a naked swordsman at speed. Is that a thunderbolt held by the man, it is disputed; is the man therefore Zeus? The identification, in spite of all the discussion (for bibliography see p. 12), would fit, given the assemblage I have been plotting. Zeus, as god, is representative of the divinity of encounter with the other, of the realm of arbitration, group and contest (the ceramic bowl and stand, convivial container), of the experience of violence clashing – speed and explosion of the thunderbolt. There too is the animated physique and speed of the runner.

Vermeule remarks on the character of war in Homer: 'there is an almost baroque magnificence in the physical ruin of Homer's heroes . . . death is made more marvellous by the poet's ingenious methods of puncturing the shell of flesh or smashing the protective white bones' (Vermeule 1979: 96–7). There are many vignettes of spear and weapon thrusts through a human anatomy held in a rich epic vocabulary. Blood, brain and intestines flow freely. The scenes 'offer, in a richer variety of action and more subtle orchestration than any comparable poetry in the world, devices for placing in front of us in unforgettable style the fragility of the human casement and the animal nature of human ambition and weakness' (*ibid.*: 99).

The experience of war expressed in the literature of the German *Freikorps* is one of speed and explosions, the surge of the charge, contact with the 'other' through the penetration of the weapon.

> The man longs for the moment when his body armour will explode, strengthening his rigid body-ego; but a body such as his cannot atomise, as does the mass, by allowing itself to be penetrated, fragmented, and thus destroyed. His body atomises only if he himself erupts outward. He desires to

> move beyond himself, bullet-like, towards an object that he penetrates. But
> he also desires to survive.
> (Theweleit 1989: 179)

Here is that combination of opposites that is the soldier male: hard armour and muscle, drilled, damming the threat within of the flood of disruptive energy and intestinal mush. The only release from the dam is the act, the rush of killing or dying, penetration or explosion; hot blood is the only thing permitted to flow (*ibid.*: 185).

Further to the distinction I have introduced between the world of household and work, and that of war and violence, the lifestyle of the soldier, Deleuze and Guattari (1988: 395f) write of the difference between tools and weapons. Weapons have a privileged relation with projection; the projectile is primarily weapon: 'anything that throws or is thrown is fundamentally a weapon, and propulsion is its essential moment. The weapon is ballistic'. The tool is more introceptive or introjective, preparing 'a matter from a distance, in order to bring it to a state of equilibrium or to appropriate it for a form of interiority'. Another and key difference is the relation of tool and weapon to speed. With Virilio (1986), it can be said that weapons and speed go together, and the projective character of weapons is the result. Deleuze and Guattari qualify the distinction with argument that the tool is more to do with displacement and gravity in a world of work: 'work is a motor cause that meets resistances, operates upon the exterior, is consumed and spent in its effect, and must be renewed from one moment to the next' (1988: 397). In contrast, that of the weapon and weapons handling is a field of 'free action', also

> a motor cause, but one that has no resistance to overcome, operates only
> upon the mobile body itself, is not consumed in its effect, and continues from
> one moment to the next. Whatever its measure or degree, speed is relative in
> the first case, absolute in the second.

There are some important points here with wide reference and I will quote further.

> In work, what counts is the point of application of a resultant force exerted by
> the weight of a body considered as 'one' (gravity), and the relative
> displacement of this point of application. In free action, what counts is the
> way in which the elements of a free body escape gravitation to occupy
> absolutely a nonpunctuated space.
> (*ibid.*: 397)

The point I take is that understanding a tool or weapon requires relating it to the assemblage of which it forms a part, here specified in terms of productive work and free action. Of course, a weapon assumes a world of production for its existence, but its specificity lies elsewhere, in an assemblage which for Deleuze and Guattari includes force considered in itself, no longer tied to anything but number, movement, space and time, and when speed in the abstract accompanies displacement. Here then is a relation between the experience of speed, weapons and violence. And further details are added to the distinctions between domestic society and the war machine.

Reference may be made back to the conception of the artifact introduced earlier in this thesis, founded in a philosophy of internal relations, and using this idea of assemblage (non-identity). The self-evidence of a category of artifact, such as spear or axe, is refused. The tool or weapon is here constituted not by an abstract definition of (a particular) tool or weapon, but by their origins in particular practices or projects. There is no 'society' or 'culture' put upon the material artifact; the artifact always already delegates actions, representing the material 'output' of the interpretive decisions of those who desired, made and used the artifact. There is no hierarchical separation of technology and society, or the material and social, as the artifact is found in the practices within which it is constituted, used, consumed, experienced.

The only artifacts to appear in Korinthian painting, apart from clothing are, to repeat: weapons, with and without men to use them; armour; shields; tripods, bowls and stands (*agalmata*); horse bridles; chariots. There is also a net and a cart. Associations of this artifactual world are with violence and war, bloodletting, and the speed of the race. Gernet presents also the field of reference of *agalmata*: religious awe or *aidos* (1981: 121), encapsulating wealth, the gift, luxury, sacred power, even mystery and portent (*ibid.*: 141). Tripods, shields and their devices, and rich textiles may be of this order. And also horses themselves (*ibid.*: 115; Schnapp-Gourbeillon 1981: 169–73). There was a cult of Athena's golden bit at Korinth (Gernet 1981: 131). Detienne and Vernant (1978: Chapter 7) detail an elaborate set of associations of the horse in myth, conceived as a creature of chthonic powers:

> In Greek thought the Gorgon symbolised one essential aspect of the horse. Many features of its behaviour – such as its highly strung nature, its neighing, its sudden movements of panic, its mettlesome disposition, its unpredictability, the foam at its mouth and sweat on its flank – reveal the horse to be a mysterious and disquieting beast, a daemonic force. In religious thought there are striking affinities . . . between the frenzied horse, the Gorgon, and the man who is possessed.
> (*ibid.*: 191)

Again the references to the world of masculine sovereignty are intensified.

Lifestyle and an aesthetics of the body

πλεκτοὺς δ' ἀμφιτιθεῖ στεφάνους,
ἄλλος δ' εὐῶδες μύρον ἐν φιάληι παρατείνει·
κρητὴρ δ' ἕστηκεν μεστὸς ἐυφροσύνης·
ἄλλος δ' οἶνος ἑτοῖμος, ὅς οὔποτέ φησι προδώσειν,
μείλιχος ἐν κεράμοις, ἄνθεος ὀζόμενος·
ἐν δὲ μέσοις ἁγνὴν ὀδμὴν λιβανωτὸς ἵησιν, . . .
βωμὸς δ' ἄνθεσιν ἂν τὸ μέσον πάντηι πεπύκασται

One puts our garlands on,
another passes fragrant myrrh on a dish.

The mixing bowl is set up, full of cheer,
and still more wine stands ready (they say it will not give out),
soft wine, in earthen jars, with the scent of blossom.
In the middle of all, frankincense gives out its holy fragrance . . .
The altar, in the centre, is thickly garlanded with flowers.
Xenophanes West B1

ἕρπει γὰρ ἄντα τῶ σιδάρω τὸ καλῶς κιθαρίσδην

counterbalanced against the iron of the spear is sweet lyre-playing.
Alkman Davies 41

Korinthian ceramic design comes to be part of a discourse of masculine sovereignty defined in relationship with a world of the everyday. I have traced an assemblage of reference and connection around animal and bodily form (stylised and animated), violence and contest, speed and energy, the floral, and geometric and figurative schemata. Connection can also be seen with the sort of juxtapositions made here by Xenophanes and Alkman: flowers, perfume and the symposion; weaponry and the music of association. A primary theme is that of lifestyle: experiences and meanings centred upon the sovereignty and identity of a warrior lord, an heroic *agathos*, expressing himself in an aesthetic field, but an aesthetic of expression which goes beyond restriction to a narrow class grouping.

There is a complex of overlapping relationships between masculine and feminine; war and the *oikos*; excess and nutrition; otherness, divinity and the domestic; death and everyday anonymity; the warrior group and sexual reproduction; risk and transgression of law and convention; social and personal identity and the loss of self; integral creatures and monsters; integration (structured formation) and dismemberment; animals as reflections and strange unknowable animals; sovereignty and subordination. Mediating elements are violence, conflict and confrontation, and the graphical body or form (of people, of animals, of monsters, of flowers). Birds too seem to occur in a mode of mediation.

The imagery assumes a concept of lifestyle separate from work and production, just as the *arete* of the *agathos* presupposes the time of leisure (Adkins 1972: esp. 32–3). Lifestyle is a sphere of (high) culture and freedom of action separate from the toiling masses.

Korinthian potters made a distinctive and quite rapid shift to design which works with these values and forms, the building blocks of a particular lifestyle. The imagery is, as I have attempted to show, focused upon a subtle and complicated *aesthetics of bodily form*. A question follows: what is the significance of this visualisation of connections between lifestyle and an expressive aesthetic of the body? I have already introduced the general argument of Donlan, Murray, Kurke and others that aristocratic politics made a shift into a (contested) *ideology* of lifestyle, indeed were based upon the organisational power of the male group gathering for feasting and entertainment in the symposion. More particularly I have drawn upon the work of Bataille (esp. 1985a) who related the rise of militarism and fascism in the 1920s and 1930s to his concepts of sovereignty, transgression and a repudiation of the everyday. Bloch too has provided (1991: *passim*) commentary upon the ideological focus of fascism in a world of myth removed from the everyday. For Benjamin (1979) fascism was the transformation of politics into an aesthetics of expression; expression was a key for Bataille also in the understanding of fascism. I have indicated at length how Theweleit (1987, 1989) analyses the militarist *Freikorps* of post-war Germany as mobilising a political and aesthetic ethos centred upon the body and upon gender. The purpose of setting these interpretations of militarism next to my encounter with archaic Korinth is not to imply analogy or that Korinthian design is the articulation of a proto-fascism. I wish rather to show how this complex of expression around images and evaluations of the body, gender and lifestyle is a pervasive and often powerful ideological field with which we live still today. However, before I can elaborate upon and provide further support for this thesis I will halt the flow and draw together observations made so far of the aryballos from Boston.

Aryballos Boston 95.12: a summary interpretation
In a violent but balanced encounter the man meets and faces the monstrous double of man–animal. The *agalma* of stand and bowl mark the environment as special, exotic, removed from the everyday and pertaining to a marginal space of religious awe and the power or value of male association. So too do references to the floral. As prize perhaps, the *agalma* refers to arbitration and judgement and to the emergence of winners and losers, the dominant and subordinate. Birds, through their associations, mark the exotic and mediate forces of mortality and divinity, wild and domestic, molar and molecular. The mobile naked swordsman adds another connotation of the body and the energy or speed of violence. Above, in the shoulder frieze, is a violent and separated world of the animal, but brought to stylised order. This is all far from a lower culture of labour in the fields, and is the sphere of action of a lord defining a (gendered) self through risk and an expressive order of violence.

The old formulae of parallel linearity and predictable angularity are present in the frieze layout; referenced too in the black upon pale ground slip painting are the security and certainty of traditional ceramic manufacture. But these serve essentially to highlight the shift to a comparative excess of detail in scrutinised miniaturism and massive deviation into curve (vegetal, animal, energised) and inclination (the 'decorative' devices), all in a workmanship of risk. This forms a counterpoint with the visualised themes.

Part 2   Korinthian ceramic style: eighth through seventh centuries BC
Animal art and the decorative: is there a case to answer?
I have presented a series of associations running through the design of Korinthian pottery, focused through one particular aryballos with figured painting. But, as has been indicated, many (later) pots have scenes containing only animals; so many are simply coursing hounds. Many other pots are sub-geometric, with little figurative imagery. Taken on their own, these do not seem to make sense in the same way as the more complex designs. A conventional judgement is that they are 'simply decorative'

(Whitley 1991b: 196–7 is a recent example). The related question is how much of Korinthian design is covered by the visual ideology of masculine sovereignty: is it only applicable to a few fine pieces? Am I guilty of overinterpretation?

The concept of decoration or the decorative is central to this issue. I have elsewhere presented a general critique and argued for the careful qualification of this term (Shanks 1996a: 41–3). Here I will recap and expand with some statistics taken from the Korinthian pottery (full treatment may be found in my dissertation, Shanks 1992e: 145–7 and Appendix Two).

The decorative is a term rooted in a concern with meaning. So, to call, for example, a line of painted animals decorative (as in Figure 3.27) may be understood in the following ways.

> The design has been borrowed from, is an imitation or adaptation of a source whose (original) meaning has been lost.
> The painted design is of purely aesthetic significance, having no functional, or other meaning. The term ornamental may be considered appropriate here, with the scene considered to be a supplement to form. The ornamental artifact may be one whose surface finish or appearance is elaborated beyond simple functional requirements.
> The design is a sort of visual cliché, a stock or formulaic scene whose origins are to be found in convention or tradition.

This concept can be argued to be misleading or redundant on the following grounds.

First, any surface could be described as decorative. Everything has a surface or outside; and every surface has a finish of some sort. Finishes may vary, some may be described as more or less elaborated; the potter-painter may choose to invest more or less time and interest towards the end of the production process. But finish is not supplemental; it is the dimension which supplies form. The term decorative may be used for an artifact which displays more concern with elaboration and labour investment in the final stages of production. But a simple textured surface could equally be described as decorative. The initial choice of material, such as fine Korinthian earthenware, may well imply (or *intend*) a certain finish; the process of production (black figure firing, for example) also. A process of production is not often an accidental amalgam of separable activities: black figure surface and painting requires a set of practices from clay extraction to brush manufacture. In this way the finish is *internally related* to production. So I argue that the term 'decorative' has no specific field of reference, because everything can be described as decorative or decorated. The decorative is simply the appearance of the form of an artifact.

The aesthetic is a field which cannot be separated from production and function. This is the corollary of the first point. It is inappropriate therefore to have a concept of the decorative referring to a special field of aesthetic finish, in contrast to the communication of a substantive meaning. The aesthetic is not well conceived as an abstracted and separate field of activity (as in Art, 'beauty' or 'taste'). The aesthetic is that which pertains to perception; it is an adjectival concept, not substantive.

Nothing could ever be described as purely decorative. In the idea of the decorative iconic meaning is subordinated to form and tradition. But can there ever be a limit case of a purely decorative or formal surface empty of meaning? I would argue that there cannot, because a graphic or design always implies at least the conditions of its production. The decorative must always be the outcome of a set of relations of (artistic) production, and these can never be without meaning, purely 'technical' or functional. A pair of miniature sphinxes upon a Korinthian aryballos implies the fine brush and slip, the manufacture of both, the acquisition of the skills necessary to paint them, the knowledge of firing process, the belief that such a design will enhance the surface and help the sale of the pot, and much more. All this can hardly be called meaningless or gestural.

Invoking the decorative does not explain why certain stock scenes were chosen rather than others, nor why they came to be conventional or traditional in the first place. An argument such as that of Carter (1972) that certain eastern conventions were adapted to answer a desire to depict action and narrative does not explain that desire.

So-called decorative pots need to be considered in context, in their relationship with more complex designs, because they share a mode of production and many design features. This point is given added force by acceptance of the previous point that a design always implies its mode of production.

The category of the decorative is rooted in a particular ideology and metanarrative of design and making. It characteristically involves radical division between labour and reason:

decorative	meaningful
formulaic	purposive
tradition	beauty
craft	art
application	decision
ornament	form
artisan	artist

The humble artisan is eclipsed by the genius of the creative individual – a hierarchy very particular to the west (Lucie-Smith 1981). This set of oppositions is part of the root of the capitalist division of labour into management, reason and decision over labour, operations and execution of tasks (the classic exposition is Braverman 1974). It is ideologically related to class interests. This is not the place to pursue this line of critique (further comment can be found throughout Shanks 1996a; consider also the implications of Vickers and Gill's argument (1994) about ideologies of art in relation to Greek ceramics). Here I point out merely that the discourse to which this distinction belongs allows two routes to understanding the decorative: through an abstract aesthetics of beauty and form, appreciating how some decorative devices are better or more 'beautiful' than others; or through tracing the 'life of forms', the creation, use and transmission of graphical conventions, devices, schemata. Both tend to problematic idealism (argument over the nature and appreciation of 'beauty') and/or a detachment of design from production and its social origins. In this context I do not hold with the latter.

Statistically the argument that Korinthian scenes are simply decorative does not hold.

If the animal frieze were to be described as decorative, choice of motifs could be said to be governed by an 'aesthetic' interest, rather than one concerned with iconic meaning. Certain animals would be chosen not because of what they were but because of how they looked, how they added to the surface finish perhaps. But given the linear character of the figured scenes and the stylised nature of the animals, I suggest that it would be very difficult to argue that a bull next to a lion looks better than a ram next to a goat: they belong to a *similar* aesthetic standard or taste. The animals are stylistically interchangeable. A *pattern* of animals (alternating or repeated groups, for example) may be described as decorative, and I will consider this option in a moment. Another variation of the idea of the decorative would be if the friezes were constructed on the basis of a *random* selection of animal figures (all animals being equivalent in their absence of meaning); a decorative animal frieze could be one which revealed a random selection of animal figures. This may be extended to cover the human figures too, which rarely can be identified as characters from myth. So, the idea of the decorative may imply that, given a graphic convention of linear friezes, the figure types have an equal chance of selection. This is not statistically valid for the sample of Korinthian pots I have been studying. Korinthian design is not decorative in the sense of painting which makes no reference to subject matter.

The relative numbers of animals and humans in the later scenes (Figure 3.35) make it clear that there is in no way an equal chance that the main types of animal will be painted. In later friezes, for example, there is a clear preference for lions, and not for rams. I claim that it is not feasible to argue that the lion was more aesthetic or decorative.

Let us assume instead the relative numbers of creatures. According to an idea of the decorative as random selection, the pattern of encounters between them might then be expected to be according to overall proportions. On the basis of the probabilities of a particular animal occurring (according to observed numbers) were calculated expected interactions between different types of animal. Chi squared was calculated to test for difference between observed and expected interactions. All the chi squared values are significant at 0.01, that for birds at 0.1: the null hypothesis of no difference between observed encounters and those expected if random is rejected (Shanks 1992a: Appendix 2, Table 5.6). Later figured friezes cannot be called decorative in this sense. This test was not possible for earlier friezes because of the sample size.

A sense of the decorative may mean that the *combinations* of animals appearing in scenes show no bias or skew. (A combination is a set containing r items from a larger group of n items. Different orders of the same r items are not counted separately.) Given basic figure classes of animals, monsters, birds, people and dogs, there are thirty-one possible combinations of figures in later friezes (account not being taken of

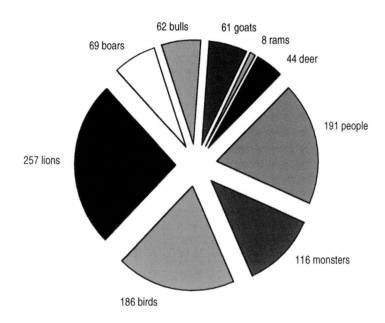

Figure 3.35 The numbers of animals and people appearing in the later Korinthian painted ceramic friezes.

a figure type occurring twice). Each frieze combination might therefore be expected to have little more than a three per cent chance of being painted: there would then be thirty-three or thirty-four of each frieze (according to the total number of friezes in the sample). This is nothing like that observed. It is very clear that the combinations of figures which appear in later friezes cannot be explained by this concept of the decorative, a choice of figures which makes no reference to what they depict. The discrepancy between the types of frieze that might be expected and those actually observed is summarised in Figure 3.36.

There is even more discrepancy between observed and expected types of earlier frieze. A quantitative analysis such as that just presented for later friezes is not useful given the smaller number of friezes. But there occur only thirty different kinds of figure combinations out of a possible 127 combinations (of birds, monsters, animals, floral/ornament, fish, people and dogs). Many likely combinations (given the observed numbers of particular creatures) hardly occur at all, such as birds and animals, (only two cases in 174 friezes, given 267 birds and 149 animals).

So there is a clearly skewed choice of certain types of animal and combinations. Now the decorative may also be held to refer to *patterns* of animals such as alternating figures chosen with reference to the aesthetic (pattern) rather than meaning. But even here the clearly skewed choice is significant *a fortiori*.

So, using the concept of the decorative is not a good way to approach the relationship of figurative to sub-geometric design, more complex to less complex painting.

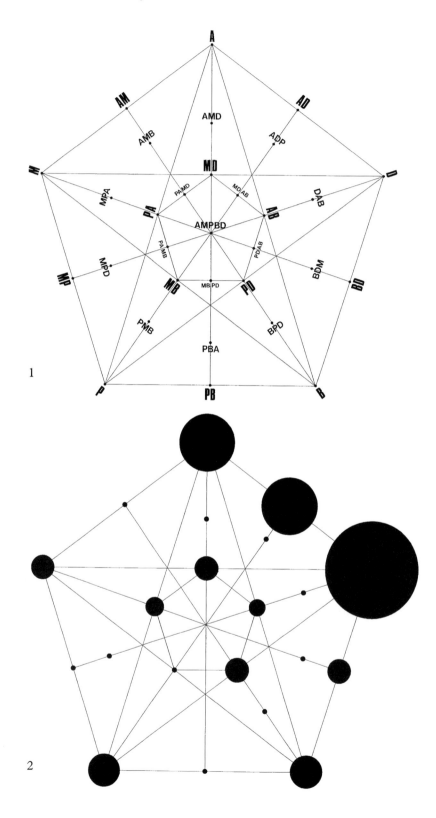

1

2

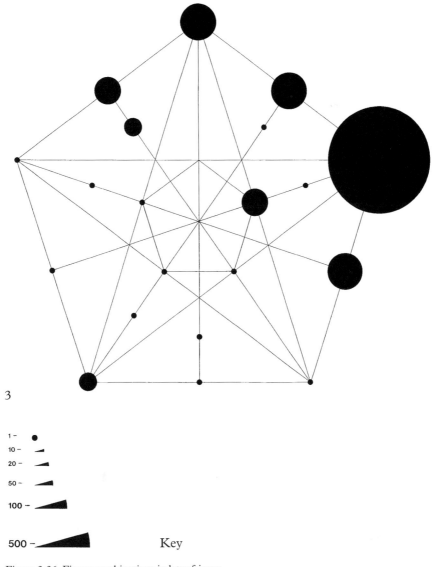

3

1 – ●
10 –
20 –
50 –
100 –

500 –   Key

Figure 3.36 Figure combinations in later friezes.
1 possible figure combinations of
   A animals
   M monsters
   P people
   B birds
   D dogs
2 expected frequencies
3 observed frequencies.

A short note on anthropologies of art

So, how is the Korinthian 'sub-geometric' design to be understood? It is on the basis of critique of such concepts of the decorative that Tilley and I have argued for a de-centring of the individual, and a conception of art and style as social production.

> To de-centre the individual is to view artistic production as a social and material rather than an individual and psychological process, and to explain the work of art with reference to its location and reception in society, to the institutional sites of its production and consumption . . . Viewing the artist as a cultural *producer* rather than cultural *creator* requires that artistic production, rather than being conceived as a form of practice radically different from other cultural practices, deriving from a unique creative impulse, should be regarded as being in principle a form of production no different from others . . . Art is primarily an historical rather than an aesthetic form. (Shanks and Tilley 1992: 147–8).

To consider art as social production breaks with those problematical oppositions between decoration and meaning, artisan and artist, ornament and form, and indeed style and function. The separation of design into figurative (carrying (iconic) meaning) and sub-geometric is to be abandoned. To consider the decoration of a pot is to consider the *practices* which produced the pot. There is no *necessary* hierarchy or division of practices in the production of the pot. So the surface finishing of a pot should be set in context of the whole design (decoration is not supplemental adornment). There is no necessary division between the painting of figurative and abstract design, myth and decoration, surface and form. These categories are not oppositions but are a *continuous* field of possibility within the making of a pot. There are structures of meaning which are beyond the potter–painter and their aesthetic encounter with beauty and style, structures which are the medium and outcome of their potting and painting. Beyond the individual: it may be better to think less of intentional individual potter–painters than social or cultural *machines* producing Korinthian pottery – machine-like assemblages of practices, values, meanings, tastes, kilns, potters, traders, ships . . . such as I have been exploring. This supplies further context to the argument presented in Chapter One.

Let me now widen this argument, which has anyway been implicit in the interpretation presented so far. Support may be found for this position, I contend, in a series of Marxian-derived writings on art and cultural production (for example Bennett 1979; Eagleton 1976; Macherey 1978; Wolff 1981, 1984). Anthropologies of art summarised by Layton (1991) and by the authors gathered by Coote and Shelton (1992) also indicate the complexity of social mediation involved in understanding artifact design. Visual art can be thought as a 'focus' for cultural activity, and rather than aim to indicate the function or meanings expressed by an artifact (the latter I have termed the fallacy of representation), it is better to consider how it works for a particular society, tracing the 'life of signs in society' (Geertz 1983: 109). Morphy's rich interpretations of Yolngu art (for example 1992) trace a series of connections running through myth, place, design and making, time (the ancestors), an aesthetic of spiritual shininess, and ritual, with meanings changing in different contexts and connections reorientated around analogy and metaphor. I read this as an example of the heterogeneity of cultural assemblage.

Of course a sub-geometric aryballos with a linear painted surface is different from that figured aryballos with which I began. The question is how to interpret the painting of the sub-geometric, given the proposed shift to a conception of art as production. Where do the linear aryballoi fit into the Korinthian machine?

Pattern and order, texture and accent
From a survey of the anthropological literature Tilley and I suggested (1992: 150–5) that much art in small-scale societies is less about representing particular aspects of the social world than it is to do with principles of order and how order should be. As Forge puts it:

> In an art system such as Abelam flat painting, elements, in this case graphic elements modified by colour, carry the meaning. The meaning is not that a painting or carving is a picture *of* anything in the natural or spirit world, rather it is *about* the relationship between things.
> (Forge 1973: 189)

Some studies, notably those of Adams (1973), Hodder among the Mesakin Nuba (1982: 125–84), Vastokas and north-west coast Indians (1978), and Fernandez (1966) lend support to the proposition that there is a link (involving transformation) between principles of order in art and principles of the social order, worked through social relations. I also argue that a key dimension is balance of power. Art and style may be ideological, that is taking a particular position with regard to a conflict of social interests. Artifacts may be focal points for the translation of interests. Or, if the principles upon which society relies (principles which mediate social practices and help define social reality) incorporate contradiction, these contradictions may be displaced or encountered through a graphical or stylistic medium (consider Berger *et al.* 1972).

So this shift to a conception of art as practice, the challenge to absolute definitions for terms such as abstract and figurative, form and ornament, decorative and iconic, may involve attention to order (and disorder). Non-figurative 'decoration' or figurative work such as an animal frieze, the sub-geometric, is much more interpretable in this context. A field of order and disorder: focus is particularly upon textured patterns, and, taken with more complex figurative painting, there are continuities and discontinuities, accents of detail set off by a smoothing of ceramic surface, a function of the geometric and floral patterns. This is not arbitrary, but a mediation of wider social principles. The patterns and textures of lines of stylised animals, floral garlands, chequerboard strips may be considered to help establish ambience, atmosphere, aura, impression, an interplay of deflection and attraction of inspection, the organisation of area (see Gombrich (1979) on graphical pattern and order).

Innovation, variability and change

Let me approach the textures and patterns from another direction. In Chapter Two the scale of production of Korinthian pottery was considered as part of investigation of the generation of style and stylistic change. The questions are of commissioning and creativity: where do the designs come from? Were some sections of society commissioning new designs which advertised a graphic and corporeal ideology; were the designs more of an invention of the potters themselves? These two issues (of the place of the earlier Geometric canon and of the generation of style) are of course related in Korinthian pottery. Both are to do with the relation between tradition and change (including the category of risk which I introduced), and the nature of innovation and creativity. The designs changed. To what end?

As has long been acknowledged by the use of the term sub-geometric, the issue of decorative order is about creativity and experiment in the context of older (Geometric) conventions. But the argument for a conception of style as social production also draws in wider contexts. Interpretation is taken back to the material environment of archaic Korinth and beyond, new perfume jars in the potters' workshops, lifeworlds of polis, mobility, war and dedication, questions of the consumption and deposition of these wares. This introduces the following chapters.

I will now consider some details of innovation and variability in ceramic design as a prelude to some general comment.

Korinthian late Geometric pottery had a limited graphical vocabulary: in Coldstream's definitive account (1968: 99–100, 102–4) can be counted eighteen different design elements (lozenges, triangles and the like). There are forty design elements in Neeft's more detailed listing of late Geometric Thapsos pottery (1981). In my sample of Korinthian pottery from the late eighth century and after there are 232 different floral and geometric designs, and 104 figure types (Figs. 3.6 and 3.9–3.12). The potters of Korinth dramatically increased the graphical variety displayed upon their pots within a generation of 700 BC.

The variability does not remain constant. Later pots in the sample are less varied than earlier in terms of the number of designs which appear upon them: the number decreases from 172 to 113, a drop of 34 per cent. Standardised scores (division by number of friezes) indicate that the decrease is even larger than these figures suggest: the drop is from 0.13 to 0.06, down by more than half (54 per cent). A decrease in the variety of pots produced is also displayed when the number of unique earlier and later aryballoi is compared. (Unique is here defined as a pot which has a geometric or floral design or combination of designs which appears upon no other pot in the sample.) Of earlier pots 33 per cent are unique; of later 24 per cent.

Neeft (1987) found it possible to classify over 925 later aryballoi into forty-eight groups on the basis of gross decorative features, and most of these classes are variations of dog frieze, dot rosettes and linear banding. Many earlier pots are also strongly linear, with the surface below the shoulder covered with fine horizontal and parallel lines, but there is variation around this 'type' with the many different designs upon the shoulder. Over half of earlier aryballoi are of this sort, with lines and one or two geometric or floral devices upon the shoulder.

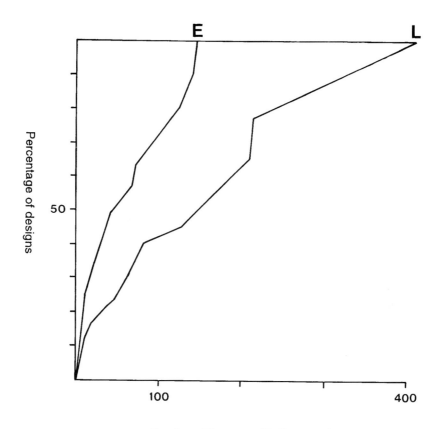

Figure 3.37 Cumulative graph: the number of times a graphical element is used – comparison between earlier and later friezes.

Compare the number of times a particular graphical design is used in earlier and later friezes. The cumulative graph (Figure 3.37) clearly shows a change, with more designs used less often upon earlier pots.

There is another change – in the number of designs (geometric, floral, animals and people) which appear in each of the friezes (running dogs and repeated geometric or floral designs excluded). Most friezes (59 per cent) of the later pots have three or four elements to them; there is less modality in the earlier friezes: more variety in the number of elements appearing in a frieze (this is clearly shown in Figure 3.38).

Geometric and floral design are used differently by the potters with time. One in eight of earlier friezes has a geometric or floral design, compared with three in one hundred later. One in three of later friezes has geometric or floral design in a minor position ('filling ornament'), more than a threefold rise from the earlier pots. (The significant strength of this change of use and relationship between major and minor positioning is indicated by scores of 0.3 for phi-squared and 0.9 for Yule's Q (Shanks 1992a: Appendix 2, Table 3.1)).

Proportionately fewer designs appear repeated to form a frieze or in a panel upon

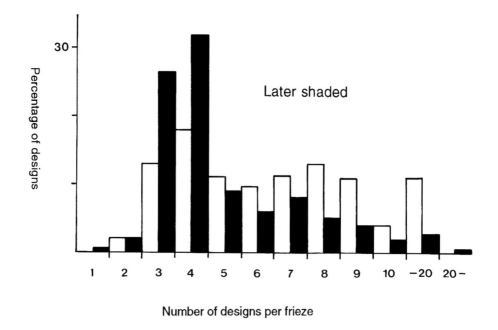

Figure 3.38 The number of designs per frieze; earlier and later compared.

later pots: drops of more than 40 and 75 per cent respectively. With respect to the occurrence of geometric and floral ornament with people and animals, there is a marked rising preference for animal friezes with or without geometric or floral designs in a minor position (70 per cent of later friezes are like this, 24 per cent of earlier).

There are also clear changes in the type of designs used. Triangles, many in friezes around the shoulders of aryballoi, drop out of use by later potters (from 17 down to 1 per cent of friezes), while the use of check and dot rosettes to form textured friezes and as minor ornament shows a 2.5- and 7-fold rise. Lozenge forms come to be used less and take a minor position. Petal forms still appear in friezes around later pot shoulders, but less so (from 9 per cent to 4 per cent of all friezes). Vegetal triangles (with linear hooked apices) continue to be a frequent feature, repeated as friezes, or as major or minor ornament.

There is considerable variety in the types of early figured pots: forty types of surface design (use of linear banding, floral and geometric design, counting also different combinations of basic frieze elements) for 153 pots (standardised: 0.26). Animal friezes clearly dominate later figured pots, and there is much less variety: forty-six types (as above) for 757 pots (standardised: 0.06: drop of 77 per cent). The variety of frieze type also drops from thirty combinations (as defined above) of animal, monster, birds, people, dogs, snakes and abstract elements (standardised: 0.17) to twenty (standardised: 0.02: drop of 88 per cent). The character of figured frieze and pot changes markedly: there are only eleven out of thirty-nine frieze types

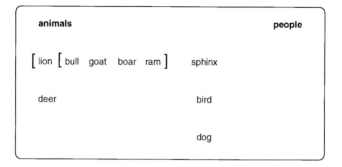

Figure 3.39 Animal classification. Violent animals interact among themselves, but rarely with people. Birds and monster forms (mixing lion, bird and person) mediate. Deer occur on their own, as do (domestic) dogs which may chase birds. The sphinx is, in its associations and character, dog–bird.

which occur both on earlier and later pots; there are only nine types of pot out of sixty-seven found in both earlier and later times.

Many earlier pots are decorated in a way which recalls the subjects of Korinthian Geometric design: bird friezes, and with non-representational designs (different from Geometric designs but still non-representational). I have noted the predominance of linear surface with decorated shoulder. But there is great variety, and the friezes have more elements combined in more complex ways than later. This may be termed a period of experiment upon the Geometric and new ideas of the design of ceramic surface, but this does not catch the detail.

Animals, including dogs, appear in 1,019 of 1,045 (98 per cent) later figured scenes. I have shown how these friezes can in no way be called a random mix. And in the associations and connections I followed arising from the aryballos in Boston, I noted significances to do with masculine identity, violence and the domestic. I will refine some of those points.

Consider again the interactions between the main types of animal. The main ways that animals interact in a way which is not expected from the overall proportions of animals are:

 people are separate and do not mix much with animals
 birds occur with sphinxes
 lions are with boars, bulls and goats more than expected
 deer occur with deer more than expected
 boars oppose boars.

These patterns of interaction are not so clear upon earlier pots, though there is a series of friezes which show deer on their own. So, to end, the classification of animals in Figure 3.39 is suggested to apply particularly to later friezes.

An overview of Korinthian ceramic design
The Geometric tradition

A parallel linearity and *striation*: a stratified or horizontally sectioned surface.
90°, 45° and 60° rotation or angularity.
Horizontal flow around the pot.

Lines providing dimensions (length across the pot and number in parallel).

A metric scheme (the distances between the lines).
Multiple brushes reproducing designs.
A workmanship of certainty.
Fine and uniform slipped surface.
Surface as texture, repelling attention, all background.
Only slight accents of detail: panels and creatures, a bird, a snake's head.
A tight and restricted graphical vocabulary.
Symmetry.
Repetition.

The Geometric is a ceramic surface which can be described as a space of *qualities*.

Abstract decoration with a line subordinate to texture.
Geometric articulation.

The new order

Tradition combined with innovation:
- an open or *smooth* (contrast striated) space is opened in (geometric) texture – space for the friezes;
- a workmanship of risk in free-hand painting and incision of figures;
- allied with a retained workmanship of certainty.

New pot shapes, particularly the aryballos, miniature and for perfume.

A new graphic line:
- the curve – fluid roundness in contrast to geometric ideal of the circle;
- inclination (in contrast to 90°, 45° and 60° angularity);
- petal form (a combination of both of the preceding).

An enlarged graphic vocabulary:
- new designs irrupting within a geometric field;
- diversity augmented through variation and agglomeration of graphic forms.

The painted forms *approximate* to an idea (of a creature or flower), in contrast to *reproducing*, for example, a lozenge net, or parallel lines.
The friezes have little or no background.
The miniature friezes may request close-range attention.

The figured friezes are a special world, in contrast with the domestic:

- referenced are lifestyle and masculine sovereign identity, a culture of violence and contest;
- a significant theme is that of fixity and stylisation in contrast with fluidity and heterogeneity or 'otherness';
- this is worked out in relation to body form (of people, flowers and animals), and action or inaction (battle, coursing hounds or stylised lions, for example);
- different species play differing roles in this scheme – significant is the mediatory role of birds.

Developed is a space of the *affective*: movement, actions upon another, experiences of speed and violence, inclination, charged with meanings.

This involves an aesthetics of the body and corporeal form.

The drawing in friezes may not so much provide dimension and sketch the contours of a pot, but follow a point (a visual ideology).

Korinthian design uses figurative decoration and a line at times 'free' or abstract (freed from fixed shapes and explorative).

There is a general appeal to the person, self and identity:
- visual imagery articulated through the looking of the viewer;
- an aesthetics of the body (imagery and perfume);
- a visual ideology of lifestyle and masculine identity.

Characteristics of the earlier changes

Greater graphical variety.

Graphical variety occurs alongside pot bodies decorated with parallel (Geometric) linearity.

Greater variety of scene structure, pot design and types of figure.

Continued use of panels and repeated designs, as in Geometric.

Frequent use of parataxis: juxtaposition which poses questions of connection to the viewer (articulation through looking), and which ties the scene not to a singular meaning but to a collective assemblage.

Play on figuration, transformation and association: artifacts, birds and the floral.

There are backward references with the appearance of birds and snakes.

Geometric and floral designs are used in major positions in figure friezes – free-standing floral designs particularly.

Triangle and petal shoulder friezes suggest the pot as flower.

Later changes (mid seventh century)

Less variability in types of pot and figure scene, people and monster types and poses, bird types and in geometric and floral design.

More figured friezes.

Dog friezes with rosettes upon linear aryballoi predominate.

Stylised animals predominate.

Less use of parataxis; more scenes have clearly recognisable subjects.

Increased use of geometric and especially floral designs (rosettes) in minor positions (filling ornament).

There is continued and prominent use of linear (or banded) surface texture.

Check and rosette friezes – textures – increase.

Floral forms are articulated into garlands separated from figure friezes.

These display intricate and complicated interweaving – an interplay of curve, petal and texture – the new and old graphic.

Garlands appear around the shoulders of pots.

Ideology and creativity   The scenes of animals, birds, people and exotic ornament were a distinct contrast with the preceding and contemporary geometrically covered pot surface. New pot shapes, the aryballos particularly, were (re)introduced by potters. With a celebration of a workmanship of risk within controlled limits of conventional linear banding, the potters painted free-hand silhouette and outlined figures. Incision and polychromy both added another element to this display of dexterity and regulated precision. In figured earlier designs, potters played on old subject matter, transforming Geometric water birds, retaining wavy-line snakes, but expanding with elaboration, and introducing rich exotic flora. New themes of violence, soldiering, the animal and avian worlds, monsters and strangeness, symbols of the special, are juxtaposed in parataxis in the open linear field. The logical connections and lines of connotation between the themes conform with what becomes clearer later. It is a loose and hazy flow around a special world which is antinomial to marriage, reproduction and the domestic. There is some play with transforming designs: standing tripods through protomes, standing florals through cabled garlands. The introduction of incision is play on figuration.

The variety of figures on earlier pots is greater than that seen later, and, even with the predominantly linear sub-geometric aryballoi, there are few coherent classes of decoration, other than a general one of linear surface with decorated shoulder. There is clearly an explicit conception, size and look of the aryballos – 'the way it should be'. This conception, or prototype, is provided with slight variations of decoration, producing uniqueness in conformity with the generic aryballos. The figured pots, such as the aryballos from Boston already discussed, are at the extreme of such a scale.

I emphasise the workmanship of risk allied to an iconography which in its juxtaposed elements sets up questions and sparks off lines of association, rather than providing clear ideological messages (the ideological field is clearly one under construction). This means that the risk, ambiguity and elaboration of form and figure are more of an affirmation of the potter's creative self. This could be connected with the great variation upon the modality of earlier designs.

Risk in mode of production and execution, convention transgressed; risk and transgression too in the ideological associations traced to the lifestyle of the hero. The analogy or ideological system may well have appealed to potters themselves, to those who were to take the potters abroad from Korinth, and to those who acquired them as gifts to gods or for the dead (consciously or unconsciously) and to which I will come soon. I argue that the connection between the figured scenes, technique and ideology is a significant one, but it cannot be claimed that the style was anything more than a *marginal* play with figured scenes: there are too few pots with figured decoration. Nor do the (relatively inexpensive) pots represent a powerful ideological argument for an ethical order of aristocratic masculinity. The imagery is often restrained, ambiguous, 'open' to interpretation. The pots figured according to risk and transgression communicate a few potters (perhaps with 'commissioning' others) experimenting with an expressive field of 'individual' identity and aspiration to a sovereign masculinity defined through the body and its corporeality. This ambiguity and interpretability suggests a *contested* ideological field, or one of certain themes such as action, gender, personal space, transgression, identity and sovereignty, undergoing negotiation and definition.

Nor does a model of emulation work easily, whereby Korinthian pots would be produced for an aspiring class or social group, imitating some visual precedent associated with a higher class. Apart from the lack of precedents, there is a clear *emergence* of the visual ideology, its clarification after experiment in its earlier stages: the imagery does not arrive ready-made. I also have argued that the imagery coordinates with its *ceramic* medium, quick to produce and therefore cheap. The techniques of production and surface decoration are an interplay of the fixed and stylised and the fluid and heterogeneous, risk and security, temporalities of tradition and innovation.

The popularity and predominance of sub-geometric is the continuity of a certain taste from the Geometric. The highly regulated design is of an artifact done in *style*, that is an evident intention achieved with evident success. It implies the continuity of standards of (technical) practice, ways of producing the ceramic, whereby the manner has an aesthetic importance of its own, independent of what is made or how it is consumed. Its qualities are of competence, assurance and security (Pye 1980: 71). With the continuity of design from plain and linear to elaborately figured, there is flexibility in an openness to interpretation while offered is an option of acquiring an expression of an emergent visual ideology.

Most later pots are still linearly decorated, but there is not the variability around decorative models as there is on earlier aryballoi. The continuity of design represented by the sub-geometric or linear pots with their textured surfaces and few accents of detail (inviting close scrutiny) communicates security. The co-existence and implied comparison with figured pots makes the later linear vessel doubly secure – it resists the change, variety, heterogeneity. That many later friezes work with a restricted graphical vocabulary, again as in the Geometric canon, further reinforces this. The linearity continues the backward and conventional reference, aryballoi in accordance with traditional manner of finish and decoration, but many pots make a brief and restrained reference to the hunt and domestication through coursing hounds, and to the exotic in the floral designs. In the figured scenes structure is much clearer, as is communication of the ideological components of violence, excess and the mediation of the animal in a world of aristocratic masculinity. The scenes set fewer overt questions. Exotic flora are contained within controlled shoulder garlands. Animals are marshalled and regulated; there is less use of incongruous juxtaposition. Both earlier and later pots display an excess over the linear Geometric. The earlier pots may look closer to Geometric, but later figured scenes are more regulated and formulaic.

Against a background of conservative pottery design, the figured painting was an experiment with a risked potter's hand in an ideological field of aristocratic lifestyle and value. It is very unlikely that this was the 'culture' of the potter, yet a ceramic and iconographic medium was adapted to express it. I suggest that the potter's own class background is perhaps retained in the earlier play on themes and design which questions and opens space rather than expresses with ease and clarity: consider the figurative play with birds, heads, helmets, flowers and tripods. This is the mark of the potter's creativity. But the ideology of the decisive hand and risk of creative self and integrity in the fine miniature brush work and incision can be interpreted as within the bounds of the depicted conceptual world. So too is the general interplay of stylisation and experiment with variety and heterogeneity.

The creativity of these Korinthian pots is their heterogeneity. With a new graphic line and imagery they are an irruption of an affective and smooth space, in contrast with a continuation of the striated or stratified texture and canon of the Geometric. The small perfume jars displaying this miniature figuration intimate a field of the personal, point to a political aesthetics of the body, appeal somewhat to notions of self and identity. This is the potential of the new material environment: decorated surfaces which do not repel attention, but provide a different ambience in a different way, and even attract attention to pose and answer questions. The later textures, stylised animals scenes, security of the Geometric and realm of clear signification (scenes with recognisable themes), are a taming of the heterogeneity and creative exploration.

Geometric tradition cannot be disassociated from the changes at the end of the eighth century: there is an essential interplay of continuity and transgression. The term protokorinthian is accordingly inappropriate. Furthermore the vectors of association that I have traced in the 'cultural assemblage' that is Korinthian design, the social and ideological contexts mean that it makes no sense to term these pots protokorinthian, as if somehow they escape to prefigure what is to come. This terminology belongs to an entirely different conception of style, one which finds development, the ripening of artistic styles, and then their fading. The term is useful perhaps only as a label, convenient in conventional discourse, for pots produced from late eighth to seventh centuries in Korinth, and even here it is unsatisfactory because it has to be prefixed with sub-geometric to encompass the continuity of geometric design which is an essential component of what the potters were doing in Korinth.

Many pieces of the collage presented in this chapter have pointed away from Korinth to imaginary and real worlds beyond – mobility and travel, sanctuaries and cemeteries, consumption and deposition. These are the topics in the life-cycle of Korinthian design taken up in the next two chapters.

4

Consumption: perfume and violence in a Sicilian cemetery

Korinthian pots were taken to many sites abroad, in Greece and the West. A total of 1,121 pots in the sample (58 per cent) have a recorded provenance, coming from more than ninety sites including Korinth itself. These are almost entirely cemeteries in Greece, the Aegean and Italy (both Greek colonial and 'native' sites) and sanctuaries (mainly Greece and the Aegean). Sites and pot numbers are shown on Figures 4.1 and 4.2.

There are only eighty-seven pots from the production site of Korinth; more than 78 per cent of the provenanced pots (in the sample) were exported. It seems an inescapable conclusion that the production of pottery at this time was dominated by 'external' contacts and consumption. This conclusion may be conceived in a weaker or stronger way: either pots just happened to end up away from Korinth, or the pottery was designed for export. The proportion exported would seem to support the latter stronger conclusion. I will be examining these possibilities.

The importance of studying how artifacts were used, what Ruth Cowan (1987) has called the 'consumption junction', and how they came to be deposited in the archaeological record, seems clear in a contextual archaeology. For archaeological example, Whitley (1987, 1991b, 1994b) and Morris (1987) have presented studies of dark age Attic (and other regional) burial practices which aim to establish a dark age and archaic social structure read from careful delineation of the patterning found in archaeological remains (through statistical analysis of mortuary practices and combinations of grave goods). Their work has confirmed the value of exploiting contextual associations. But this is not the place to present such a study, for a number of reasons.

I am not willing to read society off from material culture patterning, for reasons outlined in Chapter One and associated with what I have termed the fallacy of representation. *A fortiori*, the use in such studies of multivariate statistical analysis to establish material culture patterning needs very careful qualification (Shanks 1992d). I have also indicated in Chapter One problems with the definition of context, arguing for indeterminate association rather than a conception of the context, for example, of an item of Geometric pottery as being solely the grave within which it happens to be found. Account needs to be taken of the fragments and ruins with which archaeologists work: I have been attempting to illustrate that it is indeed debatable whether the aim should be reconstruction of ancient 'social structure', taking the form of a conventional sociology or anthropology, arguing instead for the development of specifically archaeological forms of interpretation and narrative (see also Shanks 1992b, 1995a, 1995b).

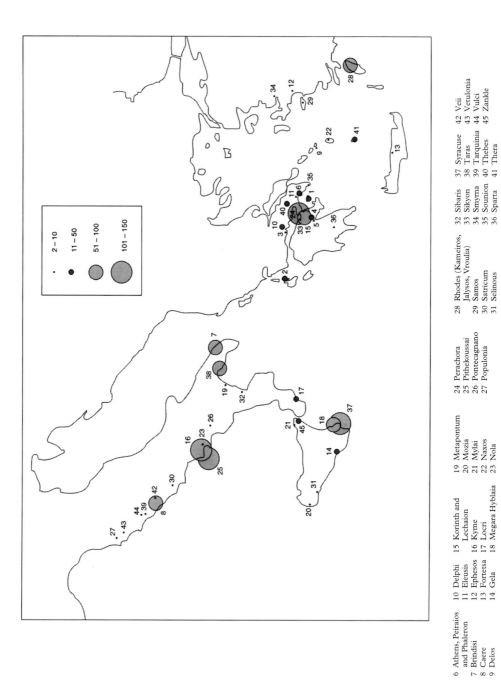

Figure 4.1 The distribution of Korinthian pottery in the first half of the seventh century BC.

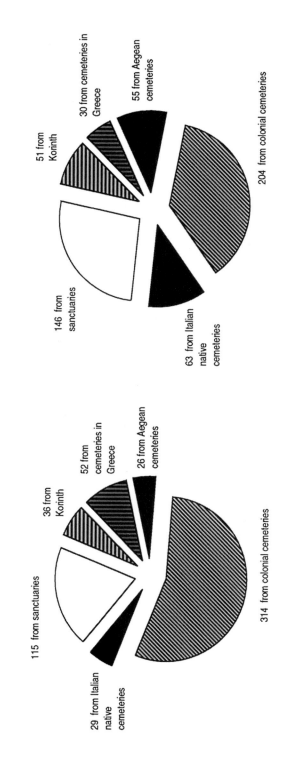

earlier

115 from sanctuaries

29 from Italian native cemeteries

36 from Korinth

52 from cemeteries in Greece

26 from Aegean cemeteries

314 from colonial cemeteries

later

30 from cemeteries in Greece

55 from Aegean cemeteries

51 from Korinth

146 from sanctuaries

63 from Italian native cemeteries

204 from colonial cemeteries

Figure 4.2 The main types of provenance of Korinthian pottery of the seventh century BC.

The life-cycle of the Korinthian aryballos leads out through its consumption in the hands of trader or colonist to its deposition. The assemblage that I have been sketching can be extended with further textures and associations, but a detailed study of the cemeteries and sanctuaries of the eighth and seventh centuries would require another book. However, it is also clear that broader conclusions are quite in order, for a consistent picture emerges.

Perfume and the body

κἀλειφόμην μύροισι καὶ θυώμασιν
καὶ βακκάρι· καὶ γάρ τις ἔμπορος παρῆν.

I drenched myself with unguents, sweet scents
and myrrh, for there was a merchant or so at hand.
Semonides West 16

ἔνθα δὲ χηλοὶ
ἕστησαν, ἐν δ' ἄρα τῆσι θυώδεα εἵματ' ἔκειτο.

there chests
stood, in which garments as fragrant as incense lay stored.
Odyssey 21.51–2

The majority of the Korinthian pot shapes are accepted as accoutrement to drinking wine (cups and jugs), or they are small closed shapes which contained perfume. Aryballoi are the most numerous and conspicuous pots in terms of the figured decoration. I have no need to further elaborate the connotations and associations of cups and ewers: they fit easily into the ideological field I have been exploring. The drinking of wine may be easily related to the ideologies of that institution which I have already discussed, the symposion, the male drinking group, which comes to be such a significant feature in later Attic iconography (Lissarague 1990). Wine came to be a defining element of masculine society (Murray 1990). Here however, I wish to expand upon the place of perfume, sketch out its cultural space.

Were these aryballoi really perfume containers? Ancient Korinth was famed for its perfume, as has already been mentioned. Pliny (*Natural History* 13.5), writing much later of course, remarks that Korinthian perfume had long been popular. Plutarch (*Timoleon* 14.3) records Dionysios of Syracuse in exile, wandering the perfume boutiques of Korinth. But this is circumstantial evidence. Some earlier aryballoi are quite delicate and might therefore be supposed to be unsuitable for carrying expensive oil. Payne, in contrast, commented (1931: 4) that the early aryballoi are so delicate as to make them suitable *only* for perfume. However, most are very robust, as is shown by their preservation.

Payne noted that an aryballos from Akrai in Sicily (Payne 1931: 288, Cat. No. 486) smelled of scent when opened! Here we are getting closer. Biers, Searles, Gerhardt and Braniff have conducted analyses of residues in plastic or figure vases produced in Korinth in the seventh and sixth centuries BC – small closed containers

Figure 4.3 The face of the perfumed panther. An aryballos from the Argive Heraion.

which may well be suspected of carrying perfume (Biers *et al.* 1995; Biers *et al.* 1988). Gas chromatography and mass spectometry revealed traces of camphor and various components of fats and oils perhaps related to perfume. There was docosane, a hydrocarbon found in plant material such as maize tassels and flowers, and the oleoresin of an evergreen tree was detected in two vases. Several ancient authors, including Pliny (*Natural History* 12.62), say such a substance was used in perfumery. In a poster session at the 96th meeting of the Archaeological Institute of America, Atlanta, Georgia 1994, Biers, Gerhardt and Braniff claimed, on the basis of analysis of the organic residues of twenty-four vases, that the contained perfume was pungent rather than floral and perhaps had insecticidal properties.

So let us assume that these vessels were perfume jars (Cook 1966: 232–3; Payne 1931: 3–4).

There is quite a lot of evidence relating to perfume in the ancient world (Faure 1987). Forbes (1965: 34) lists the ingredients for twenty-eight ancient perfumes. After Dioscorides of the first century AD, Shelmerdine (1985: 11–16) gives account of processes of manufacture. Astringent plants were heated in oil to provide a base. Stronger aromatics were then added and strained repeatedly. Another method, later termed *enfleurage*, used animal fats to extract oils or essences (Dioscorides 2.76) (perhaps those animal fats found in the organic residues are traces of this (Biers *et al.* 1988)).

A Bronze Age perfume industry and traffic in the Aegean is very well attested (Bunimovitz 1987; Shelmerdine 1985). There is considerable textual evidence for movement of resins and perfumed oils (Knapp 1991: 32–47). Haldane (1990: 57–8) reports remains of coriander seeds, flower parts, pomegranate skin and safflower seeds in the Ulun Burun shipwreck (Turkey) of the late fourteenth century BC and suggests that the coriander and pomegranate could be used in preparation of the astringent oil base for perfume.

The associations of sweet smells in early poetry have been outlined by Lilja (1972): gods, religious uses, eros, stored clothes, symposia, anointed corpses. The gender contrast with Korinthian pottery is interesting: most references to perfume in ancient poetry are in association with women, not men (*ibid.*: esp. 63–4). Archaic perfume thus belongs perhaps with gender redefinitions in a field of ideological negotiation. Lilja (*ibid.*: Chapter 4) could find no distinction between unguents and other manufactured perfumed substances: ancient perfume was associated with olive oil.

Working from a wide range of ancient literary sources and in classic structuralist manner, Detienne (1977, 1979: Chapter 2) has interpreted the cultural field of ancient perfume as culinary, gendered, economic and physical or physiological, relating also to animals and sex (seduction and the perfume of the panther, already mentioned above (see p. 100)). Perfumes were associated with spices (through their scent, strange and exotic origins). They had culinary associations as scents and perfumes were sometimes conceived as the food of the gods; there was a hierarchy of foods from perfumes to the raw anthropophagy of lower orders. Perfumes were aphrodisiacs, instilling the drying heat of passion, and thus can be associated with conceptions of gender, because woman was conceived as hotter and more moist than the male (in order to resist the drying effect of passion's heat). Mason has supported these references to gender in an interpretation of Hesiod's presentation of the birth of woman and sacrifice. Pandora, 'gift' from Zeus to men, was like fire (Mason 1987: 153–4), and the circumstances of her arrival in the world of mortality brought death, sacrifice, the need for sexual reproduction and agriculture (previously men were closer to divinity in the lack of these). Agriculture and sexual reproduction were linked in mythical origin: the need to plough a furrow went with the need to sow seed in the woman (see also DuBois 1988). Foods and basic needs changed in Hesiod's mythical origin of sex and gender. The connections go further. Hesiod's misogyny has woman as a combination of active and passive: lack of industry and lust for sex. This is that contrast between the absent female in Korinthian ceramic design, and the presence of dangerous warrior women and other monsters.

The space of perfume is thus a complex one. Although based upon olive oil, it is treated and transformed. Thus it is outside of agriculture and associated foods, belonging with divinity, and with a culinary code which distinguishes gods from men from lower and animal orders. As hot aphrodisiac it is sexually charged, coming between male and female. Perfumed oil is also of the body, and I have described how Korinthian design can be interpreted as a locus for definitions of the body. Applied to the skin, it cleans and enhances. Perfumed oil belongs with a concern with the body, its appearance and personal condition.

This is all particularly appropriate to its consumption in cemeteries and sanctuaries: gift to gods, perfumed oil for the body of the dead. Appropriate also for voyaging outside the polis of agriculture and marriage, in the time and space of the marginal adult male, the trading time outside the agricultural cycle, in search of wealth and personal sovereignty.

Cemeteries and sanctuaries: the shape of consumption

Export to cemeteries and sanctuaries: the numbers of pots found in other contexts (domestic, for example) are so low (for full details see Shanks 1992e: Appendix 1) that I have added them to the regional counts for cemeteries in Figure 4.4 or the published details of provenance and context are uncertain and I have simply excluded these pots from interpretation of consumption patterns.

I make reminder again that Korinthian pottery is an object of discourse. The dominance of cemeteries and sanctuaries may, of course, be an illusion, the product of research priorities and preferences of classical archaeology, product also of differential preservation. Fieldwork over the last century and a half has concentrated upon public buildings in settlement centres, temples included, and upon the great sanctuaries. Cemeteries have attracted attention because they are likely to yield a good return of artifacts for effort invested, an important consideration for artifact and museum-centred interests. Korinthian pottery has been found at settlement sites (for example, Megara Hyblaia: Vallet and Villard 1964. But even if Korinthian pottery was consumed in domestic contexts too, this does not alter the fact that major modes of consumption were as grave goods and as offerings in religious contexts away from Korinth. It seems very reasonable to continue interpretation based upon this fact.

Cemeteries and sanctuaries in early archaic Greece

Snodgrass, in his analysis of the emergence of the polis (1980a: esp. 52–65), has emphasised the importance of religious developments, the growth of communal sanctuaries in which was invested considerable wealth, a shift of attention away from the individual grave. Simply in terms of quantities of goods, the sanctuaries were a major part of the archaic economy. He has also noted (*ibid.*: 105) a shift from dedicated tripods to weapons, after about 675. Tripods were replaced somewhat by oriental cauldrons but he connects the rise in dedicated weaponry with hoplites and their possible place in the city state. As well as a focus for dedication, some sanctuaries were the site for games and contests. Of course, Olympia is infamous.

Morgan (1993: 26–7) has outlined what she sees as the gradual accretion of sanctuary and religious functions to the state. The formalisation of athletics, contest and funerals represented a taming or curtailment of elite spheres of activity. The transfer of arms and armour from graves to sanctuaries represents an ideological statement of the place of military force in the state.

The material ambience of some sanctuaries is markedly cosmopolitan with dedications of many local styles and forms (Snodgrass 1980a: 52–65 for a summary). This was the case at Perachora for example (see p. 187), as also at the Samian Heraion where has been found a diversity of goods, especially from the east, which came in quantity after the eighth century (Kilian-Dirlmeier 1985: esp. 236–40; Strøm 1992 on eastern goods in Greek sanctuaries generally).

For De Polignac (1984, 1994) sanctuaries were rallying points, locales for the exchange of hospitality and alliances, like fairs (Gernet 1968). Games and dedication particularly made of them theatres of ostentation (De Polignac 1994: 17), with individual and inter-state rivalry a function of the loose clan structure I have described above (*ibid.*: 13). The import of goods, including eastern exotica, is a prominent feature of the mobility represented by sanctuaries, meeting points for local populations and those travelling from further afield. Morgan mentions the likelihood of itinerant craftsmen (1990: 37). Local populations, Greeks and foreigners, sacred and profane goods and activities: I have already mentioned in Chapter Two the marginality which may be associated with sanctuaries – they were connective locales for the meeting of different worlds. This may also be seen in the siting of the pan-Hellenic sanctuaries (Delphi, Olympia, Isthmia and Nemea) in marginal, inter-state areas (Morgan 1993: 31).

The sanctuaries received gifts and pillage, but not all artifacts found in the sanctuaries are votive. There is considerable evidence for sacrifice and burning, cooking and eating from early times onwards. At early Isthmia 'the material record indicates that drinking and dining were the principal activities . . . emphasis seems to have been placed on communal dining rather than on the display of wealth, and no investment was made in building' (Morgan 1994: 113; see Gebhard and Hemans 1992: 13–15). Consensus is that communal dining was a significant part of cult activity (Bergquist 1990; Kron 1988; Tomlinson 1980, 1990).

With respect to mediation and travel between worlds, consider also that in the famous rich warrior grave (45) at Argos, dated to about 710 BC, were found, with the weaponry and armour, twelve iron cooking spits and two firedogs in the shape of warships (Courbin 1957: 370–85). Other similar firedogs are known from four warrior graves in Crete and Cyprus (Coldstream 1977: 146). Mason, in discussing Hesiod's cosmogony and account of the origins of sacrifice (1983), isolates a culinary semantic field (separating mortals and immortals *via* operations performed upon grain and meat, particularly in sacrificial rites) and connects it with gender and economic distinctions. The fire, smoke and aroma of sacrifice draw perfume too into the culinary field. Eating and cuisine may be connected with personal identity – what it is to be a person.

Design and provenance

When compared with the overall pattern of consumption, as represented by Figure 4.2, the consumption of *figured* Korinthian pots (those with figured work covering more than one third of the surface), as represented in Figure 4.4, reveals an interesting regional variation: more figured pots were going to sites in Greece and the Aegean than to colonies and sites in Italy and the West. So, whereas 64 per cent of all earlier production ended up in the cemeteries of Italy, only 43 per cent of figured wares went the same way. These figures are 54 and 39 per cent for later pots, 59 and 40 per cent for all pots. The relative proportion of figured pottery which went to the cemeteries and sanctuaries of the mainland and Aegean is larger, by corollary: for example, 25 per cent of total production ended in sanctuaries (mostly Greece and Delos in the

Aegean), but 38 per cent of the figured ware was for the same places. Phi-squared values indicate that this association between figured friezes and site is not a strong one, but it is consistent. It is possible to say that the people of the colonies of Italy, non-Greeks too, who deposited Korinthian pots in graves, were not so inclined towards the figured pots, were more conservative in terms of ceramic style.

Simple inspection of the figured designs from the main sites seems to indicate that some themes or subjects may be associated particularly with one site or type of site.

Earlier pots with scenes containing people occur exclusively in Greece and the islands, and mainly in cemeteries.

There are no earlier pots with birds from the mainland and island cemeteries.

Pots with geometric and floral ornament occur mainly in sanctuaries.

The distribution of particular motifs according to site type and region is shown in Figures 4.5 and 4.6. The points just made are clearer in these figures. However, there is otherwise a great deal of similarity from region to region and site type to site type. The slight deviations from what would be expected if all the regions and site types used the same pots, favouring the same kinds of design, are clear and as mentioned: they are to do with the occurrence of people and the geometric or floral in the scenes. Overall, the figures upon Korinthian pots say little about where they were consumed or ended up. (Discussion and statistics: Shanks 1992a: 184–5 and Appendix 2, Tables 6.6 and 6.7.)

The lack of images of people upon the pots in the colony cemeteries explains the appearance of relative conservatism I have just noted as may perhaps the lack of birds on pots from Greek and island cemeteries. Scenes involving people are the most explicit rendering of the visual ideology I am interpreting. Birds are the main figurative element of late Geometric style, and a stylistically forward-looking preference may have wished to avoid their use. The high number for geometric or floral ornament in the sanctuaries is almost entirely explained by a series of plates or dishes from Perachora and Aetos.

So the conclusion seems reasonable that there are no obvious and significantly different preferences for particular design elements, apart from a relative conservatism in the west regarding earlier peopled scenes. There is indeed a remarkable homogeneity in the distribution of figured frieze components and types.

The question of the relation between source, trader and destination is raised by an interesting observation. Many Korinthian pots are found in the same context (grave or votive or sanctuary deposit) as other pots which are *exactly* the same, and these pots are often the only examples of that particular design. There are forty-two such earlier pots and sixty-two later: 7 per cent and 11 per cent of earlier and later pots with a provenance. To express this more effectively, given the immense variability of Korinthian design described above, if two or more pots are exactly the same, there is a one in seven to one in six chance (or higher) that they will be from exactly the same site and context. (These figures are perhaps more significant given the poor quality of archaeological samples and that 42 per cent of the sample pots have no reliably recorded provenance.) This suggests that Korinthian pots were taken straight from

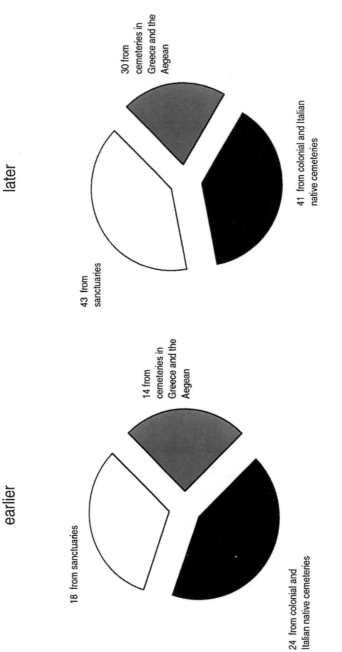

earlier

18 from sanctuaries

14 from
cemeteries in
Greece and the
Aegean

24 from colonial and
Italian native cemeteries

later

43 from
sanctuaries

30 from
cemeteries in
Greece and the
Aegean

41 from colonial and Italian
native cemeteries

Figure 4.4 Figured Korinthian pots and their provenances.

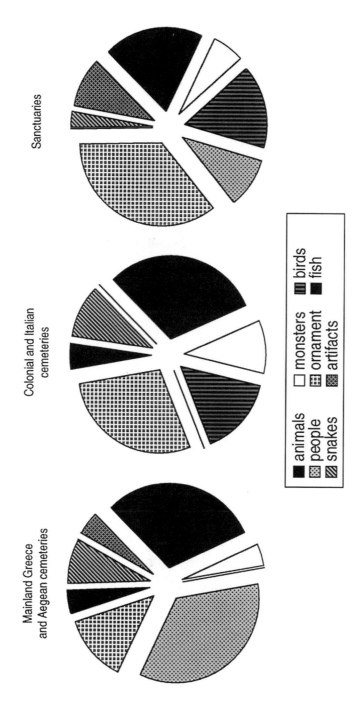

Figure 4.5 Components of the earlier Korinthian friezes and their provenances.

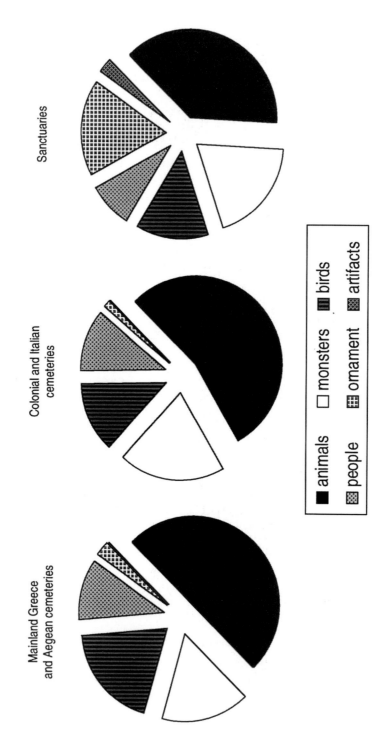

Figure 4.6 Components of the later Korinthian friezes and their provenances.

potter to consumer, and that there was little circulation or use of the pots outside their offering as grave or sacred gift. The remarkable homogeneity just noted could be interpreted in support of this, that the pots were acquired for their use as grave good, votive offering or some other use in a sanctuary.

The consumption of Korinthian pottery at some particular sites

This is a general picture. But what of particular sites? There are sufficient numbers of pots in the sample from several individual sites to enable a quantitative comparison of different designs. The sites are Korinth itself, the sanctuaries of Perachora and Aetos on Ithaka, the Attic cemetery at Phaleron, and cemeteries at Pithekoussai, Syracuse (Fusco) and Kyme. These are well-enough published to enable reliable judgement about the context of deposition. Figures 4.7 and 4.8 present the data.

The general impression of a relative conservatism in the cemeteries of Italy regarding figured frieze pots is not apparent when all different types of pot design are considered. For the earlier period the proportion of plain linear decoration (following an old Geometric canon) at Perachora is high, while the new figured friezes appear quite popular at the Korinthian colony of Syracuse. Dog-frieze pots feature much higher in later colony cemeteries than in the sanctuaries – proportionately twice as many. The decorated plates from Perachora and Aetos are again evident in the proportion of pots with geometric or floral ornament. Aetos also appears both earlier and later to have used relatively more different non-figurative designs, in marked contrast with the other sanctuary, Perachora; this may be an effect of the small sample size. Later sites are otherwise consistent in terms of the relative variability of design represented by the number of non-figurative design elements.

The most distinctive observation to be made of the Korinthian pots found in these sites is the marked contrast between Korinth and all the other sites (due to the presence of pots with simple and all-over black surface, with little or no decoration).

I am not eager to push hard the data in the absence of major and obvious differences and with relatively small sample sizes. There are indeed local differences such as those I have just listed, but the overall picture is:

> a preponderance in all sites of linear pots with little extra decoration;
> a large increase in the number of dog-frieze pots in the colony cemeteries;
> a general rise in all sites in the presence of figured pots;
> a difference between the pots consumed at Korinth and those elsewhere.

These are all general points which have already been made about the development and changes in the design of Korinthian pot design. There may well be a degree of conservatism in the use of Korinthian pots in colony cemeteries: in addition to the point made earlier, I add that dog-frieze pots are a restrained reference to the themes I have interpreted. But overall there is a clear picture. Design and composition give little clue to the provenance of different pots and designs; there is a marked homogeneity or consistency in the pattern of consumption. Apart from at Korinth itself.

It would be interesting to consider not just surface decoration but also the forms used at different sites. However, the different types of pot have not been consistently

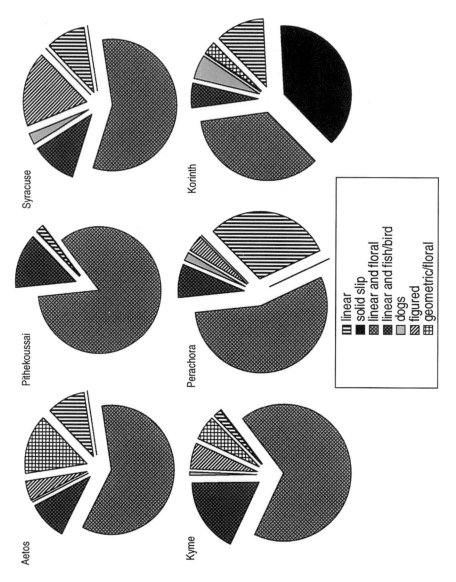

Figure 4.7 Types of earlier design from different sites.

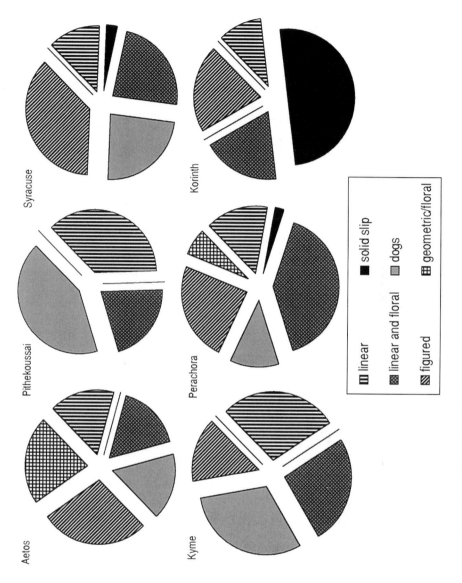

Figure 4.8 Types of later design from different sites.

published. Often only representative pot shapes and designs have been recorded, with little statistical information given about those omitted. This applies particularly to pots decorated more simply and linearly. It therefore makes conclusion about the character of Korinthian design according to site difficult and unreliable. This is another reason why I am not happy with extracting too fine detail from the data just discussed.

I have so far been able to make some comments about general consumption, and there are no new lines I might follow, no major additions to that cultural assemblage which is Korinthian design, though the picture has clarified. That the production of Korinthian pottery at this time in the early state was dominated by export, and the character of home consumption was different has been recognised before. Johansen's synoptic work (1923) and Payne's on Korinthian pottery generally (1931) were much concerned with provenance but simply in terms of establishing for certain the source of the style of pottery known from so many sites in Greece and the west. That some types of Korinthian pottery (geometric Thapsos and protokorinthian) were for the 'export' trade has been argued for example by Roebuck, (1972: 117–21) and Coldstream (1977: esp. 186–7, 242). Salmon (1984: 110–11, n. 64) makes a distinction between pots which accompanied Korinthians for purposes which could not be served at home (such as dedication), and a true 'export' market or purpose. His point is that the distribution of types probably depends upon the nature of the sites that have been excavated in the west and in the Korinthia: 'the shapes which Roebuck claims were made for export were especially suitable for dedication (Thapsos cups and protokorinthian cups and aryballoi), whether in sanctuaries or in graves: that will explain why they are found only rarely at home' (*ibid.*: n. 64). But what makes a pot 'especially suitable for dedication'? This is the key question. And how can pots carried by Korinthians be distinguished from pots carried by others? Is it a worthwhile distinction at all, a valid archaeological question? I will consider this question of 'export' in Chapter Five. Here I observe that the quantitative analysis reported above indicates that particular types of pot do not seem to have been designed for particular places or for particular forms of use or consumption, other than Korinth itself. But this is a substantive rather than quantitative observation in the sense that it is not just that most pots happened to end up abroad, but that Korinthian design included internal reference (in what I have termed its cultural assemblage) to travel, mobility and the mediation of marginal states and spaces.

Korinthian pots travelled to sanctuaries and cemeteries. What was the character of these types of site and how were the pots used with other artifacts? I will now move in and discuss some particular sites.

Cemeteries

Phaleron   The cemetery at Phaleron (Pelekides 1916; Young 1942), used from the late eighth century, was perhaps the poorest in Attika, in terms of things buried with the bodies. Many of the burials had no grave goods at all. For the eighty-seven excavated graves there were six methods of interment, with burial in urns reserved for small children. Many of the graves cannot be dated with any certainty, because of the lack of grave goods. Young (1942: 24) found that mainly the child burials contained articles with chronological (therefore stylistic) significance. Most of the offerings are small even miniature and, in comparison with large mortuary ceramics elsewhere, of poor quality (see summary comment in Coldstream 1977: esp. 117). There is a mixture of local Attic pots and Korinthian, the former often apparently under influence from the latter. The forms are mixed open cups in fine fabric, some aryballoi, oinochoai, and some pots in coarse fabric.

Pithekoussai Settlement and the associated cemetery of this Euboean establishment date from the middle of the eighth century (Buchner and Ridgway 1993; Ridgway 1992b for bibliography). There was a variety of mortuary practices. Children and people aged up to eighteen to twenty were buried in coffins in trenches with grave goods; infants were given *enchytrismos* burial (in amphorae and other large containers). Cremations of adults of either sex were made upon a pyre with or without grave goods and then the remains were taken to the place of burial and sometimes covered with a tumulus (as were some inhumations), sometimes with further grave goods. Some adults of either sex also received inhumations in trench graves without grave goods. Two-thirds of the excavated burials are pre-adult.

Grave goods are mainly pottery, imported and local, and personal ornaments in metal. Rhodian pottery is of the characteristic *Kreis- und Wellenband* style of globular aryballoi – the pots claimed to be of Phoenician manufacture by Coldstream (1969). There are Levantine aryballoi and one north Syrian protome variety too (Ridgway 1992b: Fig. 12, from grave 215-4). Korinthian aryballoi are numerous. There are local copies, such as those found at Kyme (see Neeft's groupings (1987)). There is the same variety of imported *lekythoi*, including also Argive monochrome. Oinochoai are local and Korinthian. Cups include Thapsos *skyphoi* and those Korinthian *kotylai* with very thin walls (metal skeuomorphs?). The amphorae used in the *enchytrismos* rite are mostly local coarse ware, but looking like Near Eastern types; one in ten are Korinthian, Euboean, Chiot and Phoenician imports. Though a Euboean foundation, Euboean pottery is relatively rare.

The excavations have recovered the largest collection of paste scarabs of Egyptian type found in a Greek cemetery (Hölbl 1979: Vo. 2, 177f, Nos. 740–856). The red and green serpentine scaraboids of North Syrian or Cilician types (the Lyre-Player group) are prominent and are also found all over the contemporary Greek world (for analogous types in Rhodes and Cyprus see Bosticco 1957: 228). Most occur with babies and children. Some are local imitations (Hölbl 1979: Vol. 1, 215f).

The personal ornaments include bronze fibulae conforming to the Villanovan sequence; arm bands and pendants are also closely related to Italian types. There is some patterning to deposition of metal grave goods: silver personal ornaments tend to appear in adult cremations; bronze appear in child inhumations. More generally, in all this variety arrangement of graves in family plots seems evident (Ridgway 1992b: 52–4) with also clear distinction of age grades by rite. No graves exceptionally rich in goods have been found as yet to prompt the usual archaeological interpretations of social hierarchy.

The cemetery's material culture is in marked contrast with the dump of material excavated on the acropolis (its origins are uncertain). There arybolloi are virtually absent while kraters are common. Thin-walled *kotylai* are much rarer and there is a range of shapes for dining and drinking, though the imported pieces are drinking accoutrement.

Kyme   Across the bay of Naples from Pithekoussai, the colony of Kyme was settled sometime in the second half of the eighth century (*Monumenti Antichi* Vol. 22, 1913). The nineteenth-century excavations of the cemetery yielded a considerable amount of pottery which can be found in many museums, but little was systematically recorded. There seems to have been a distinction between adult cremation in stone-covered bronze cauldrons and child inhumation. One notable cauldron is of a North Syrian type with bull's head protomes (Amandry 1956: 242–3, Pl. 28). Its profile looks similar to cauldrons at Eretria. Local pottery sometimes closely imitated the main imported type, Korinthian. There are some oil containers from Euboea and Rhodes. As at Pithekoussai oriental scarabs occur only in inhumation graves, presumed to be of children. Metal offerings were also made of fibulae, beads, bracelets and rings, many of silver.

The rich graves did not contain pottery. Consider tomb 104 of the Fondo Artiaco plot. This is a cist tomb. Cremated ashes with jewellery were placed in a silver box inside two cauldrons which contained also purple linen cloth. The box was covered by an Etruscan bronze shield accompanied by two bronze cauldrons one inside the other upon a conical stand. One cauldron with lotus handles is reminiscent of a Cypriot type from two centuries earlier. Other grave goods included horse bits, ironmongery, bronze spearheads, a carp's-tongue sword of Italian type, two more silver vessels, a Phoenician piriform jug, a *kotyle* of Korinthian shape, an oversized electrum fibula of Villanovan style, and an Etruscan orientalising silver fibula.

Coldstream's discussion of the grave (1994: 55) is an ethnic speculation about the relative involvement of Italians, Greeks and Phoenicians, familiar in traditional archaeology's culture history. He pits Strøm's supposition of locals being predominant (Strøm 1971: 147) against Buchner's Greek colonists (Buchner 1979).

Syracuse (Fusco)   In the 730s some Korinthians founded Syracuse (Hencken 1958; Orsi 1893, 1895), the site taken from local Sicels. Burial was similar to that of Korinth. Inhumation in rectangular graves, rock-cut or sarcophagi, was the usual practice in the earliest and main colonial cemetery of Fusco. Bronze pins were offered, necklaces, rings, fibulae, and a horse figurine has been found. There were also bronze bowls and cauldrons. Hencken (1958) has plotted many connections or similarities between the metalwork offerings and examples across Greece, Italy and Western Europe. There were scarabs and other orientalia too, but not as many as at Pithekoussai. Imported pottery was mostly Korinthian – aryballoi, cups and oinochoai. Again there were local copies of perhaps Argive and Korinthian style.

Sanctuaries

Perachora   The development of the sanctuary of Hera Akraia across the gulf from Korinth can be traced from the beginning of the eighth century at the latest (Dunbabin *et al.* 1962; Payne 1940; Salmon 1972; Tomlinson 1977, 1990, 1992).

In the eighth century there was an apsidal temple by the harbour and a 'sacred pool' associated with dining (Tomlinson 1994: esp. 334–5). A second temple by the seventh century is postulated, though there is no direct evidence. A rectangular building on an upper terrace has been identified as a diningroom by Tomlinson (1977: esp. 197) and given a seventh-century date (Tomlinson 1992: 333, after Immerwahr 1990: 16). A polygonal terrace wall of approximately the same date attests to site development. There was also the trace of a building near the 'sacred pool'.

Remains of the sanctuary's goods show that it was especially flourishing in the seventh and sixth centuries and was indeed one of the major Greek sanctuaries at this time, with finds exceeding those of Delphi. Artifacts excavated include pottery, mainly Korinthian, *koulouria* (ring-shaped ceramic cakes), known also from Kerkyra and later Solygeia in the Korinthia, jewellery (including thin sheet gold), pins, figurines and ivory seals bearing figurative designs. There are over 900 objects in Egyptian style, mostly scarabs. Of the eighth to seventh century bronzes 80 per cent are of eastern origin (74 per cent Phoenician and 6 per cent from Greek Ionia) (Kilian-Dirlmeier 1985: 215–54). There is no evidence of tripod or armour dedications.

Interesting finds were remains of ceramic models of houses or temples (Fagerström 1988: 155–7; Payne 1940: 34–51, Pl. 9). Others have been found at another sanctuary closely associated with Korinthian goods, Aetos (Robertson 1948: 101–2, Pl. 45a–g). These models may represent an interest in (new?) architectural designs. For Morgan (1994: 129–35) they symbolise trade (the sanctuaries' site and cosmopolitan material culture), household and territory (again the site within the Korinthian chora), an association between the *oikos* and marriage links (the mediatory role of sanctuaries) (*ibid.*: 133).

Aetos   Out west, *via* the Korinthian Gulf, from around 800 BC dedications were made on the island of Ithaka at Aetos (Benton 1953; Robertson 1948). No temple or religious building has been confirmed and the name of any deity is unknown. This has led Morgan (1988: 315–16) to doubt that Aetos was simply a sanctuary, more a 'central place' with some cult functions; but it remains accepted as such. Finds came from three terraces upon which votives seem to have been dumped. As well as Korinthian and local pottery, there are beads, ornaments, amulets in the form of miniature bronze vessels, scaraboid seals from Asia Minor, ivory seals and hammered bronze horse figurines.

General points about the consumption of Korinthian pottery in sanctuaries and cemeteries
I have indicated that a detailed contextual interpretation of the consumption of

Korinthian artifacts is out of the question on the grounds that it would require another volume. It is also the case that variability of publication is a problem, as are the poor stratigraphical contexts of the excavated sanctuaries (most material is recovered from indiscriminate dumping). Even large samples from cemetery sites such as Pithekoussai are clearly skewed. It is nevertheless quite possible to make some pertinent points.

I begin with three truisms of theory.

> Burial practices are more about the living than the dead; they are the *social* practices of members of society.

> Mortuary practices, at the junction between active living members of society and the dead, frequently take the form of a *rite of passage*, or part of such a rite, between two or more social states or conditions.

These two points are the basis of most anthropological and archaeological investigation of mortuary practices (see, for example, Huntingdon and Metcalf 1979; archaeological discussion in Chapman and Randsborg 1981; Shanks and Tilley 1987: esp. 42–5; see also Morris 1987).

> Objects dedicated to divinity at a sanctuary, votive offerings, objects placed with the dead are all *gifts*. Reference is also made to *value* in every case of dedication or offering. The giver or receiver may value and desire the gift. The gift may not be valued by the giver – those pots given to the dead may be cheap and worthless, but nonetheless reference is made to value if only in that the act of giving is considered appropriate and right. This notion of the value of a sacred or grave gift may be an abstract one of 'wealth' or 'expense': hence our common-sense notions of 'rich' and 'poor' sites and graves. Abstract value (for example that of a commodity) is detached from the object itself. But another sense of value is that of the gift. Here the value of an object is that it is inalienable in the sense that it is not separated from people and social relations, but people and things may interpenetrate, with people implicated in the things they give, and objects taking on the attributes of people. To give something may well be to give a part of oneself.

I suspect that it is because of a dichotomy between these two notions (abstract commodity object and gift implicated in the social) that much analysis of mortuary practices in archaeology holds a premise that the mortuary domain represents society, and often pragmatically uses grave goods as some sort of index of abstract wealth and therefore social rank or status (for example Whitley 1991). The subtlety of people's treatment of the dead and consequent difficulty of interpretation, anthropological or archaeological (see the classic cautionary tale of Ucko 1969), is ignored in a methodological imperative to find 'society' *via* a dichotomous conception of the object or artifact (for a discussion of such mortuary analyses of Morris and Whitley in Dark Age and Archaic Attika see Shanks 1992d). My treatment here of Korinthian pottery and its cultural assemblage of production, travel and consumption is an attempt to relocate artifacts in an *indeterminate* space (created in a particular interpretive encounter) which is beyond radical distinctions between commodity and gift, the economic and social. I refer back to my discussion of the character of an artifact (its ontology) in Chapter One.

And now to the points which emerge from considering the consumption of Korinthian pottery in these cemeteries and sanctuaries.

> There is, through the eighth and seventh centuries, (often increasing) 'wealth' and energy invested in cemeteries and sanctuaries.
>
> The material invested in cemeteries and sanctuaries is usually a cosmopolitan mix of local products, artifacts from the east Greek world, some Greek places such as Korinth, Euboea, Argos and Rhodes, and includes also goods from or references to beyond this milieu – orientalism and the east.
>
> This represents a reference to mobility, mediation and travel, whether of goods or people, in relation to cemetery and sanctuary, death and divinity.
>
> Many goods here are special or exotic in some way: imports, brought from afar. The cauldrons recall the discussion I presented of the special character of tripods and bowls; here they are connected directly with the body. The local copies of imported ceramics implies that the imports were of stylistic value in some way.
>
> These sites of consumption can be interpreted as making persistent reference to social, cultural and conceptual *edges*: the colonies are at the edges of the Greek (next to the non-Greek world), importing also and making reference to eastern, non-Greek articles; death is at the junction of life and death, society and nature (hence the rites of passage); sanctuaries mediate mortality and divinity.
>
> The *person* or social individual is consistently implicated in this consumption of Korinthian pottery. Here it is important to note that the individual is not automatically referenced in mortuary practices; there is no cross-cultural regularity which has the social individual or person referred to in the treatment of the dead. (I assume that there is no need to support this point here: consider collective burial and see the arguments about the individual in Shanks and Tilley 1987: Chapter 3). There is the notion of the gift forming a link between giver and receiver; most of the articles given are small, or miniature (the scrutiny of inspection rather than public view), and pertain perhaps to the person – perfume for massaging or anointing the body, pins, rings, amulets and (personal?) seals for adorning the body. And the different treatment of adult and younger dead implies a distinction between the adult full member of society and those who have not yet become so, have not yet become a *social* person or individual.
>
> There is remarkable consistency, a *koine*, across different sites with respect to these listed characteristics. My presentation should be enough to establish that this is not a function of the coarseness of the archaeological sample.

The gift and identity through self-alienation

One interpretation of the consumption of goods in these places is that external relations and stylistic origins (the exotic goods, imports from Greece and mother-cities of distinctive and non-local style) are being used to construct a self-image of a society or community as an entity in relation to some 'other'. Arafat and Morgan (1989: 335) write of a 'Mayflower complex' wherein elite status in colonial communities was maintained by stylistic reference back to pre-colonial origins (also Morgan 1993: 20). They rightly point to long-lasting local demand and local copies of imported items (often almost indistinguishable from Korinthian). But there is no need to invoke differences of class or rank. I could find no immediate correlation between pot deposition and anything which Arafat and Morgan might interpret as representing ranked society, although in the absence of detailed quantitative analyses and with limited data.

In these particular arenas of consumption, people are perhaps bringing themselves to encounter the edges of their local and immediate social experience, and in so doing this local social existence is given identity and form. In using pots from Greece, both traditional and innovative in style, in referencing a wider international milieu with which the community exchanges, in using these goods in confrontation with death and divinity, the ultimate 'other', society constructs itself. In the colonies, this self-construction of identity is in the face of other people who are non-Greek. With death and the sacred belong those origins and exchanges which mark the beginnings and edges of the community which is burying or making the offering. Such a process would, of course, be particularly appropriate in situations such as new colonies or societies undergoing change, where identity was under re-evaluation or doubt.

The relative, but slight, conservatism of the colonies regarding peopled scenes, and later conservative preference for dog friezes may be explained by the use of goods to construct identity. Pots which make reference to Greek stylistic origins and are less stylistically innovatory may be more attractive in these new communities than those which stretched stylistic taste in a way that was perceived excessive, yet the interplay of tradition and innovation is fundamental to the significance of this style.

This sort of process of cultural construction is very familiar in anthropological accounts of how society is constituted in and through exchange. A community may assert its own internal viability through the idea of it being positively valued by others who come with their goods. But external relations (so important to self identity) may be manipulated by certain groups to the detriment of others: some people may have a monopoly on these important relations with the 'other' and thereby is established a social hierarchy. It is not far to that other process, 'prestige-goods' economy, to which so much reference has been made in social archaeology. Here social elites carefully control access to foreign goods which are the means of display of status, wealth and power: people and certain articles are reciprocally the agents of each other's value and estimation.

But the assemblage of goods and practices in these cemeteries and sanctuaries indicates that there is a great deal more going on. I think of the literature (from Malinowski 1922 to Leach and Leach 1983 and Strathern 1988) surrounding one of the classic cases of exchange network, the *Kula* ring in the Melanesian archipelago, and the difficulty of explanation in simple terms. The inadequacy of separating economic, ritual and political factors is clear and is discussed in Chapter Five. Here in the archaic Mediterranean exchange and relationships with an 'other' are under-standable as processes of self-alienation (the use of exotic goods which have no intrinsic relation with the giver as gifts to an 'other') and construction of identity. Miller has discussed (1987: Chapter 4) the work of Munn on Walibiri iconography and on Gawa canoes in the *Kula* ring to show the absolute necessity of (material) culture for the establishment of all human relations, and to discredit the idea that people's relationships with things (such as in technology, style and exchange) can be separated from some prior form of social relation (such as the political or religious). In such an understanding a Korinthian pot is not just the product of art or an article for exchange or trade. My introduction and use of the concept of cultural assemblage and general economy, developed and established through encounter with Korinthian design, has affirmed these points, that these artifacts are to be understood as the locus of a field of social practices, references and meanings.

Writing the body

Five ceramic pieces:

One and two:
] Εὐάντας | Χαι [
] κεας | ’Ανγάριος | [
] αυϜιος | Σοκλες | [
] κλιδας | ’Αμύντας [
] τοι Μαλέϙο | και [

] τελε [
] λος | χ[
] Χαιρία[ς
] λεος [

A list of names, incised by a potter.
Graffiti on two sherds from the same pot. Potters' Quarter, Korinth. Earlier.
Jeffery 1990: 130, No. 1; Pl. 18; Lorber 1979: 10–11, No. 2.

Three:
A Korinthian alphabet incised above its Euboeic equivalent.
Graffiti on a conical oinochoe from a grave at Kyme. Earlier.
Jeffery 1990: 130, No. 2; Pl. 18.
Lorber 1979: 11–12, No. 5.

Four:
side: Θόας Δ[ίας] Τελέ[σ]τροφος]μαιναϙ[ο
base:]ξε[ ]δεια[

A pyxis from Aegina. Later. Various figures, horses and a man, with painted names.
Base marked out like a wheel with an incised name in each quarter.
Jeffery 1990: 131, No. 4, Pl. 18.
Lorber 1979: 7–10, No. 1.

Five:

Painted nonsense inscription upon the shoulder of an aryballos from Megara Hyblaia. Earlier.

Lorber 1979: 11, No. 3.

Graffiti are a feature of orientalising design. Some of the earliest examples of Greek writing, a syllabic script of Phoenician origin, appear incised or painted upon pots (Jeffery 1990). There are names, marks of property (this belongs to so and so), abecedaria and nonsensical inscriptions, writing for the sake of writing. Another early use of writing is to mark graves.

I have referred to the crucial distinction between the gift and commodity, drawing attention to the character of the unalienated artifact, not abstracted from social relations as is the commodity form, but reflecting and shaping the identities of other social actors involved in the life-cycle of the artifact. Some anthropologists studying Melanesian exchange (Strathern 1988) have argued that Melanesians do not conceive of objects and people as independent entities, and that both acquire their identities from the relationships in which they are involved (for extensive archaeological use of this argument see Tilley 1996).

Writing marks a pot with labels of those social actors with whom it is associated. And more. Painting or inscribing a name fixes an identity and sometimes a relationship. If this is a major use of writing, the very act of writing anything (nonsense or abecedarium) may signify the same impulse. So these early examples of writing may be associated with a condition of objectification and not alienation, signifying social attachment to material forms such as grave goods, dedications to divinity and grave-markers, the unalienated artifact wrapped in redefinitions of self and identity.

A stylistic repertoire and the translation of interests

The exotic and 'other' – the movement of artifacts – contact with this realm of the external – death and the divine – the person – identity. These features consistently recur at the points of consumption of Korinthian artifacts. I suggest that they relate closely to that series of references I have already interpreted within Korinthian style. From production to iconography and style, through its transport, and to deposition as gift to dead or divinity with other personal and transported articles, Korinthian pottery is one of several material forms which provide a medium for the transient present to be subsumed beneath larger and transcendent experiences. These are to do with the personal, death, the divine, animal and bodily form, an expressive aesthetics, the exotic and 'other worldly', and masculine sovereignty.

Modes of burial and offering, personal goods (from perfume jars to bracelets), imports and exotics which have travelled far: this is a *repertoire of style*, a set of goods and practices which can be drawn upon, which were considered appropriate for certain social practices. The stylistic repertoire is implicated in powers and identities, personal and social: lifestyles. This explains why the particulars of the consumption of Korinthian do not differ widely, even given the immense distribution of these wares. For the primacy lies not with the particular destination of a pot, so much as with the stylistic repertoire to which it belongs and which transcends in wider

Table 4.1. *A 'family grave plot' at Pithekoussai*

number	type	body	goods
199	cremation	adult female	gold-plated silver hair rings silver-ribbed bracelet local oinochoe
575	inhumation enchytrismos	baby	Levantine amphora bronze ring bone pendant scarab
574	inhumation	young boy	two Lyre-Player seals local oinochoe
578	inhumation enchytrismos	baby	local amphora
577	inhumation	adult	no grave goods

experiences. One of these experiences is of mobility or the travelling of artifacts (and, by extension, people). I raise the possibility that the primacy lies not in destination but in stylistic repertoire, and also the *carrier or trader* and the experience they represent. This may be another source of value.

This is all to question the radical differences often drawn between domestic, mortuary and votive uses of artifacts. Others (for example Tomlinson 1992: esp. 346, 349–50) have similarly questioned the distinction between votive pottery and that used at sanctuaries, for example for dining, albeit in a sacred context. Patterns of distribution do not differ widely; in that these apparently separate fields are drawn together in the cultural work, we might write of the *translation of interests* effected by Korinthian design.

Because of the argument I have presented against the independence of the economic in interpretations of an artifact, and also because of the way Korinthian design disperses into power, ritual and conceptual realms of death and the animal, I am unwilling yet to write of Korinthian pottery being 'traded'. The pots clearly *travelled*; they incorporate a spatial vector and principle of mobility and mediation. It is to this that I move in Chapter Five. I can now investigate to what extent travel connects with this cultural assemblage.

But to end let me consider Ridgway's discussion of some graves at Pithekoussai (Ridgway 1992b: esp. Chapter 6). Under an historical metanarrative of traders and colonisers, locals, Greeks and Phoenicians, residents and itinerants, he homes in upon one grave (575) and its family plot (*ibid.*: 111f). The amphora used in this *enchytrismos* burial bore three semitic inscriptions. Ridgway connects this with the Lyre-Player seals and Rhodian aryballoi and speculates on the possible traders, based in the east, sending their vessel to a compatriot in Pithekoussai. Superimposed upon one of the inscriptions is a roughly drawn triangle interpreted as an all-purpose semitic symbol known all over the Mediterranean. Ridgway interprets this as an appropriate action on the part of a Phoenician resident reusing the amphora in a burial rite.

The 'family group' of grave 575 is listed in Table 4.1.

Ridgway's family is thus held to consist of a mother, two babies, a young boy and a servant (the adult without grave goods). But what of the father of this archaic nuclear family? The plot was disturbed in antiquity by two seventh-century cremations: 'their presence has probably deprived us of a cremation burial that we would have been able to identify as almost certainly that of an adult male of Levantine origin' (*ibid.*: 114).

Ridgway infers Levantine residents from other imports and adopts a line of argument for another family plot (graves 166 and 167 and inhumations beneath) similar to that just described: mixed goods of imports, local imitations and local styles, are held to represent immigrants mixing with Greeks and locals.

Style is here held to directly reflect ethnic identities. Quite simply, this is not a valid archaeological inference (see pp. 206–7 on ethnicity). Another line of argument which I support would consider that it does not matter whether they were Phoenicians, Levantines, Greeks or locals. Instead the archaeological evidences are of a discourse of social mobility and identity whose components are the elements of the stylistic repertoire sketched so far, negotiated within the burial of a family member. Particular experiences of bereavement are translated through rite and deposition, style and ornament with a constituting interest in identity and belonging. The eastern pottery vessel appears 'unalienated' as the otherness of body, the vessel's mercantile trade marks an appropriate reference to the investment in the movement of goods and in a personal space of amulet seals and bodily adornment. The transitional or mediatory state is effected in the gesture of the new mark over the three which came with the amphora. Other nearby burials display different interpretations or workings with the same themes. In however slight a way the links lead off into the cultural assemblage which has so engaged me in previous chapters.

5

Trade and the consumption of travel

I have mapped a route through the contexts and references of Korinthian pottery, through production and consumption, art and style (Figure 1.4) – a cultural assemblage of uses, meanings, lines of dispersal away from what may be conceived as the artifact in itself. I have yet to fully consider the movement of pots and other goods away from Korinth, the question of the mode of distribution. Such is the purpose of this chapter: the matter of 'trade'.

The general trend in archaeological considerations of the movement of goods, a most visible aspect of the archaeological record, has been more sophisticated anthropological models of forms of exchange and distribution (from the seminal work of Renfrew 1969, 1972, 1975; through Ericson and Earle 1982), in the context of those anthropologies of regional links (world systems and prestige goods) mentioned in the previous chapter. Nevertheless, simple descriptive accounts of 'trade' allied with a common-sense understanding of its economic working (traders taking goods from point of surplus to point of demand) is still evident in many conventional archaeologies and ancient histories of archaic Greece. Salmon's monograph on Korinth takes such a line (Salmon 1984: Chapters 7–10).

The rich associations and textures of the cultural assemblage that is Korinthian design can be interpreted as relating to social and personal identity, building new experiences into the city state, providing a stylistic repertoire and visual ideology which goes far beyond the conventional boundaries of the economic, hence my references to Bataille's concept of general economy. The term 'trade' already seems too narrow. I will build on this point, arguing that a narrow and economic definition of trade (as simply the mechanism whereby goods reach their destinations) is inadequate in accounting for the distribution of Korinthian wares. With respect to anthropological modelling through archaeological sources, my work on archaic Korinth suggests that forms of (archaeological) narrative which contrast with those of cultural and social anthropology may be needed.

Homo economicus and *homo politicus*: minimalist models of archaic trade

νῆες ἐν πόντωι θοαί
πολλὸν δ' ἱστίων ὑψώμεθα
λύσαντες ὅπλα νηός

fast ships at sea
let's untie the sheets and slacken the ship's tackle.
Archilochos West 106.1–2

A trend in approaches to the archaic Greek economy which has developed in the discipline of ancient history has been a more anthropologically sophisticated understanding which questions the easy application to early Greece of concepts and models of economy and trade drawn from study of more modern economic systems of medieval Europe and after. Theoretical impetus has come from Marxian analysis and social history, as in the work of Finley (for example 1973), and from the anthropologically derived work of Polanyi (1957), Hasebroek (1933) and others. Many issues crystallised in the long-running debate between *formalist* or *modernising* accounts of the ancient economy and those which are described as *substantivist* or *primitivist*. Formalist models use general and formal concepts which are not necessarily related to the substantive field of reference, to the particular society studied. Primitivist models use concepts which take account of the character of the particular society studied, that is pre-modern or 'primitive'; the basic point is that there is no general category of the 'economic', but that it is embedded in wider society and varies according to society type. I trust that it is clear that my work immediately questions a common-sense or modernising conception of the economic context of Korinthian pottery. Therefore a short sketch of a substantivist or primitivist model of the archaic economy (and particularly with respect to trade) is in order here (I draw on Austin and Vidal-Naquet 1977; Finley 1973; Garnsey *et al.* 1983; Humphreys 1978).

The picture of the ancient economy presented in a substantivist model is of the self-sufficiency of relatively small and cellular social and economic units (from farms to towns), based on agriculture and depending little on inter-regional trade. High overland transport costs meant that no region could undercut another in the production of cheap essentials, and export was dominated by prestige or special items. With a low status accorded to traders and craftsmen, wealth and status lying in land, and with little investment in productive techniques or in large-scale production, the economy was consumption- rather than production-led. Towns were therefore centres of consumption rather than production, and with wealth and status lying in the ownership of land, consumption followed the stylistic tastes of landed wealth and the landed aristocracy.

The production of Korinthian pottery was almost certainly undertaken on a small and household basis, and I have given estimates of the scale of production and export. That design works with the tastes and ideologies of what may be termed an 'aristocratic' interest in male sovereignty, though subject to experiment and negotiation, is also clear from my interpretation. I have also shown in Chapter Four the close link between production and consumption: the notion that there is little intervening between design and consumption in cemeteries and sanctuaries, because mode of production and the visual ideology and significances of deposition correlate so closely. This is to play down the independence of mediating distribution and exchange.

Snodgrass (1983) has presented a powerful argument that the scale of archaic trade was small and cannot be characterised as commerce. He cites the following evidence which indicates that there was no class of Greek trading ship before the late sixth century, and that oared warships were the means of distributing goods.

Figure 5.1 From archaic ceramic plaques found at Penteskouphia, near Korinth.

Pictures of archaic ships carrying goods for trading are all penteconters indistinguishable from war galleys (for example upon the Penteskouphia plaques from
the Korinthia: (*Antike Denkmäler* 1887: Pl. 8.3a 1898, Pl. 29.12), and ships
which are clearly merchant vessels are not found depicted until 525 BC at the
earliest (Morrison and Williams 1968).
Herodotos (1.163) has archaic Phokaians using pentekonters and not a form of
merchant ship for trading.
Miniature ships dedicated at archaic Samos were all war galleys (Kyrieleis 1980:
89–94).

Related arguments for his minimalist model of archaic trade include the following.

Trade would seem not to involve an independent class of traders. The Berezan
letter (of about 500 BC) would seem to indicate trade operated by wealthy
land-owning shipholders and their dependants or agents. Bravo, in discussion of
the implications of the letter (1975, 1977), has drawn attention to the fact that
the two most common early terms for trader, *emporos* and *phortegos*, both imply
collaboration between traders and others. It can also be added that Millett
(1991) traces early Greek credit, which could have been central to the logistics
of early trading ventures, to a devolved form of reciprocal gift-giving between
aristocratic patrons and their clients.
When Herodotos (4.152) has the whole crew of the trading ship of Kolaios of
Samos making a tithe dedication, cooperative enterprise and shared profits are
indicated, not management and control by a merchant.
Hesiod (*Works and Days* 618–94) generally has trade as a complement to agriculture: a landowner setting off to make some profit from his surplus.

Snodgrass gives quantitative estimates of the scale of archaic trade in stone and metals, the two heavy materials shipped in any quantity. It was relatively slight. Metalworking sites (such as at Pithekoussai, Motya and Bassai) were consistent with industries dedicated to local needs; the operation of commerce in the field of metals would seem to have been cut to the minimum by the location of a network of foundries serving local needs. 'As in so many aspects of the archaic economy, the practice . . . was to support oneself as far as was feasible from internal resources, of labour if not of materials' (Snodgrass 1983: 25). He argues that most artifacts would have travelled with their owners; for example, many exotic imports appear as dedications in sanctuaries – brought with visitors. As regards marble (which, given the sources and quarries, must have travelled) and statuary, Snodgrass reckons that the stone would have been purchased at the quarry by the sculptor, and would have travelled as their property; 'there is no . . . marble trade' (*ibid.*: 25). He summarises:

> If 'trade' is defined in the narrow sense of the purchase and movement of goods without the knowledge or the identification of a further purchaser, then it seems that a substantial component of archaic Greek maritime shipments could not be classified as trade.
> (*ibid.*: 26)

Snodgrass draws substantially on the model of the ancient Greek economy of Humphreys (1978) to which I refer in the heading for this section (followed also by Rihll 1993). In Marxian and Weberian tradition she has the economic institutions and functions of the city state dependent upon the political realm: hence we might look as much to a *homo politicus* as well as a *homo economicus* in understanding the early polis. The importance of war and the war-band is proposed as Humphreys traces a complicated interaction between travel and guest-friendships of nobles, war, raiding, piracy and the development of trade. On analogy with the medieval war-machine (Duby 1973) trade is to be studied in the context of other forms of the transfer of goods such as war, raiding, hospitality to strangers and gift-exchange. These are matters of lifestyle (of aristocracy) within which particular demands and desires are generated. Lifestyle and wealth depended upon ownership of land, establishment of the *oikos*. And war and exchange involved more than the transfer of goods; they were concerned with the mobility of manpower, soldiers and others travelling abroad, and slaves acquired and imported. Humphreys (1978: 161–2) places great emphasis upon slavery, an institution assumed by both Homer and Hesiod. With land owned inalienably and transmitted by inheritance, there were inevitably imbalances in the relationship between land and manpower, with some *oikoi* having too little land for its members, some *oikoi* too little manpower to work their land. Inheritance is important here also as a source of friction and threat to the *oikos*: fathers might well quarrel with sons over the division of land and the time this took place. The interest of inheriting sons was to persuade the old man to give up and hand over land which could become the basis of their own *oikos*, after marriage too. Hesiod (*Works and Days* 331–2) has quarrels between fathers and sons as wicked crime against the family, and he advises men not to marry before the age of thirty (*ibid*.: 695–6). So the availability of labour becomes crucial:

> Wherever imported slaves, bought or captured, are used to supply the extra labour needed on land which the owning family cannot work with its own manpower, a potential outlet for the surplus labour produced by other families is blocked. Given the scarcity of agricultural land in Greece, the use of slaves in farming meant, at least potentially, the need to drain surplus free labour off the land into emigration or alternative types of occupation. (Humphreys 1978: 162)

These other occupations were war, seafaring, raiding, colonisation, attendance perhaps at the sanctuary games – opportunities to establish personal alliances, display prowess, dispose of and acquire goods. Fighting, travel and seafaring were the main political outlet for young men who had not yet received their inheritance or who may have had little or no land to inherit. Travelling and joining a colony was also a means of acquiring land which had become unavailable at home. Illegitimate and therefore landless Archilochos led the life of seafarer and mercenary before settling as hoplite and landowner in the colony of Thasos.

Their separation from the *oikos* and from marriage, and their association with younger men and others who were not full land-owners and heads of households, makes war and travel *marginal* and ambiguous. They are also complements to agriculture, rather than alternatives. They fit into the slack agricultural seasons, would belong to a space in the life-cycle of the male member of a city state between adolescence and land-ownership. Travel and war were means of acquiring mobile wealth and slaves to provide status when a land-owner, perhaps even wealth to purchase land for an *oikos*. These activities are thus also a means of *social* mobility – providing opportunities for the enrichment of lifestyle, for acquiring the expensive equipment of a hoplite, for acquiring the trappings of a landed aristocracy in the absence of their inheritance.

It is appropriate here to mention the grave (No. 79), admittedly pre-archaic (sub Protogeometric II), found in the 1994 excavation season of the Toumba cemetery at Lefkandi, Euboea (Popham and Lemos 1995). Given the discussion of mobility, war and exchange, a list of the contents of what the excavators call a 'warrior–trader' will suffice.

cremation in a bronze cauldron
stone balance weights
a bronze weighing balance (?)
Syrian cylinder seal (an antique of 1800 BC)
three vases from Cyprus
two bichrome jugs from Phoenicia
earrings
bronze krater
remains of monumental standed craters

Any household might own a small boat, and use it for local trading, *cabotage*, as perhaps envisages Hesiod. But both Snodgrass and Humphreys stress the point that the only ships depicted in archaic times (and therefore used for trade) are those sea-going war galleys which would have belonged with the wealth and lifestyle of the aristocracy:

> In an age when political success depended upon personal resources and prestige, noblemen travelled abroad to make influential friends, to contract marriage alliances with leading families in other states, and to gain fame by winning at the Olympic, Pythian, Nemean or Isthmian games; some voyaged further afield to visit the wonders of the East (Solon) or to serve eastern monarchs as mercenary soldiers.
> (Humphreys 1978: 166)

So shipping is not so much an 'occupational role' as an aspect of lifestyle, embedded in reciprocal obligations (rowing for the experience of travel and opportunity of acquisition; discharging perhaps the obligation to return a gift, to repay a visit).

> πολλὰ μὲν δὴ προυκπονέαι Τηλέμβροτε,
> ἐνταῦθα μέν τοι τυρὸς ἐξ Ἀχαΐης
> Τρομίλιος θαυμαστός, ὃν κατήγαγον

> you've made quite some preparations Telembrotos,
> now here's a fabulous Tromilian cheese
> which I brought back from Achaia.
> Semonides West 22–3

Travel and *mobility*

Humphreys stresses *a priori* the need to integrate an understanding of archaic trade into a holistic view of the circulation of men, women and goods. She considers archaic Greek trade as part of a much wider context of exchanges between the Aegean and the world beyond. This regional approach has been followed by Purcell (1990) whose ideas may be profitably associated with those of Andrew and Susan Sherratt (Sherratt and Sherratt 1991, 1993). Challenging easy conceptions of trade and colonisation, Purcell relates the redistribution of local resources, mercenaries, slaves, demography and the movement of luxury goods by means of a general concept of *mobility*. In contrast to the self-sufficient cellular household, Purcell stresses the extensive regional systems to which communities in the eastern Mediterranean belonged, systems which extended to include key relationships with imperial powers of the Near East. For Purcell mobility is a function of a varied and broken ecology and its necessity of interdependence: 'instead of autonomous enterprises and isolated producers, the object of attention is now whole ecological systems which exploit varied resources in highly complex and flexible ways, and which maintain large and ramified social groups' (Purcell 1990: 42). Colonisation, mercenaries and slavery are operations performed by and upon the resource of manpower: the relocation of surplus. This is not necessarily a result of population increase and too many people: 'we do not have to assume significant demographic growth in any individual community; the effect is the better deployment of available resources, intensification . . . as a general response to new political demands' (*ibid.*: 47–8). Imperial powers of the Levant were a 'source of movement', requisitioning systems creating social and economic demand for all sorts of goods and people from abroad, the central part of centre and periphery relationships. From the Levantine coastal margin in the first half of the first millennium developed the Phoenician *koine*, a network of routes and communities over the Mediterranean, many already long-established. Into this network moved the Greek aristocracy in the eighth century, intensifying links and a mobility which served their interests and demands.

Purcell provides an easy prime-mover, ecological diversity, for the social changes he considers. But this ecological determinism may be discarded without seriously damaging the observations on the connections between economy, war and travel. Although the independence of a household economic unit is opened to question, trade is subordinated to wider concepts of movement and mobility, and the economic evaporates into a cultural field of travel, social links, obligations and dependencies.

This is an historical field too: the inter-regional links of the eastern Mediterranean were long established, as emphasised by Purcell (also Kochavi 1992; Morris 1992; for summary comment Sherratt and Sherratt 1991); I have already made reference to the case of Lefkandi: (Popham 1982, 1994; Popham *et al.* 1980). The Aegean in the second millennium was linked with many communities abroad. The Aegean states were in an international milieu from the start. Those Greeks setting out in the eighth century from Korinth were accessing *again* links, experiences and meanings (of the external, the exotic and the East). They may not have been Korinthian of course. This does not substantially affect my sketch. Indeed carriers who came from outside Korinth would add to the 'international' character of this 'trading assemblage'.

Experience and the constitution of geographical space
Malinowski's classic ethnography of the Trobriand islanders, *Argonauts of the Western Pacific* (1922), gives account of the Kula ring, the great cycle of Melanesian gift-exchange. Travelling in their canoes on long journeys, the Kula voyagers enact the adventures of mythical culture heroes (Helms 1988: 46) endeavouring in the Kula to affirm their individuality, freedom and fame through travel, esoteric knowledge and the exchange of extraordinary goods – shell armbands and necklaces. Authority too, displayed in the exchange deals pulled off, the artifacts owned, the knowledge and know-how acquired (Scoditti and Leach 1983: 272).

In Trobriand cosmology the geometric form of the circle (necklaces, armbands, the Kula 'ring') stands for complete knowledge of the cosmos, realisable, but never actually attained, by journeying men, given that only they have the capability of knowing the world through travel, diving under the sea, exploring the terrestrial world of caves, climbing mountains. In their travel, which is as much ritual as opportunity for entrepreneurial gain (Uberoi 1971: 141–7), men's names become associated with shells, so the Kula hero may hope to achieve ultimate prestige through immortality, the circulation in space of Kula goods transformed by naming and association into personal preservation in time unending (Scoditti and Leach 1983: 271–2).

Trobriand earth and distant lands of Kula contacts, bridged by the ocean, correspond to inner and outer experience (Montague 1980: 74–8, 83–6). The outer world of experience is like stone, solid, substantial, directly visible, and includes the living people of the Trobriands. Inner experience is amorphous, like the wind, only indirectly perceptible (noises and scents), full of movement, and ghostly. Foreign lands, being out of sight, are associated with inner experience, and foreigners, though they appear solid, are conceived as amorphous beings, just as the ocean appears solid but dissolves into movement in the Kula voyage.

Mary Helms has provided an invaluable comparative ethnography of the experiences of trade, exchange and travel in her book *Ulysses' Sail* (1988). As well as an economic activity, the travel in trade is variously experienced as fun and enjoyment, opportunity for companionship and establishing self-identity. Its ritual defines an ideological field as much as an economic function, involving goods often conceived sacred, because invested with so much social significance. Travellers, delvers into the unknown, frequently engage in competitive rivalry through their Kula goods and through displays of knowledge which negotiate social standing and authority. A major argument in relation to the mobility of people and goods is that geographical displacement needs to be associated with other forms of distance, including cosmologies, mentalités and what may be termed the conceptual space of lifeworld.

The conceptual space of archaic Korinthian design

Here then I trace a continuity between geographical space and mental maps, but involving also secular cosmologies and ideologies of social distance. Beginning with Figure 1.1, the ruined fragments of archaic Korinthian lifeworlds have helped me construct images of the new scales of building, personal and public spaces redefined, the old space of the *oikos* augmented and transformed. Sanctuary sitings, the Perachora headland, the narrowing of isthmus with Akrokorinthos and Korinthia as backdrop, are highlighted by new building projects and public activities – designed vistas. With continued haptic experiences of the touch of smooth fine ceramic comes surface treatment and scale which brings the aryballos or cup close, just as the lack of graphical accent of geometric pattern repelled close attention. These may be termed new vectors or scales of phenomenological reach: spaces of personal and cultural definition, encounters with alterity.

The conceptual space of Korinthian ceramic imagery is one which works upon alterity and in relation to the fields of the domestic and gender. The presentation of masculine sovereignty is one of ambivalence and mediation between different states such as animal, human and divine (summarised perhaps in the figures of bird and fighting soldier); referenced are distinctions to do with particular conceptions of masculine and feminine identity.

The stylised wild animals and figures representing bodily control, the scenes of violence and references to soldiery, the absence of the everyday and of agriculture, the connections with the east and with travel can be interpreted as delineating a world which belongs with that of the mercenary who moves away from home, inhabits spaces removed from the household and polis. I related this sort of masculine sovereignty to a war-machine – concepts, meanings, powers to do with permanent war and the identities by which it is sustained. Standardised hoplite weaponry can be related to techniques of the body: postures, disciplines, articulated in arts, practices and lifestyles.

The glory of praise achieved through travel, a form of *kleos*, might well be accompanied by the acquisition of *keimelia,* treasure (Morris 1986: 8, 9; Finley 1978: 60–1). Kurke (1991: esp. Chapters 1 and 2) has outlined the relationship of the general economy of the archaic *oikos* to its moral geography. The hero, representative of his *oikos,* was bound to its space, marked by the house itself, its land and the presence of ancestors. The symbolic capital of the *oikos* was its treasury of *kleos* (renown), crystallised in its *keimelia* and *agalmata.* But the renewal of the ancient and ancestral *kleos* of the *oikos* took the hero away to acquire deeds and exchange *agalmata.* The result was what Kurke terms the 'loop of *nostos* (homecoming)'. This is typified by Odysseus, his travels and (inevitable) homecoming. It is exemplified in a new genre and idiom by Pindar's odes, celebrating the victory and homecoming of aristocratic athletes; here though, Pindar's art is its mediation of individual *kleos* and a new civic pride and duty.

The ships for long-distance travel, supplied ultimately by landed wealth, belong with lifestyles of display, war, raiding and movement into spaces beyond the local and everyday. Its material culture and world of experiences constitute a repertoire of style. The colonies, cemeteries and sanctuaries mark out the space of the polis, conceptually and in terms of territory and geography. Colonies are at the edge of the Greek, or at least (by definition) beyond the limits of the mother city. Their independence is ambiguous: dependent upon mother city in origin, but a pristine design of polis in new lands. This is related to the ambiguity of the colonial founder, social outcast, but later colonial hero, found in ancient accounts and dealt with below. Cemeteries mark the boundary of living community and the dead; they may also be found at the edges of the community. Sanctuaries may have identified the limits of the polis; they mark the boundary between human and divine. Korinthian pottery, in its design, travel and consumption significantly as gift (to dead and divinity) is an *actualisation of ambivalence.* The gift mediates giver and receiver, establishes a link between them, and their equivalence, but also the subordination of receiver to giver. An object inalienable from the social relationships by which it is constituted, it objectifies the link between giver and receiver, representing the giver to the receiver. The gift is both the person of the giver and object. Hence the gift marks ambivalence (Mauss 1954; Richman 1982). Korinthian ceramics in their design, exchange and consumption, their conceptual space, mark the boundaries.

The Phoenicians, east and west

δὴ τότε Φοῖνιξ ἦλθεν ἀνὴρ ἀπατήλια εἰδώς,
τρώκτης, ὃς δὴ πολλὰ κάκ' ἀνθρώποισιν ἐώργει·

ὅς μ' ἄγε παρπεπιθὼν ᾗσι φρεσίν, ὄφρ' ἱκόμεσθα
Φοινίκην, ὅθι τοῦ γε δόμοι καὶ κτήματ' ἔκειτο.

Then there came a Phoenician, knowledgable and wily,
a greedy rodent who had done a lot of bad things to men.
He won me round with his clever reasoning so we went to
Phoenicia, where he had his houses and goods.
Odyssey 14.288–91

Tyre, the crowning city, whose merchants are princes, whose traffickers are
the great and honourable of the earth.
Isaiah 23.8

Analysis of the places where scarabs and similar traded objects have been found,
reveals discrete and separate distributions: for example the Perachora material
(Greece) is stylistically separable from Campanian imported orientalia (Italy) (Markoe 1992: 81 based on Hölbl 1979 I: 214–15, 220–1). Markoe (1992) and Ridgway
(1992a) both consider that this pattern of distribution of imported goods and of
mineral sources reveals an important role for Phoenicians in Italy, shared spheres of
commercial interest with Italians and Greeks. Sherratt and Sherratt (1991, 1993)
give much importance, in their social system for the first millennium, to enterprising,
entrepreneurial Phoenicians, a professional mercantile cadre. What is to be made of
these Phoenicians?

Aubet (1993) has developed a systemic model of the Phoenician city states and
their trade. As Purcell emphasised the motivation for Phoenician activities clearly
had a great deal to do with Assyria. Tiglath-Pileser III (745–727 BC) and his
successors Shalmaneser V and Sargon II built a military ring around an independent
Tyre, one of whose kings, Mattan II, was forced to pay tribute amounting to 150
talents of gold (some 4,300 kg) (Aubet 1993: 73). For Aubet, tribute, rather than
outright domination, was a way of exerting control and directing Phoenician interest
while respecting autonomy (*ibid.*: 74). Assyrian demand was for raw materials,
particularly metals. Phoenicia was no mere vassal of Assyria. Accordingly Aubet
looks to the internal dynamics of Phoenician society for understanding their trading
interests and activities.

Aubet (1993: Chapter 4) closely examines the historical sources for the mechanisms of Phoenician trade in the first half of the first millennium BC in the light of
historical and anthropological models of the ancient economy, such as were outlined
above (see pp. 200–1). The sources are surprisingly meagre:

an account given by an Egyptian Wen-Amon of a journey from Egypt to Phoenicia
and dated to about 1070 BC (text translated in Aubet 1993: Appendix 2);
biblical sources – the Hebrew prophets, particularly the oracles against Tyre in the
books of Isaiah and Ezekiel (sources gathered in Aubet 1993: Appendix 3);
a diplomatic document (a treaty between Baal of Tyre and Asarhaddon of Assyria
and dated to 675–671 BC);
the Homeric epics.

Aubet finds no evidence for any clear evolution of trading systems, for example the development of private mercantile enterprise from state controlled exchange and distribution. Nor is there any opposition between reciprocity or gift exchange in a ceremonial economy in which rank and status prevailed, and mercantile trade concerned with profit and market. So the formalist–substantivist distinction is not a *formal* opposition. Instead Aubet finds there was a mixture of exchange relationships involving eastern imperial monarchies, the Phoenician monarchy, oligarchic elites organised into trading partnerships, and private independent ventures, often as much piracy as trade.

> The essential question is not whether Phoenician trade in the ninth to seventh centuries was basically a private or a state undertaking . . . public trade and private initiative, almost always associated with the search for profits and the desire for gain, were perfectly complementary. It was a synchronous process in which both the private sector and the palace were looking for profits and in which the palace needed the private merchant as much as the trader needed the protection of the palace.
> (Aubet 1993: 95–6)

Other notable features of Phoenician activity include a pronounced family orientation – the guilds or mercantile consortia behaved like family brotherhoods. Epigraphic evidence indicates that there were price/market fluctuations and operations. The temple acted as a financial body, lending on interest, and was fully involved in trade: religious institutions were fully embedded in the economy.

Archaic trade in Homer, much asssociated with 'Sidonians', Phoenicians and other foreigners, is clearly individual enterprise, not organised, but casual, nevertheless also associated with management by Phoenician monarchs, their gift-exchange and hospitality (Aubet 1993: 102–7). Homer's attitude to trade is the characteristic Greek and aristocratic one of disapproval of mercantile activity (*emporie*) in contrast to *prexis* or *ergon* trade (as in Hesiod), more akin to piracy. Such (*prexis/ergon*) trade was mentioned above (in discussion of Humphreys pp. 197–8) as complementary to the agricultural cycle. *Emporie* was left to the *emporos*, a specialised professional, often seen as untrustworthy and foreign. These professionals were not sailing in sleek war galleys: large Phoenician merchant vessels, the ships of Byblos, are known from the middle of the third millennium BC (*ibid.*: 146–8).

To illustrate the heterogeneity of trading activities consider the silver krater of Achilles and its life-cycle recounted in the *Iliad* (23.740f). It appears offered as a prize in the funeral games of Patroklos. Of Sidonian manufacture it was carried by Phoenician traders, set up in various harbours (*stesan en limenessi Iliad* 23.745), presumably for sale, but was given as gift to king Thoas of Lemnos. It later served as ransom for one of Priam's sons held by Patroklos. Odysseus won it in the games and took it back to Ithaka. Such items are called *keimelia* – things to be stored and treasured, not used, and there to be given as a gift, but they may be bought or stolen too.

The issue of the Phoenicians is intimately involved in questions of orientalising contact between Greece and the east. To some, the archaeological links seem so close that resident or itinerant 'foreign' craftsmen have been proposed, making their goods of eastern style in Greece (Boardman 1980: 57f; Burkert 1992: 21–5; Dunbabin 1957: 40–1; Filippakis 1983; Markoe 1992: 68–9; 77–9, 84; Muscarella 1992: 44–5; Ridgway 1992: 111–18, 1992a; Treister 1995). For Coldstream this involved direct foreign investment with Phoenician perfume manufacturing or bottling facilities on Rhodes (1969), Kos (*ibid.*: 2), and Krete (1979: 261–2, 1986: 324; discussion by Jones 1993; see also Frankenstein 1979). Phoenicians have been proposed to be living at Kommos on Krete because of what looks to the excavator like Phoenician cult (Shaw 1989).

The basis of these suppositions is almost entirely stylistic interpretation – that some sort of prolonged contact or presence was necessary for Greek style or goods to be so influenced, for certain orientalia to be present in the quantities observed. I will question the validity of this link between style and ethnicity in the next section. I conclude this section with the general picture to emerge from Kopcke and To-kumaru's synoptic edited book (1992) on Greek Mediterranean links from the tenth to eighth centuries BC: there was mediation and heterogeneity rather than a bifurca-tion of Greek and 'barbarian', gift-exchange and mercantile activity.

The orientalising cauldron

I suggest that the question of whether Greek or Phoenician traders/carriers were responsible for the movement of goods is inappropriate. Cutting instead through to stronger *archaeological* inferences, concepts of mobility and movement, heterogene-ity and mixture (whether of goods or people or ideas) are enough. The Mediterra-nean thus becomes in these times a cauldron of cultures (Morel 1984; Morris 1992; Purcell 1990: 33; Snodgrass 1994: 2).

Colonies were mixtures of Greek and non-Greek, and the Greek itself was not homogeneous:

> The description of, say, Syracuse, as 'a Corinthian colony' need mean little
> more than that the *oikist* and his immediate entourage came from Corinth.
> Does not Archilochos, with his cry that 'the ills of all Greece have come
> together in Thasos' (West 102), imply such a picture?
> (Snodgrass 1994: 2)

Ethnicity and identity are concepts which apply to a dynamic condition of contesta-tion and negotiation in the face of 'otherness'; this is shown in a startling way by Clifford's portrayal of contemporary identity in Mashpee (1988) and Hebdige's classic work on sub-cultural style in the 1970s (1979). The relationships between ethnicity and material culture style are neither simple nor direct. This has been one of the main findings of archaeological theory and ethnoarchaeology of the last twenty years (consider the papers in Conkey and Hastorf, 1990, and, for classical archaeol-ogy, the work of Hall (1993, 1995)). Hence orientalising Korinthian design is not well understood as an interaction between east and Greek. This is the root of many false lines of questioning which assume clear ethnic and national distinctions in material culture: Greek or Phoenician originality, movement of people or goods?

Colonisation and its discourse

A major dimension, indeed evidence, of mobility is colonisation. It is not my intention here to review the discussion about Greek colonisation in the eighth and seventh centuries. It is not necessary. After Carol Dougherty's presentation (1993) of ancient accounts of colonial foundations, consider rather the extant historical sources on colonisation, its discourse, and analogies with the cultural assemblage formed by Korinthian design.

Plutarch on the founding of Syracuse:

> Melissos had a son named Aktaion, the most handsome and modest young man of his age. Aktaion had many suitors, chief among them Archias, a descendant of the Herakleidai and the most conspicuous man in Korinth, both in wealth and general power. Archias couldn't persuade Aktaion to be his lover, so he decided to carry him off by force. He gathered together a crowd of friends and servants who went to Melissos's house in a drunken state and tried to take the boy away. Aktaion's father and friends resisted; the neighbours ran out and helped fight the assailants, but, in the end, Aktaion was pulled to pieces and killed. The friends then ran away, and Melissos carried the corpse of his son into the marketplace of Korinth where he set it on display, asking reparations from those who had done this. But the Korinthians did nothing more than pity the man. Unsuccessful, Melissos went away and waited for the Isthmian festival when he went up to the temple of Poseidon, decried the Bakchiadai and reminded the god of his father Habron's good deeds. Calling upon the gods he then threw himself from the rocks. Not long after this plague and drought came down on the city. When the Korinthians consulted the god about relief, they were told that the anger of Poseidon would not subside until they sought punishment for Aktaion's death. Archias heard this because he was one of the delegation consulting the oracle of Apollo, and he decided, of his own free will, not to return to Korinth. Instead he sailed to Sicily and founded the colony of Syracuse.
> *Moralia* 772e–773b

A frequently found narrative form in the founding of colonies is that of an act of murder, followed by expulsion of the murderer as act of purification (in consultation with Delphic Apollo), then the creative act of foundation of a colony by the exile. With features of radical break with mother city, mediation through the otherness of divinity, and sanction of creative sovereignty, the threat of disorder is withheld by expulsion of the threatening element which in turn, after contact with divinity, becomes a source of vital sovereignty – the new colonial city state. I have commented above on similarities with the narrative form of tyranny and reconstructions of ideologies of sovereignty. The sovereignty of the *oikist* (transferred to the state in

McGlew's account (1993)) is reflected also in the planned layout of colonial settlement:

> Politically, this planned element is one of the reflections of the power of the
> *oikist*; but culturally it is even more significant, in that it shows the Greek
> mind grappling with entirely fresh problems.
> (Snodgrass 1994: 8; see also Malkin 1987: 135–86)

Colonies play upon their separateness from mother city in design and material culture. Another archaeological dimension of this discourse is the competition and emulation to be seen in mortuary practices between the colonies, and less between mother cities and colonies (Shepherd 1993) (though there are links, for example at Syracuse, mentioned in the previous chapter). Awareness also of indigenous practices complements this negotiation of sovereignty.

The consumption of travel

According to Alkaios, his brother Antimenidas fought as mercenary for the Babylonians and killed a giant:

ἦλθες ἐκ περάτων γᾶς ἐλεφαντίναν
λάβαν τώ ξίφεος χρυσοδέταν ἔχων

you have come from the ends of the earth
with the hilt of your sword ivory bound with gold.
Alkaios Lobel and Page 350.1–2

καὶ δή ᾽πίκουρος ὥστε Κὰρ κεκλήσομαι

Now I'll be called an auxiliary, like a Karian.
Archilochos West 216

Morgan (1988: 336) reminds us that there is no evidence for us to associate aristocracy with early trade, a position supported for Korinth by Snodgrass: 'the legendary wealth and power of the Bakchiad aristocracy seems to have begun improbably early for it to have been founded in commerce' (1980a: 147).

For the eighth century Morgan comments:

> Korinthian involvement in the Gulf was probably limited to small scale
> activity by private, non-aristocratic, individuals for personal motives; even if
> aristocrats were the group who needed, and eventually acquired, metal, it
> seems unlikely that they went out to get it themselves. Trading was unlikely to
> have enhanced the status of participants.
> (Morgan 1988: 336–7)

In the interpretation of Korinthian design I have developed there is no need to depend upon aristocratic traders. Design has been treated as a nexus of interest and ideology, as well as social practices, intimately involved with definitions of self and class. But aristocracy is not simply a social *rank*; as a *class* it is a set of relationships and modes of translation of interest, and I have attempted to elucidate some of these. Accordingly it is a mistake to use archaeological sources to construct historical narrative of the sort 'aristocrats sailed out from Korinth to acquire goods'.

The shipping of Korinthian pottery is less well understood as commerce or trade. How far archaeology has come from traditional distribution maps and suppositions of trade is debatable: I perceive a failure to develop clear links between artifact distributions and conventional anthropological models of trade and exchange. This is why I have used instead the concept of cultural assemblage.

Recall those mercenaries up the Nile carving their names upon an Egyptian colossus. Trade is thus not abstract movement of these pots produced in Korinth, but is an experience of travel intimately linked with the ideologies of sovereignty and identity, and which implicate wealth, lifestyle, marginal and ambivalent states of masculine sovereignty and aristocratic powers. I have found that production and design in Korinth has close conceptual links with consumption, and that particular destinations made little difference to the selection of particular pots from the considerable variety available. There are some indications that pots were going to specific destinations without circulating in a wider social and cultural field. I have found it reasonable to propose that the mode of distribution is part of the same wide cultural assemblage as design and consumption. Travel and mobility are part of Korinthian design, the repertoire of style. The pots were indeed designed for travel.

In his lost epic of the seventh century BC, the *Arimaspea*, reconstructed by Bolton (1962), Aristeas of Prokonnesos related a journey north beyond the known world. He told of the Issedonians, whose women were treated equally to men, of a world of griffins, gorgons, the *graiai*, swan-maidens, cannibals and amazons. There were to be found the *Arimaspoi*, one-eyed horsemen, and a land of ever-falling feathers. His journey began, it would seem, when he was drawn to travel after apparent death and resurrection, in a trance-like state. Bolton (*ibid.* esp. 125–6, 132–56) connects this with shamanism, divine possession and altered states. Death and otherness, altered states, the avian, monstrous and threatening gender roles beyond, at the edge, reached through the fascinations of travel – is it coincidence that here again are key elements of this cultural assemblage and its metanarrative?

6

Art, design and the constitutive imagination in the early city state

Through the fragments of practices and lifeworlds a series of dispositions and stories can be traced. Much of what I have had to write could be said to do with the changing culture of the archaic city state and its ideologies of sovereignty, but it is not enough to leave it at that, for ideology, and indeed the class structure involved in the new discourses of sovereignty, are *relationships*; they are worked through people's practices. In the same way the aryballos both signifies and connects or translates: this is its social work, permeated by reworking, contradiction and contestation. Interpretation and uncertainty are endemic to social production, both past and present.

Archaeologists are dealing with the constitutive imagination – the making of goods and the building of worlds to live in. But the new imagery of Korinth is not simply an imaginary or decorative world, part of something like Renfrew's 'projective system' of society, as Snodgrass suggests for Attic Geometric figures scenes (Snodgrass 1979: 128). I have discussed the heroic ethos of late dark age Greece. Consider Gernet's comment (Gernet 1981: 144) that myth is not a way of thinking with images, but is the images themselves in a field of the affective. I read this as doubting the distinction between image and theme represented, or between 'generic signal' and ethos represented. Veyne (1988) has also presented an interpretation of Greek myth as only secondarily referring to a distinction between truth and fiction, reason and fantasy. Myth is instead primarily pragmatic, establishing *relationships* between poet and audience, for example in the case of Pindar (Kurke 1991). Neither true nor false, myth has an illocutionary force which cannot be reduced to content, being instead about themes such as anonymous authorship, repetition, the learned. This is again an argument for seeing beyond the opposition of representation and reality into the constitutive imagination.

The traditional hereditary and exclusive aristocracy in Korinth were in trouble by the eighth century BC; this much is certain from the literature. The old ways were not working; people were not subscribing to conventional legitimations rooted most probably in birth and wealth. Archaeological evidences of the material cultural lifeworld of Korinth indicate how the political was being redesigned to involve an aesthetic field of lifestyle.

I pick up the point that power is about having allies and translating interests, and that material culture may be effective in doing this. Attention was shifted in Korinth to recruitment and mobilisation of new resources. There are coordinated in a new way from the eighth century orientations towards war and violence, represented by the design of weaponry and graphical depiction of violence, and by what is done with weaponry – discipline, the aesthetics of wounding, the dedication to divinity, for example. Religion becomes the focus of communal energies, of the display of new craft skills, a public arena of *expenditure* – the wealth of patrons or indeed of a community, dedications offered to divinity. There were developed new visual and architectural environments. The new expenditures were made in a nexus of religion, trade and travel. Powers over movement and space find expression in fields of mobility and mediation, shipping and sanctuaries..

Ceramic design, the emergence of a new taste regarding the form and decoration of ceramic fineware, is clearly part of a new display of expenditure and investment in war and religion, travel and trade too, and part of the new and increasing visual environment. This new environment provided a frame and gave cues to the possibility and appropriateness of actions, particularly the actions of the propertied class, those with the wealth and leisure to experience and exploit new opportunities. It was now appropriate to use wealth to build a large public and monumental temple with finely worked and decorated surfaces, to invest energy in that which was beyond the local community and to travel with fine and decorated perfume jars. The body, self and gender are important themes in these new developments. Other conceptions, for example of a productive field gendered feminine, were set in opposition or marginalised. To accept, find significance in, enjoy figured design is to enter an ideological world of masculine sovereignty, a world which determines the powers of a minority over others, and the mechanisms whereby this may be achieved. The new developments involved redefinition or reworking of the material and conceptual resources at the base of elite practice, new orientations for the energies of the propertied class and its community.

Here, in this expressive politics, this repertoire of style, are the elements of an efficient technology of power. Technology may be defined as a nexus of knowledge and technique and to do with knowledgeable agents achieving interests and desired ends. Technology refers to many disparate fields of *applied (systems of) knowledge*. Just as a worker employs or makes reference to a technology (body of applied knowledge and its objects) in achieving ends, so too we may conceive a social agent employing a technology of social power in achieving ends. How do we get our way in social life? What are the bodies of applied knowledge (i.e. practical and not propositional)? You can beat someone (skills and tools may well be relevant here). You may make a speech (rhetorical skills relevant here). Technologies of power include some or all of the following:

> systems of wealth and property which enable projects to be realised;
> tools, to operate upon raw material and realise a design;
> weapons and war-machines, to be used (symbolically too) to enforce interests;
> environments or settings for particular kinds of project and action;
> knowledges and information, as the basis of actions with and upon others;
> concepts and practices of the self and body, ideas of the powers and limits which
>   are appropriate to both;
> systems of rhetoric and persuasion as essential to the translation of interest;

aesthetic systems which indicate the appropriateness of action and which may also work in translating interests by establishing metaphorical links.

I trust it is clear how this listing relates to the cultural assemblage built in archaic Korinth.

The efficiency of this particular technology lies in flexibility and scope, and in the provision of opportunities for richly textured experiences and gratifications. That we may recognise its workings now is a testament to that efficiency: it works.

This new technology of power centred on *expression*, a transformation of power into an aesthetic and expressive field. This involves a discourse of sovereignty. Artifacts and new cultural experiences make visible, rework, articulate, embody and clarify, sometimes even obscure, a series of links between violence, masculinity, what I termed otherness or alterity, divinity, animal and bodily form, and links with the absences – the domestic everyday and feminine. I have shown how these may be central to a relationship of dominance and subordinance, between an overlord and an underclass. I outlined a cultural complex, masculine sovereignty, and showed the importance of lifestyle and particular conceptions of self and body – aesthetic fields. Their representation in visual form draws attention to these ideas and dispositions. And however slight the importance of Korinthian imagery may have been in the beginning, this visual environment grew. That the designs also seem to clarify in the relations they represent suggests that there was no established set of ideas and dispositions to be represented, but that the design of pottery grew with the realisation of the significance of these powers and their technologies.

Korinthian ceramics display traditional manufacture and design, but also deviation from these into risk and the moment of manufacture, above all a new visual field. This is a new articulation of tradition and innovation and implicates ideological time in the way just described – past and pregnant futures, and the moment of decisive encounter.

Birth is not at all central to the working of technologies of power which foreground style, the aesthetic, display, expenditure and reference to gender and conceptions of body and self. The old aristocratic *oikoi* and retainers worked as well, if not better, with these expanded dimensions of cultural practice. Birth may still have been referenced, but was dispensable. Tyranny at Korinth usurped the recently elaborated technologies of power while retaining reference to the weight of tradition in the notion of monarchic rule (Kypselos as *basileus*). Here again is that mixture of tradition and innovation.

But we are not seeing simply the development of an aristocratic ideal. Various projects were at work. Someone with the requisite wealth and aspiration would not have come to a potter with a demand for a new class of goods, so much as an *interest*, a sensitivity to the expression of themes to do with style, violence, war and animal and human form, as well as the old certainties of traditional style. This interest may have been generated elsewhere, but found (partial) realisation in the responses of the potters over the years, who produced figured Korinthian wares, designs which clarified and gave form to the new technologies of power, just as did the weapons systems, the stone *kouroi*, ships, stories and experiences of travel.

The potter, attending to the need to dispose of their products, translated the growing interest in figurative imagery and an exotic visual environment into an iconography upon miniature vessel forms, developing a new workmanship of risk rather than certainty, with expressions of self and creativity. Their wares supplied the symbolic economies of new lifestyles, networks of distribution and consumption.

All potters need an outlet for their products (other than in the exceptional case of pottery done for the pleasure of the potter). The relationship here is not so much one between a potter and a market, but one between a potter and an *interest*. A simple relation of positive feedback between potter and interest accounts for the development of the style. But the lack of definition to this interest, in times when power and style had not been expressed in this way, gave a relative autonomy to the potter, enhanced by the lack of heavy demand, and by the relative social and technological independence of the potting *oikoi*. This gave space for the exploration of a new and explicit (political) aesthetic. The resultant energy is carried on through the later development of Korinthian and Greek ceramic design.

Korinthian design was, then, not the output of the creative genius of Greek potters meeting with ideas and artistic schemata of the east. It is not part of some overarching evolution of style. The pots were the result of an accidental meeting of interest in an aesthetics of sovereignty or power and a conservative and specialised technique of production and firing.

Trade abroad is deemed meaningful even in the ideology of pottery design, intersecting orientalia, movement beyond the domestic, agencies of shipping to new colonies, experiences of adventure and travel in a Mediterranean *koine* of mobility and interregional links, and the miniature wares were also suitable for restricted cargo space.

Some may have interpreted the pots and imagery as part of their interest in aspiring to new sovereignty through expressive lifestyles and their accoutrement. The colonist in Italy placing a perfume jar in a grave was uniting all sorts of things – feelings for the dead, Greek identities and links with Greek cities (pots from mother city Korinth), traders, a cultural edge of eastern and exotic motifs, a visual imagery and attendant experiences of masculine and aristocratic sovereignty, decorative order and securities of tradition. The colonist translated these into their own project of attending to the dead, dealing with identity, death and the otherness it represents.

Korinthian pottery from the late eighth century was part of a heterogeneous mixture woven through the projects of potter and consumer to get away from the old political ways and struggles, a network of connections, a manifold and insidious cultural assemblage. The focus on and through the body is a powerful and flexible metaphoric idiom, allowing augmentation and easy translation into various projects. This flexibility and multiplicity is the root of a popularity attested by the growth of production into the sixth century and export across the Mediterranean. In the intimate association with this cultural assemblage was the power of Greek aristocratic interest. Therein was also what we call the polis.

BIBLIOGRAPHY

Abercrombie, N., Hill, S. and Turner, B. S. 1980. *The Dominant Ideology Thesis*. London: Allen and Unwin.

Adams, M. J. 1973. 'Structural aspects of a village age', *American Anthropologist* 75: 265–79.

Adkins, A. W. H. 1960. *Merit and Responsibility: a Study in Greek Values*. Oxford: Clarendon Press.

Adkins, A. W. H. 1972. *Moral Values and Political Behaviour in Ancient Greece*. London: Chatto and Windus.

Adorno, T. 1976a. 'On the logic of the social sciences' in T. Adorno, H. Albert, R. Dahrendorf, J. Habermas, H. Pilot and K. R. Popper (eds.), *The Positivist Dispute in German Sociology*. London: Heinemann.

1976b. 'Sociology and empirical research' in T. Adorno, H. Albert, R. Dahrendorf, J. Habermas, H. Pilot and K. R. Popper (eds.), *The Positivist Dispute in German Sociology*. London: Heinemann.

Adorno, T., Albert, H., Dahrendorf, R., Habermas, J., Pilot, H. and Popper, K. R. 1976. *The Positivist Dispute in German Sociology* (G. Adey and D. Frisby, trans.). London: Heinemann.

Ahlberg, G. 1971. *Fighting on Land and Sea in Greek Geometric Art*. Stockholm: Skrifter Utgvina av Svenska Institutet i Athen.

Althusser, L. 1971. 'Ideology and ideological state apparatuses' in *Lenin and Philosophy and Other Essays*. London: New Left Books.

Althusser, L. 1977. *For Marx* (Ben Brewster, trans.). London: Verso.

Althusser, L. and Balibar, E. 1970. *Reading Capital* (Ben Brewster, trans.). London: New Left Books.

Amandry, P. 1956. 'Chaudrons à protomes de taureau en orient et en Grèce' in *The Aegean and the Near East: Studies presented to H. Goldman*. Locust Valley NY: Augustin.

Amyx, D. A. 1983. 'Archaic vase-painting vis-à-vis "free" painting at Corinth' in W. G. Moon (ed.), *Ancient Greek Art and Iconography*. Madison: University of Wisconsin Press.

1988. *Corinthian Vase Painting in the Archaic Period* (3 volumes). Berkeley: University of California Press.

Amyx, D. A. and Lawrence, P. 1975. *Corinth 7.2: Archaic Corinthian Pottery and the Anaploga Well*. Princeton NJ: American School of Classical Studies at Athens.

Anderson, P. 1976. *Considerations on Western Marxism*. London: Verso.

1980. *Arguments within English Marxism*. London: Verso.

Andrewes, A. 1956. *The Greek Tyrants*. London: Hutchinson.

Antike Denkmäler 1887. Volume 1.1. Berlin: Deutsches Archäologischen Instituts.

1898. Volume 2.3. Berlin: Deutsches Archäologischen Instituts.

Antonaccio, C. 1993a. 'The archaeology of ancestors' in C. Dougherty and L. Kurke (eds.), *Cultural Poetics in Archaic Greece: Cult, Performance, Politics*. Cambridge: Cambridge University Press.

1993b. *An Archaeology of Ancestors: Hero and Tomb Cult in Early Greece*. London: Rowman and Littlefield.

1994. 'Placing the past: the Bronze Age in the cultic topography of early Greece' in S. E. Alcock and R. Osborne (eds.), *Placing the Gods: Sanctuaries and Sacred Space in Ancient Greece.* Oxford: Clarendon Press.

Arafat, K. and Morgan, C. 1989. 'Pots and potters in Athens and Corinth: a review', *Oxford Journal of Archaeology,* 8: 311–46.

Arato, A. and Gebhardt, E. (eds.). 1978. *The Essential Frankfurt School Reader.* Oxford: Blackwell.

Arnold, D. E. 1985. *Ceramic Theory and Cultural Practice.* Cambridge: Cambridge University Press.

Aubet, M. E. 1993. *The Phoenicians and the West: Politics, Colonies and Trade* (Mary Turton, trans.). Cambridge: Cambridge University Press.

Austin, A. A. and Vidal-Naquet, P. 1977. *Economic and Social History of Ancient Greece: an Introduction.* Berkeley: University of California Press.

Bapty, I. and Yates, T. (eds.) 1990. *Archaeology after Structuralism.* London: Routledge.

Barrett, J. 1988. 'Fields of discourse: reconstituting a social archaeology', *Critique of Anthropology* 7: 5–16.

Bataille, G. 1977. *La Part Maudite: Essai d'Économie Générale.* Paris: Seuil.

1985a. 'The psychological structure of fascism' in *Visions of Excess: Selected Writings 1927–39.* Minneapolis: University of Minnesota Press.

1985b. 'The notion of expenditure' in *Visions of Excess: Selected Writings 1927–39.* Minneapolis: University of Minnesota Press.

Beard, M. 1991. 'Adopting an approach' in T. Rasmussen and N. Spivey (eds.), *Looking at Greek Vases.* Cambridge: Cambridge University Press.

Beazley, J. 1928. *Attic Black Figure: a Sketch.* London: British Academy.

Benjamin, W. 1979. 'Theories of German Fascism: on the collection of essays "War and warrior" by Ernst Jünger', *New German Critique* 17: 120–8.

1982. *Das Passagen-Werk. Gesammelte Schriften. Volume V.* (ed. R. Tiedemann). Frankfurt am Main: Suhrkamp.

Bennett, T. 1979. *Formalism and Marxism.* London: Methuen.

Benson, J. L. 1953. *Die Geschichte der Korinthischen Vasen.* Basel: Benno Schwabe.

1984. 'Why were the Corinthian workshops not represented in the Kerameikos of Corinth 750–400?' In H. A. G. Brijder (ed.), *Ancient Greek and Related Pottery.* Amsterdam: Allard Pierson.

1985. 'Mass production and the competitive edge in Corinthian pottery' in *Greek Vases in the J.P. Getty Museum.* Malibu: J.P. Getty Museum.

1989. *Earlier Corinthian Workshops: a Study of Corinthian Geometric and Protocorinthian Stylistic Groups.* Amsterdam: Allard Pierson.

1995. 'Human figures and narrative in later protocorinthian vase painting' *Hesperia,* 64: 163–77.

Benton, S. 1935. 'The evolution of the tripod-lebes' *Annual of the British School at Athens* 35: 74–130.

1953. 'Further excavations at Aetos' *Annual of the British School at Athens* 48: 255–358.

Berger, J., Blomberg, S., Fox, C., Dibb, M. and Hollis, R. 1972. *Ways of Seeing.* London and Harmondsworth: BBC and Penguin.

Bergquist, B. 1990. 'Sympotic space: a functional aspect of Greek dining-rooms' in O. Murray (ed.), *Sympotica: a Symposium on the Symposion.* Oxford: Clarendon Press.

Berve, H. 1967. *Die Tyrannis bei den Griechen.* Munich: Beck.

Biers, W. R. 1994. 'Mass production, standardised parts and the Corinthian plastic vase' *American Journal of Archaeology* 63(4): 509–16.

Biers, W. R., Gerhardt, K. O. and Braniff, R. A. 1995. 'Scientific investigations of Corinthian "plastic" vases' *American Journal of Archaeology* 99(2): 320.

Biers, W. R., Searles, S. and Gerhardt, K. O. 1988. 'Non-destructive extraction studies of Corinthian plastic vases' in J. Christiansen and T. Melander (eds.), *Ancient Greek and Related Pottery*. Copenhagen: Ny Carlsberg Glyptotek and Thorvaldsens Museum.

Binford, L.. 1972. *An Archaeological Perspective*. New York: Seminar Press.

    1983. *In Pursuit of the Past*. London: Thames and Hudson.

    1987. 'Data, relativism and archaeological science' *Man* 22: 391–404.

Bintliff, J. 1993. 'Why Indiana Jones is smarter than the Postprocessualists' *Norwegian Archaeological Review* 26: 91–100.

Blakeway, A. 1932–3. 'Prolegomena to the study of Greek commerce with Italy, Sicily and France in the eighth and seventh centuries BC' *Annual of the British School at Athens* 33: 170–208.

    1935. 'Demaratus' *Journal of Roman Studies* 25: 129–49.

Blegen, C. W., Palmer, H. and Young, R. S. 1964. *Corinth 13: The North Cemetery*. Princeton NJ: American School of Classical Studies at Athens.

Bleicher, J. 1982. *The Hermeneutic Imagination: Outline of Positive Critique of Scientism and Sociology*. London: Routledge and Kegan Paul.

    (ed.) 1980. *Contemporary Hermeneutics: Hermeneutics as Method, Philosophy and Critique*. London: Routledge and Kegan Paul.

Blinkenberg, C. 1898. 'L'enlèvement d'Hélène représenté sur un lécythe protocorinthien' *Revue Archéologique* 33: 399–404.

Bloch, E. 1991. *Heritage of Our Times* (N. and S. Plaice, trans.). Cambridge: Blackwell Polity.

Bloch, E., Lukács, G., Brecht, B., Benjamin, W. and Adorno, T. 1977. *Aesthetics and Politics* (Ronald Taylor, trans.). London: New Left Books.

Bloch, M. 1977. 'The past and the present in the past' *Man* 12: 278–92.

Bloor, D. 1976. *Knowledge and Social Imagery*. London: Routledge and Kegan Paul.

Boardman, J. 1960. 'The multiple brush' *Antiquity* 34: 85–9.

    1968. *Archaic Greek Gems: Schools and Artists in the Sixth and Early Fifth Centuries BC*. London: Thames and Hudson.

    1970. 'Review: Coldstream, "Greek Geometric Pottery"' *Gnomon* 42: 493–503.

    1973. 'Clay analyses of archaic Greek pottery' *Annual of the British School at Athens* 68: 278.

    1980. *The Greeks Overseas: their Early Colonies and Trade* (second edn.). London: Thames and Hudson.

    1983. 'Symbol and story in Geometric art' in W. G. Moon (ed.), *Ancient Greek Art and Iconography*. Madison: University of Wisconsin Press.

Boast, R. 1990. *The Categorisation and Design Systematics of British Beakers: a Reassessment*. Unpublished PhD thesis, Cambridge University.

Böhme, J. 1929. *Die Seele und das Ich im homerischen Epos*. Leipzig: Teubner.

Bolton, J. D. P. 1962. *Aristeas of Proconnesus*. Oxford: Clarendon Press.

Bosana-Kourou, N. 1983. 'Some problems concerning the origin and dating of the Thapsos class vases' *Annuario della Scuola Archeologica di Atene e delle Missioni Italiene in Oriente* 61: 257–69.

Bosticco, S. 1957. 'Scarabei egiziani della necropolidi Pithecusa nell'isola di Ischia' *La Parola del Passato* 12: 215–29.

Bourdieu, P. 1977. *Outline of a Theory of Practice* (Richard Nice, trans.). Cambridge: Cambridge University Press.

    1984. *Distinction: a Social Critique of the Judgement of Taste*. London: Routledge and Kegan Paul.

Bourriot, F. 1976. *Recherches sur la Nature du Génos*. Lille: Lille Theses.

Bouzek, J. 1967. 'Die griechisch-geometrischen Bronzevögel' *Eirene* 6: 115–39.

Bowden, H. 1993. 'Hoplites and Homer: warfare, hero cult and the ideology of the polis' in J. Rich and G. Shipley (eds.), *War and Society in the Greek World*. London: Routledge.

Bradley, F. H. 1930. *Appearance and Reality* (second edn.). Oxford: Clarendon Press.

Braverman, H. 1974. *Labour and Monopoly Capital: the Degradation of Work in the Twentieth Century*. London: Monthly Review Press.

Bravo, B. 1975. 'Une lettre sur plomb de Berezan: colonisation et modes de contrat dans le Pont' *Dialogues d'Histoire Ancienne* 1: 111–87.

    1977. 'Remarques sur les assises, les sociales, les formes d'organisation et la terminologie du commerce maritime greq à l'époque archaique' *Dialogues d'Histoire Ancienne* 3: 1–59.

Bremmer, J. 1990. 'Adolescents, symposion and pederasty' in O. Murray (ed.), *Sympotica: a Symposium on the Symposion*. Oxford: Clarendon Press.

Bron, C. and Lissarague, F. 1984. 'Le vase à voir' in *La Cité des Images*. Paris: Nathan.

Broneer, O. 1971. *Isthmia 1: the Temple of Poseidon*. Princeton NJ: Princeton University Press.

Buchner, G. 1979. 'Early orientalising aspects of the Euboean connection' in D. Ridgway and F. Ridgway (eds.), *Italy before the Romans*. London: Academic Press.

Buchner, G. and Ridgway, D. 1993. *Pithekoussai 1:La Necropoli, Tombe 1–723*. Rome: Bretschneider.

Buck-Morss, S. 1977. *The Origin of Negative Dialectics*. Hassocks UK: Harvester.

    1989. *The Dialectics of Seeing: Walter Benjamin and the Arcades Project*. Cambridge MA: MIT Press.

Bunimovitz, S. 1987. 'Minoan-Mycenaean olive oil production and trade – a review of current research' in M. Heltzer and D. Eitam (eds.), *Olive Oil in Antiquity: Israel and Neighbouring Countries from the Neolithic to the Early Arab Period*. Haifa: University of Haifa Press.

Burgin, V. 1982. 'Photography, phantasy, function' in *Thinking Photography*. London: Macmillan.

Burkert, W. 1992. *The Orientalising Revolution*. Cambridge MA: Harvard University Press.

Burnett, A. P. 1983. *Three Archaic Poets: Archilochus, Alcaeus, Sappho*. London: Duckworth.

Calhoun, C. 1995. *Critical Social Theory*. Oxford: Blackwell.

Callon, M. 1986. 'Some elements for a sociology of translation: domestication of the scallops and the fishermen of St Brieuc Bay' in J. Law (ed.), *Power, Action and Belief: a New Sociology of Knowledge?* London: Routledge and Kegan Paul.

Campbell, D. A. (ed.) 1982–93. *Greek Lyric. Five Volumes. Loeb Classical Library*. Cambridge MA: Harvard University Press.

Canetti, E. 1962. *Crowds and Power* (C. Stewart, trans.). London: Gollancz.

Carrol, N. 1990. *The Philosophy of Horror: or, Paradoxes of the Heart*. London: Routledge.

Carter, J. 1972. 'The beginning of narrative art in the Greek geometric period' *Annual of the British School at Athens*, 67: 25–58.

Cartledge, P. 1977. 'Hoplites and heroes: Sparta's contribution to the technique of ancient warfare' *Journal of Hellenic Studies* 97: 11–27.

Chapman, R. and Randsborg, K. 1981. 'Approaches to the archaeology of death' in R. Chapman, I. Kinnes and K. Randsborg (eds.), *The Archaeology of Death*. Cambridge: Cambridge University Press.

Clarke, D. 1968. *Analytical Archaeology* (first edn.). London: Methuen.

Clastres, P. 1977. *Society against the State* (R. Hurley, trans.). New York: Urizen.

    1980a. 'Archéologie de la violence: la guerre dans les sociétés primitives' in *Recherches d'Anthropologie Politique*. Paris: Seuil.

    1980b. 'Malheur du guerrier sauvage' in *Recherches d'Anthropologie Politique*. Paris: Seuil.

Clifford, J. 1988. 'Identity in Mashpee' in *The Predicament of Culture: Twentieth Century Literature and Art*. Cambridge MA: Harvard University Press.

Cloke, P. 1991. 'Structuration theory: Anthony Giddens and the bringing together of structure and agency' in P. Cloke, C. Philo and D. Sadler (eds.), *Approaching Human Geography*. London: Paul Chapman.

Coldstream, J. N. 1968. *Greek Geometric Pottery: a Survey of Ten Local Styles and their*

Chronology. London: Methuen.

1969. 'The Phoenicians of Ialysos' *Bulletin of the Institute of Classical Studies* 16: 1–8.

1976. 'Hero-cults in the age of Homer' *Journal of Hellenic Studies* 96: 8–17.

1977. *Geometric Greece.* London: Benn.

1979. 'Some Cypriot traits in Cretan pottery *c.* 950–750 BC' in *Acts of the International Archaeological Symposium: The Relations between Cyprus and Crete ca. 2000–500 BC, 1978.* Nicosia: Department of Antiquities.

1983. 'The meaning of the regional styles in the eighth century BC' in R. Hägg (ed.), *The Greek Renaissance of the Eighth Century BC: Tradition and Innovation.* Stockholm: Svenska institutet i Athen.

1986. 'Kition and Amathus: some reflections on their westward links during the early Iron Age' in *Acts of the International Archaeological Symposium: Cyprus between the Orient and the Occident, 1985.* Nicosia: Department of Antiquities, Cyprus.

1994. 'Prospectors and pioneers: Pithekoussai, Kyme and central Italy' in G. R. Tsetskhladze and F. De Angelis (eds.), *The Archaeology of Greek Colonisation.* Oxford: Oxford University Committee for Archaeology.

Conkey, M. 1990. 'Experimenting with style in archaeology: some historical and theoretical issues' in M. Conkey and C. Hastorf (eds.), *The Uses of Style in Archaeology.* Cambridge: Cambridge University Press.

Conkey, M. and Hastorf, C. (eds.) 1990. *The Uses of Style in Archaeology.* Cambridge: Cambridge University Press.

Connerton, P. (ed.) 1976. *Critical Sociology.* Harmondsworth: Penguin.

Connor, W. R. 1988. 'Early Greek land warfare as symbolic expression' *Past and Present*, 119: 3–29.

Cook, R. 1959. 'Die Bedeutung der bemalten keramik für den griechischen Handel' *Jahrbuch des deutschen archäologischen Instituts* 74: 114–23.

1970. The archetypal Doric temple. *Annual of the British School at Athens* 65: 17–19.

1972. *Greek Painted Pottery* (second edn.). London: Methuen.

Coote, J. and Shelton, A. (eds.) 1992. *Anthropology, Art and Aesthetics.* Oxford: Clarendon Press.

Coulton, J. J. 1977. *Greek Architects at Work: Problems of Structure and Design.* London: Thames and Hudson.

Courbin, P. 1957. 'Une tombe géométrique d'Argos' *Bulletin de Correspondance Hellénique* 81: 322–86.

Cowan, R. S. 1987. 'The consumption junction: a proposal for research strategies in the sociology of technology' in W. E. Bijker, T. P. Hughes and T. Pinch (eds.), The Social Construction of Technological Systems. Cambridge: MI T Press.

Crary, J. and Kwinter, S. (eds.) 1992. *Incorporations.* New York: Zone.

Davidson, G. R. 1952. *Corinth 12: The Minor Objects.* Princeton NJ: American School of Classical Studies at Athens.

Davies, J. K. 1981. *Wealth and the Power of Wealth in Classical Athens.* Salem NH: Ayer.

Davies, M. (ed.) 1991. *Poetarum Melicorum Graecorum Fragmenta (Volume 1).* Oxford: Clarendon Press.

Dawson, C. R. 1966. 'Spoudaiogeloion: random thoughts on occasional poems' *Yale Classical Studies* 19: 50–8.

Dehl, C. 1984. *Die korinthische Keramik des 8. und Frühen 7. Jhr. v. Chr. in Italien. Untersuchungen zu Ihrer Chronologie und Ausbrietung.* Berlin: Athenische Mitteilungen Beiheft 11.

Deilaki, E. 1973. Archaiotites kai mnimeia Argolidos-Korinthias 1971–2. *Arkhaiologikon Deltion* 28(1): 80–122.

Deleuze, G. and Guattari, F. 1988. *A Thousand Plateaus: Capitalism and Schizophrenia* (Brian Massumi, trans.). London: Athlone Press.

De Polignac, F. 1984. *La Naissance de la Cité Grecque*. Paris: Editions La Découverte.

    1994. 'Mediation, competition and sovereignty: the evolution of rural sanctuaries in Geo-metric Greece' in S. E. Alcock and R. Osborne (eds.), *Placing the Gods: Sanctuaries and Sacred Space in Ancient Greece*. Oxford: Clarendon Press.

Derrida, J. 1974. *Of Grammatology* (Gyatri Spivak, trans.). Baltimore: Johns Hopkins University Press.

    1978. 'From restricted to general economy: a Hegelianism without reserve' in *Writing and Difference*. London: Routledge.

De Ste Croix, G. E. M. 1981. *The Class Struggle in the Ancient Greek World*. London: Duckworth.

Detienne, M. 1968. 'La phalange: problèmes et controverses' in J.-P. Vernant (ed.), *Problèmes de la Guerre en Grèce Ancienne*. Paris: Mouton.

    1977. *The Gardens of Adonis: Spices in Greek Mythology* (J. Lloyd, trans.). New Jersey: Humanities Press.

    1979. *Dionysos Slain* (M. and L. Muellner, trans.). Baltimore: Johns Hopkins University Press.

Detienne, M. and Vernant, J.-P. 1978. *Cunning Intelligence in Greek Culture and Society*. Hassocks UK: Harvester.

    1989. *The Cuisine of Sacrifice Among the Greeks*. Chicago: Chicago University Press.

Donlan, W. 1980. *The Aristocratic Ideal in Ancient Greece*. Lawrence KA: Coronado.

    1985. 'The social groups of Dark Age Greece' *Classical Philology* 80: 293–308.

Dougherty, C. 1993. 'It's murder to found a colony' in C. Dougherty and L. Kurke (eds.), *Cultural Poetics in Archaic Greece: Cult, Performance, Politics*. Cambridge: Cambridge University Press.

Drews, R. 1972. The first tyrants in Greece. *Historia* 21: 129–44.

    1983. *Basileis: the Evidence for Kingship in Geometric Greece*. New Haven: Yale University Press.

DuBois, P. 1979. 'On horse/men, Amazons and endogamy' *Arethusa* 12: 35–49.

    1984. *Centaurs and Amazons: Women and the Prehistory of the Great Chain of Being*. Ann Arbor: University of Michigan Press.

    1988. *Sowing the Body: Psychoanalysis and Ancient Representations of Women*. Chicago: University of Chicago Press.

Duby, G. 1973. *Origines de l'Économie Moderne: Guerriers et Paysans*. Paris: Gallimard.

Ducat, J. 1963. 'Les vases plastiques corinthiens' *Bulletin de Correspondance Hellénique* 87: 431–58.

Dunbabin, T. J. 1948. *The Western Greeks*. Oxford: Clarendon Press.

    1957. *The Greeks and their Eastern Neighbours*. London: Society for the Promotion of Hellenic Studies.

Dunbabin, T. J. and others. 1962. *Perachora: the Sanctuaries of Hera Akraia and Limenia. Volume Two: Pottery, Ivories, Scarabs and Other Objects from the Votive Deposit of Hera Limenia*. Oxford: Clarendon Press.

Dunbabin, T. J. and Robertson, M. 1953. 'Some Protocorinthian vase painters' *Annual of the British School at Athens* 48: 172–81.

Dyson, S. L. 1989. 'The role of ideology and institutions in shaping classical archaeology in the 19th and 20th centuries' in A. L. Christenson (ed.), *Tracing Archaeology's Past: the Historiography of Archaeology*. Carbondale: University of Southern Illinois Press.

    1993. 'From New to new-age archaeology: archaeological theory and Classical archaeology – a 1990s perspective' *American Journal of Archaeology* 97: 195–206.

Eagleton, T. 1976. *Criticism and Ideology*. London: Verso.

    1991. *Ideology: an Introduction*. London: Verso.

Ericson, J. E. and Earle, T. K. (eds.) 1982. *Contexts for Prehistoric Trade*. London: Academic

Press.

Fagerström, K. 1988. *Greek Iron Age Architecture: Developments through Changing Times.* Göteborg: Paul Åström.

Farnsworth, M. 1970. Corinthian pottery: technical studies. *American Journal of Archaeology* 74: 9–20.

Farnsworth, M. and Simmons, I. 1963. 'Coloring agents for Greek vases' *American Journal of Archaeology* 67: 389–96.

Farnsworth, M., Perlman, I. and Asaro, F. 1977. 'Corinth and Corfu: a neutron activation study of their pottery' *American Journal of Archaeology* 81: 455–68.

Faure, P. 1987. *Parfums et Aromates de l'Antiquité.* Paris: Fayard.

Feher, M., Naddaff, R. and Tazi, N. (eds.). 1989. *Fragments for a History of the Human Body* (3 Volumes). New York: Zone.

Ferguson, Y. H. 1991. 'Chiefdoms to city-states: the Greek experience' in T. Earle (ed.), *Chiefdoms: Power, Economy and Ideology.* Cambridge: Cambridge University Press.

Fernandez, J. 1966. 'Principles of opposition and vitality in Fang aesthetics' *Journal of Aesthetics and Art Criticism* 8: 53–64.

Filippakis, S. 1983. 'Bronzes grecs et orientaux: influences et apprentissages' *Bulletin de Correspondance Hellénique* 107: 111–32.

Finley, M. 1973. *The Ancient Economy.* London: Chatto and Windus.

1978. *The World of Odysseus.* London: Chatto and Windus.

Fittschen, K. 1969. *Untersuchungen zum Beginn der Sagendarstellungen bei den Griechen.* Berlin: Bruno Hessling.

Forbes, R. J. 1965. *Studies in Ancient Technology* 3. Leiden: Brill.

Forge, A. 1973. 'Style and meaning in Sepik art' in A. Forge (ed.), *Primitive Art and Society.* Oxford: Oxford University Press.

Forrest, G. 1966. *The Emergence of Greek Democracy.* London: Weidenfeld and Nicolson.

Fotiadis, M. 1995. 'Modernity and the past-still-present: politics of time in the birth of regional archaeological projects in Greece' *American Journal of Archaeology* 99: 59–78.

Foucault, M. 1975. *Surveillir et Punir: Naissance de la Prison.* Paris: Gallimard.

1976. *La Volonté de Savoir: Histoire de la Sexualité* 1. Paris: Gallimard.

1980. *Power/Knowledge.* Brighton: Harvester.

Fowler, H. N. and Stillwell, R. N. 1932. *Corinth 1: Introduction, Topography, Architecture.* Cambridge MA: Harvard University Press.

Fränkel, H. 1975. *Early Greek Poetry and Philosophy.* Oxford: Blackwell.

Frankenstein, S. 1979. 'The Phoenicians in the far west: a function of Neo-Assyrian imperialism' in M. T. Larsen (ed.), *Power and Propaganda: A Symposium on Ancient Empire.* Copenhagen: Akademisk.

Frankenstein, S. and Rowlands, M. 1978. 'The internal structure and regional context of early Iron Age society in south-western Germany' *Bulletin of the Institute of Archaeology* 15: 73–112.

Friedman, J. 1975. 'Tribes, states and transformations' in M. Bloch (ed.), *Marxist Analyses and Social Anthropology.* London: Malaby.

Friedman, J. and Rowlands, M. 1978. 'Notes towards an epigenetic model of the evolution of "civilisation"' in J. Friedman and M. Rowlands (eds.), *The Evolution of Social Systems.* London: Duckworth.

Frontisi-Ducroux, F. 1984. 'Au miroir du masque' in *La Cité des Images.* Paris: Nathan.

Gallant, T. 1991. *Risk and Survival in Ancient Greece: Reconstructing the Rural Economy.* Cambridge: Blackwell Polity.

Garlan, Y. 1989. *Guerre et Economie en Grèce Ancienne.* Paris: Maspéro.

Garnsey, P., Hopkins, K. and Whittaker, C. R. (eds.) 1983. *Trade in the Ancient Economy.* London: Chatto and Windus.

Gebhard, E. and Hemans, F. 1992. 'University of Chicago excavations at Isthmia 1989: I' *Hesperia* 62: 1–77.

Geertz, C. 1983. 'Art as a cultural system' in *Local Knowledge*. New York: Basic Books.

Gernet, L. 1968. 'Frairies antiques' in *Anthropologie de la Grèce Antique*. Paris: Maspéro.

  1981. ' "Value" in Greek myth' in R. L. Gordon (ed.), *Myth, Religion and Society*. Cambridge: Cambridge University Press.

Giddens, A. 1984. *The Constitution of Society: Outline of the Theory of Structuration*. Cambridge: Blackwell Polity.

Girard, R. 1977. *Violence and the Sacred*. Baltimore: Johns Hopkins University Press.

Goffman, E. 1975. *Frame Analysis*. Harmondsworth: Penguin.

Gombrich, E. 1979. *The Sense of Order: a Study in the Psychology of Decorative Art*. London: Phaidon.

Greenhalgh, P. A. L. 1972. 'Patriotism in the Homeric world.' *Historia* 21: 528–37.

  1973. *Early Greek Warfare: Horsemen and Chariots in the Homeric and Archaic Ages*. Cambridge: Cambridge University Press.

Grimanis, A. P., Filippakis, S. E., Perdikatsis, B., Vassilaki-Grimani, M., Bosana-Kourou, N. and Yalouris, N. 1980. 'Neutron-activation and x-ray analysis of Thapsos class wares: an attempt to identify their origin' *Journal of Archaeological Science* 7: 227–39.

Guralnick, E. 1978. 'Proportions of kouroi' *American Journal of Archaeology* 82: 461–72.

Habermas, J. 1976. 'A positivistically bisected rationalism' in T. Adorno, H. Albert, R. Dahrendorf, J. Habermas, H. Pilot and K. R. Popper (eds.), *The Positivist Dispute in German Sociology*. London: Heinemann.

  1987. 'Between eroticism and general economics: Georges Bataille' in *The Philosophical Discourse of Modernity*. Cambridge MA: MIT Press.

Haldane, C. W. 1990. 'Shipwrecked plant remains' *Biblical Archaeologist* 53: 55–60.

Hall, J. M. 1993. *Ethnic Identity in the Argolid 900–600 BC*. Unpublished PhD thesis, Cambridge.

  1995. 'Approaches to ethnicity in the Early Iron Age of Greece' in N. Spencer (ed.), *Time, Tradition and Society in Greek Archaeology: Bridging the Divide* London: Routledge.

Halperin, D. 1990. *One Hundred Years of Homosexuality*. London: Routledge.

Hampe, R. 1960. *Ein frühattische Grabfund*. Mainz: Römisch-germanischen Zentralmuseums.

  1969. *Kretische Löwenschale des siebten Jahrhunderts v. Chr. Sitzungsberichte der Heidelberger Akademie der Wissenschaften*. Heidelberg: Winter.

Hampe, R. and Simon, E. 1981. *The Birth of Greek Art: from the Mycenaean to the Archaic Period*. London: Thames and Hudson.

Hanson, V. 1990. *The Western Way of War: Infantry Battle in Classical Greece*. London: Hodder and Stoughton.

  (ed.) 1991. *Hoplites: the Classical Greek Battle Experience*. London: Routledge.

Haraway, D. 1991. 'Gender for a marxist dictionary: the sexual politics of a word' in D. Haraway (ed.), *Simians, Cyborgs and Women: the Reinvention of Nature*. London: Routledge.

Harris, M. 1968. *The Rise of Anthropological Theory*. New York: Cornell University Press.

  1977. 'History and significance of the emic-etic distinction' *Annual Review of Anthropology* 5: 329–50.

Hasebroek, J. 1933. *Trade and Politics in Ancient Greece*. London: Bell.

Hebdige, D. 1979. *Subculture: the Meaning of Style*. London: Methuen.

  1988. *Hiding in the Light*. London: Routledge.

Hedeagger, C. 1988. 'The evolution of Germanic society 1–400 AD' in R.F. Jones and J. Bloemers (eds.), *First Millennium Papers*. Oxford: British Archaeological Reports.

Hegel, G. W. L. 1966. *Phenomenology of Mind*. London: Allen and Unwin.

Held, D. 1980. *Introduction to Critical Theory: Horkheimer to Habermas*. London: Hutchinson.

Helms, M. W. 1988. *Ulysses' Sail: an Ethnographic Odyssey of Power, Knowledge and Geographical distance*. Princeton NJ: Princeton University Press.

Hencken, H. 1958. 'Syracuse, Etruria and the north: some comparisons.' *American Journal of Archaeology* 62: 259–72.

Henderson, J. 1994. '*Timeo Danaos*: Amazons in early Greek art and pottery' in S. Goldhill and R. Osborne (eds.), *Art and Text in Ancient Greek Culture*. Cambridge: Cambridge University Press.

Herman, G. 1987. *Ritualised Friendship and the Greek City*. Cambridge: Cambridge University Press.

Herrmann, H. -V. 1964. Werkstätten geometrischer Bronzeplastik. *Jahrbuch des deutschen archäologischen Instituts* 79: 17–71.

1966. 'Die Kessel der orientalisierenden Zeit: Erster Teil: Kesselattaschen und Reliefuntersätze' *Olympische Forschungen* 7.1.

1979. 'Die Kessel der orientalisierenden Zeit. Zweiter Teil: Kesselprotomen und Stabdreifüsse' *Olympische Forschungen* 11.

Heurtley, W. A. 1948. 'Excavations in Ithaca V: the Geometric and later finds from Aetos' *Annual of the British School at Athens* 43: 1–7.

Hill, B. H. 1964. *Corinth 1.6: The Springs: Peirene, the Sacred Spring, Glauke*. Princeton NJ: American School of Classical Studies at Athens.

Hodder, I. 1982. *Symbols in Action*. Cambridge: Cambridge University Press.

1985. 'Postprocessual archaeology' in M. Schiffer (ed.), *Advances in Archaeological Method and Theory* 8. London: Academic Press.

1990. 'Style as historical quality' in M. Conkey and C. Hastorf (eds.), *The Uses of Style in Archaeology*. Cambridge: Cambridge University Press.

1991. *Reading the Past: Current Approaches to Interpretation in Archaeology* (second edn.). Cambridge: Cambridge University Press.

(ed.) 1987. *The Archaeology of Contextual Meanings*. Cambridge: Cambridge University Press.

Hodder, I., Shanks, M., Alexandri, A., Buchli, V., Carman, J., Last, J. and Lucas, G. (eds.) 1995. *Interpreting Archaeology: Finding Meaning in the Past*. London: Routledge.

Hoffman, H. 1977. *Sexual and Asexual Pursuit: a Structuralist Approach to Greek Vase Painting*. London: Royal Anthropological Institute.

Hölbl, G. 1979. *Beziehungen der ägyptischen Kultur zu Altitalien*. Two volumes. Leiden: Brill.

Hollis, M. 1977. *Models of Man*. Cambridge: Cambridge University Press.

Humphreys, S. C. 1978. *Anthropology and the Greeks*. London: Routledge and Kegan Paul.

1980. 'Family tombs and tomb cult in ancient Athens: tradition or traditionalism?' *Journal of Hellenic Studies* 100: 96–126.

Huntingdon, R. and Metcalf, P. 1979. *Celebrations of Death: the Anthropology of Mortuary Ritual*. Cambridge: Cambridge University Press.

Hurwitt, J. M. 1985. *The Art and Culture of Early Greece 1100–480 BC*. Ithaca: Cornell University Press.

Immerwahr, H. 1990. *Attic Script*. Oxford: Clarendon Press.

Jaeger, W. 1966. 'Tyrtaios on true arete' in *Five Essays*. Montreal: Casalini.

Jeanmaire 1939. *Couroi et Courètes: Essai sur l'Education Spartiate et sur les Rites d'Adolescence dans l'Antiquité Hellénique*. Lille: Bibliothèque Universitaire.

Jeffery, L. H. 1976. *Archaic Greece: the City States c. 700–500 BC*. London: Methuen.

1990. *The Local Scripts of Archaic Greece* (second edn.). Oxford: Clarendon Press.

Johansen, H. and Olsen, B. 1992. 'Hermeneutics and archaeology: on the philosophy of contextual archaeology' *American Antiquity* 57: 419–36.

Johansen, K. F. 1923. *Les Vases Sicyoniens*. Paris: Champion.

Johnston, A. 1987. 'IG II^2 2311 and the number of Panathenaic amphorae' *Annual of the*

British School at Athens 82: 125–9.

Jones, D. W. 1993. 'Phoenician unguent factories in Dark Age Greece: social approaches to evaluating the archaeological evidence' *Oxford Journal of Archaeology* 12: 293–303.

Jones, R. E. 1986. *Greek and Cypriot Pottery: a Review of Scientific Studies*. London: British School at Athens.

Jones, S. 1974. *Men of Influence in Nuristan*. London: Seminar Press.

Keegan, J. 1976. *The Face of Battle*. London: Cape.

1993. *A History of Warfare*. London: Hutchinson.

Kellner, D. 1989. *Critical Theory, Marxism and Modernity*. Cambridge: Blackwell Polity.

Kelly, T. 1976. *A History of Argos to 500BC*. Minneapolis: University of Minnesota Press.

Kenfield, J. F. 1973. 'The sculptural significance of early Greek armour' *Opuscula Romana* 9: 149–56.

Kilian-Dirlmeier, I. 1985. 'Fremde Weihungen im griechischen Heiligtümern von 8. bis zumm Beginn des 7. Jahrhunderts' *Jahrbuch des Römisch-Germanischen Zentralmuseums* 32: 215–54.

Kirk, G. S., Raven, J. E. and Schofield, M. 1983. *The Pre-Socratic Philosophers* (second edn.). Cambridge: Cambridge University Press.

Knapp, B. 1991. 'Spice, drugs, grain and grog: organic goods in Bronze Age east Mediterranean trade' in N. H. Gale (ed.), *Bronze Age Trade in the Mediterranean. Studies in Mediterranean Archaeology* 90. Göteborg: Paul Åström.

Knorr-Cetina, K. 1981. *The Manufacture of Knowledge: an Essay on the Constructivist and Contextual Nature of Science*. Oxford: Pergamum Press.

Knorr-Cetina, K. and Mulkay, M. (eds.) 1983. *Science Observed: Perspectives on the Social Study of Science*. London: Sage.

Koch-Harnack, G. 1989. *Erotische Symbole: Lotosblüte und Gemeinsamer Mantel auf antiken Vasen*. Berlin: Mann.

Kochavi, M. 1992. 'Some connections between the Aegean and the Levant in the second millennium BC: a view from the east' in G. Kopcke and I. Tokumaru (eds.), *Greece Between East and West 10th–8th Centuries BC*. Mainz: von Zabern.

Kopcke, G. and Tokumaru, I. 1992. *Greece Between East and West 10th–8th Centuries BC*. Mainz: von Zabern.

Kopytoff, I. 1986. 'The cultural biography of things: commoditisation as a process' in A. Appadurai (ed.), *The Social Life of Things: Commodities in Cultural Perspective*. Cambridge: Cambridge University Press.

Korshak, Y. 1987. *Frontal Faces in Attic Vase painting of the Archaic period*. Chicago: Ares.

Kristiansen, K. 1984. 'Ideology and material culture: an archaeological perspective' in M. Spriggs (ed.), *Marxist perspectives in Archaeology*. Cambridge: Cambridge University Press.

Kron, U. 1988. 'Kultmahle im Heraion von Samos archaischer Zeit' in R. Hägg, N. Marinatos and G. Nordquist (eds.), *Early Greek Cult Practice*. Stockholm: Skrifter Utgivna av Svenska Institutet i Athen.

Kunze, E. 1991. 'Beinschienen' *Olympische Forschungen* 21.

Kurke, L. 1991. *The Traffic in Praise: Pindar and the Poetics of Social Economy*. Ithaca: Cornell University Press.

1992. 'The politics of *habrosune*' *Classical Antiquity* 11: 91–120.

1993. 'The economy of *kudos*' in C. Dougherty and L. Kurke (eds.), *Cultural Poetics in Archaic Greece: Cult, Performance, Politics*. Cambridge: Cambridge University Press.

Kyrieleis, H. 1980. 'Archaische Holzfunde auf Samos' *Mitteilungen des deutschen Archäologischen Instituts, Athenische Abteilung* 95: 87–147.

La Cité des Images. 1984. Paris: Nathan.

Lacan, J. 1977. 'The mirror phase as formative of the function of the I as revealed in psychoanalytic experience' in *Écrits: a Selection*. London: Tavistock.

Lampeter Archaeology Workshop (forthcoming). 'The truth about relativism' *Archaeological Dialogues*.

Larrain, J. 1979. *The Concept of Ideology*. London: Hutchinson.

1983. *Marxism and Ideology*. London: Macmillan.

Last, J. 1995. 'The nature of history' in I. Hodder, M. Shanks, A. Alexandri, V. Buchli, J. Carman, J. Last and G. Lucas (eds.), *Interpreting Archaeology: Finding Meaning in the Past*. London: Routledge.

Latacz, J. 1977. *Kampfäränese, Kampfdarstellung und Kampfwirchlichkeit in der Ilias, bei Kallinos und Tyrtaios*. Munich: Beck.

Latour, B. 1987. *Science in Action: How to Follow Scientists and Engineers Through Society*. Milton Keynes: Open University Press.

1988a. *The Pasteurization of France* (A. Sheridan and J. Law, trans.). Cambridge MA: Harvard University Press.

1988b. 'The Prince for machines as well as machinations' in B. Elliott (ed.), *Technology and Social Process*. Edinburgh: Edinburgh University Press.

Latour, B. and Woolgar, S. 1986. *Laboratory Life: the Construction of Scientific Facts* (second edn.). Princeton: Princeton University Press.

Lattimore, R. 1951. *Homer, The Iliad*, translated. Chicago: University of Chicago Press.

1960. *Greek Lyrics*, translated (second edn.). Chicago: University of Chicago Press.

1967. *Homer, The Odyssey*, translated. New York: Harper and Row.

Laum, B. 1924. *Heiliges Geld: Eine Historische Untersuchung über den Sakralen Ursprung des Geldes*. Tübingen: Mohr.

Law, J. 1987. 'Technology and heterogeneous engineering: the case of Portuguese expansion' in W. E. Bijker, T. P. Hughes and T. Pinch (eds.), *The Social Construction of Technological Systems*. Cambridge MA: MIT Press.

1991. 'Monsters, machines and sociotechnical relations' in J. Law (ed.), *A Sociology of Monsters: Essays on Power, Technology and Domination*. London: Routledge.

Layton, R. 1991. *The Anthropology of Art* (second edn.). Cambridge: Cambridge University Press.

Leach, J. and Leach, E. (eds.). 1983. *The Kula: New Perspectives on Massim Exchange*. Cambridge: Cambridge University Press.

Leitch, V. 1983. *Deconstructive Criticism*. London: Hutchinson.

Lemonnier, P. 1976. 'La description des châines opératoire: contribution à l'analyse des systèmes techniques' *Techniques et Culture* 1: 100–51.

Leone, M. 1984. 'Interpreting ideology in historical archaeology: the William Paca garden in Annapolis' in D. Miller and C. Tilley (eds.), *Ideology, Power and Prehistory*. Cambridge: Cambridge University Press.

Lilja, S. 1972. *The Treatment of Odours in the Poetry of Antiquity*. Helsinki: Societas Scientiarum Fennica: Commentationes Humaniorum Litterarum 49.

Lissarague, F. 1988. 'Les satyres et le monde animal' in J. Christiansen and T. Melander (eds.), *Ancient Greek and Related Pottery*. Copenhagen: Ny Carlsberg Glyptotek and Thorvaldsens Museum.

1990. *The Aesthetics of the Greek Banquet: Images of Wine and Ritual* (A. Szegedy-Maszak, trans.). Princeton NJ: Princeton University Press.

Lobel, E. and Page, D. (eds.) 1955. *Poetarum Lesbiorum Fragmenta*. Oxford: Clarendon Press.

Loraux, N. 1975. 'HEBE et ANDREIA: deux versions de la mort du combattant athénien' *Ancient Society* 6: 1–31.

1986. *The Invention of Athens* (A. Sheridan, trans.). Cambridge MA: Harvard University Press.

Lorber, F. 1979. *Inschriften auf korinthischen Vasen*. Berlin: Gebr. Mann.

Lorimer, H. L. 1947. The hoplite phalanx with special reference to the poems of Archilochus and Tyrtaeus. *Annual of the British School at Athens* 42: 76–138.

Lucie-Smith, E. 1981. *The Story of Craft: the Craftsman's Role in Society*. London: Phaidon.

Lunn, E. 1985. *Marxism and Modernism*. London: Verso.

Lynch, M. 1985. *Art and Artifact in Laboratory Science: a Study of Shop Work and Shop Talk in a Research Laboratory*. London: Routledge and Kegan Paul.

Maass, M. 1978. 'Die geometrischen Dreifüsse von Olympia' *Olympische Forschungen* 10.

   1981. 'Die geometrischen Dreifüsse von Olympia' *Antike Kunst* 24: 6–20.

Macherey, P. 1978. *A Theory of Literary Production*. London: Routledge and Kegan Paul.

Malinowski, B. (ed.) 1922. *Argonauts of the Western Pacific*. London: Routledge and Kegan Paul.

Malkin, I. 1987. *Religion and Greek Colonisation*. Leiden: Brill.

Mann, M. 1986. *The Sources of Social Power. Volume 1: A History of Power from the Beginning to 1760AD*. Cambridge: Cambridge University Press.

Marcuse, H. 1955. *Reason and Revolution: Hegel and the Rise of Social Theory* (second edn.). London: Routledge and Kegan Paul.

Markoe, G. E. 1992. 'In pursuit of metal: Phoenicians and Greeks in Italy' in G. Kopcke and I. Tokumaru (eds.), *Greece Between East and West 10th–8th Centuries BC*. Mainz: von Zabern.

Marry, J. D. 1979. 'Sappho and the heroic ideal: *erotos arete*' *Arethusa* 12: 71–92.

Martin, L., Gutman, H. and Hutton, P. (eds.) 1988. *Technologies of the Self*. London: Tavistock.

Mason, P. 1987. 'Third person/second sex: patterns of sexual asymmetry in the Theogony of Hesiodos' in J. Blok and P. Mason (eds.), *Sexual Asymmetry: Studies in Ancient Society*. Amsterdam: Grieben.

Mauss, M. 1954. *The Gift*. London: Cohen and West.

McGlew, J. F. 1993. *Tyranny and Political Culture in Ancient Greece*. Ithaca: Cornell University Press.

McGuire, R. H. 1992. *A Marxist Archaeology*. London: Academic Press.

McGuire, R. and Paynter, R. (eds.) 1991. *The Archaeology of Inequality*. Oxford: Blackwell.

Melas, M. 1989. 'Etics, emics and empathy in archaeological theory' in I. Hodder (ed.), *The Meanings of Things*. London: Unwin Hyman.

Mervis, C. and Rosch, E. 1981. Categorisation of natural objects. *Annual Review of Psychology* 32: 89–115.

Miller, D. 1982. 'Structures and strategies: an aspect of the relationship between social hierarchy and cultural change' in I. Hodder (ed.), *Symbolic and Structural Archaeology*. Cambridge: Cambridge University Press.

   1985a. *Artefacts as Categories: a Study of Ceramic Variability in Central India*. Cambridge: Cambridge University Press.

   1985b. Ideology and the Harappan civilisation. *Journal of Anthropological Archaeology* 4: 34–71.

   1987. *Material Culture and Mass Consumption*. Oxford: Blackwell.

Miller, D. and Tilley, C. (eds.). 1984. *Ideology, Power and Prehistory*. Cambridge: Cambridge University Press.

Millett, P. 1991. *Lending and Borrowing in Ancient Athens*. Cambridge: Cambridge University Press.

Montague, S. P. 1980. 'Kula and Trobriand cosmology' *Journal of Anthropology* 2: 70–94.

Morel, J.-P. 1984. 'Greek colonisation in Italy and the west: problems of evidence and interpretation' in T. Hackens, N. D. Holloway and R. R. Holloway (eds.), *Crossroads of the Mediterranean*. Louvain-la-Neuve and Providence RI: Université Catholique de Louvain and Brown University.

Morgan, C. 1988. 'Corinth, the Corinthian Gulf and western Greece during the eighth century BC' *Annual of the British School at Athens* 83: 313–38.

1990. *Athletes and Oracles: the Transformation of Olympia and Delphi in the Eighth Century BC.* Cambridge: Cambridge University Press.

1993. 'The origins of pan-Hellenism' in N. Marinatos and R. Hägg (eds.), *Greek Sanctuaries: New Approaches.* London: Routledge.

1994. 'The evolution of a sacral "landscape": Isthmia, Perachora and the early Corinthian state' in S. E. Alcock and R. Osborne (eds.), *Placing the Gods: Sanctuaries and Sacred Space in Ancient Greece.* Oxford: Clarendon Press.

Morgan, C. and Whitelaw, T. 1991. 'Pots and politics: ceramic evidence for the rise of the Argive state' *American Journal of Archaeology* 95: 79–108.

Morphy, H. 1992. 'From dull to brilliant: the aesthetics of spiritual power among the Yolngu' in J. Coote and A. Shelton (eds.), *Anthropology, Art and Aesthetics.* Oxford: Clarendon Press.

Morris, I. 1986. 'From gift to commodity in archaic Greece' *Man* 21: 1–17.

1987. *Burial and Ancient Society: the Rise of the Greek City State.* Cambridge: Cambridge University Press.

1988. 'Tomb cult and the Greek Renaissance: the past in the present in the 8th century BC' *Antiquity* 62: 750–61.

1993. 'Poetics of power: the interpretation of ritual action in Archaic Greece' in C. Dougherty and L. Kurke (eds.), *Cultural Poetics in Archaic Greece: Cult, Performance, Politics.* Cambridge: Cambridge University Press.

1994. 'Archaeologies of Greece' in I. Morris (ed.), *Classical Greece: Ancient History and Modern Archaeologies.* Cambridge: Cambridge University Press.

Morris, S. 1992. 'Greece beyond east and west: perspectives and prospects' in G. Kopcke and I. Tokumaru (eds.), *Greece Between East and West 10th–8th Centuries BC.* Mainz: von Zabern.

Morrison, J. S. and Williams, R. T. 1968. *Greek Oared Ships.* Cambridge: Cambridge University Press.

Mossé, C. 1969. *La Tyrannie dans la Grèce Antique.* Paris: Presses Universitaires de France.

Murray, O. 1982. 'Symposion and Männerbund' in P. Oliva and A. Froliková (eds.), *Concilium Eirene 15.1* Prague.

1983. 'The symposium as social organisation' in R. Hägg (ed.), *The Greek Renaissance of the Eighth Century BC: Tradition and Innovation.* Stockholm: Svenska institutet i Athen.

1993. *Early Greece* (second edn.). London: Fontana.

Murray, O. (ed.) 1990. *Sympotica: a Symposium on the Symposion.* Oxford: Clarendon Press.

Muscarella, O. W. 1992. 'Greek and oriental cauldron attachments: a review' in G. Kopcke and I. Tokumaru (eds.), *Greece Between East and West 10th–8th Centuries BC.* Mainz: von Zabern.

Naerebout, F. G. 1987. 'Male-female relationships in the Homeric epics' in J. Blok and P. Mason (eds.), *Sexual Asymmetry: Studies in Ancient Society.* Amsterdam: Grieben.

Nagy, G. 1979. *The Best of the Achaeans: Concepts of the Hero in Archaic Greek Poetry.* Baltimore: Johns Hopkins University Press.

Neeft, C. V. 1975. 'Corinthian fragments from Argos at Utrecht and the Corinthian late Geometric kotyle' *Bulletin van de Vereeniging tot Bevordering der Kennis van de Antieke Beschaving te s'Gravenhage,* 50: 97–134.

1981. 'Observations on the Thapsos class' *Mélanges d'Archéologie et d'Histoire de l'Ecole Française de Rome* 93: 7–88.

1987. *Protocorinthian Subgeometric Aryballoi.* Amsterdam: Allard Pierson.

1991. *Addenda et Corrigenda to D.A. Amyx: Corinthian Vase Painting in the Archaic Period.* Amsterdam: Allard Pierson.

Noble, J. V. 1988. *The Techniques of Attic Painted Pottery* (revised edn.). London: Thames and Hudson.

Oleson, J. P. 1986. *Bronze Age, Greek and Roman Technology: a Select, Annotated Bibliography.* New York: Garland.

Ollman, B. 1971. *Alienation: Marx's Conception of Man in Capitalist Society.* Cambridge: Cambridge University Press.

Oost, S. I. 1972. 'Cypselos the Bacchiad' *Classical Philology* 67: 10–30.

Orsi, P. 1893. 'Siracusa' *Notizie degli Scavi di Antichità*: 445–86.

    1895. 'Siracusa' *Notizie degli Scavi di Antichità*: 109–92.

Parker-Pearson, M. 1984a. 'Economic and ideological change: cyclical growth in the pre-state societies of Jutland' in D. Miller and C. Tilley (eds.), *Ideology, Power and Prehistory.* Cambridge: Cambridge University Press.

    1984b. 'Social change, ideology and the archaeological record' in M. Spriggs (ed.), *Marxist Perspectives in Archaeology.* Cambridge: Cambridge University Press.

Payne, H. G. G. 1931. *Necrocorinthia: a Study of Korinthian Art in the Archaic Period.* Oxford: Clarendon Press.

    1933. *Protokorinthische Vasenmalerei.* Berlin: Keller.

    1940. *Perachora: the Sanctuaries of Hera Akraia and Limenia. Volume 1.* Oxford: Clarendon Press.

Peirce, C.S. 1958. *Collected Papers Volume 7.* Cambridge MA: Harvard University Press.

Pelegrin, J., Karlin, C. and Bodu, P. 1988. 'Châines opératoires: un outil pour le préhistorien' in J. Tixier (ed.), *Technologie Préhistorique.* Paris: CNRS.

Pelekides, S. 1916. 'Anaskafe Falerou' *Archaiologikon Deltion* 2: 13–64.

Pemberton, E. G. 1970. 'The Vrysoula Classical deposit from ancient Corinth' *Hesperia* 39: 265–307.

Pickering, A. (ed.) 1992. *Science as Practice and Culture.* Chicago: University of Chicago Press.

Pinch, T. 1986. *Confronting Nature: the Sociology of Neutrino Detection.* Dordrecht: Reidel.

Pleket, H. W. 1969. 'The archaic tyrannis' *Talanta* 1: 19–61.

Polanyi, K. 1957. *Trade and Markets in the Early Empires.* Chicago: University of Chicago Press.

Pollard, J. 1977. *Birds in Greek Life and Myth.* London: Thames and Hudson.

Pollock, F. 1976. 'Empirical research into public opinion' in P. Connerton (ed.), *Critical Sociology.* Harmondsworth: Penguin.

Popham, M. R. 1982. 'The hero at Lefkandi' *Antiquity* 56: 169–74.

    1994. 'Precolonisation: early Greek contact with the east' in G. R. Tsetskhladze and F. De Angelis (eds.), *The Archaeology of Greek Colonisation.* Oxford: Oxford University Committee for Archaeology.

Popham, M. R. and Lemos, I. S. 1995. 'A Euboean warrior trader' *Oxford Journal of Archaeology* 14(2): 151–7.

Popham, M. R., Sackett, L. H. and Themelis, P. G. 1980. *Lefkandi 1: The Iron Age Settlement and Cemeteries.* London: British School at Athens.

Poursat, J.-C. 1968. 'Les représentations de danse armée dans la céramique attique' *Bulletin de Correspondance Hellénique* 92: 550–615.

Preucel, R. 1991. 'The philosophy of archaeology' in R. Preucel (ed.), *Processual and Post-processual Archaeologies: Multiple Ways of Knowing the Past.* Carbondale: University of Southern Illinois Press.

Pritchett, W. K. 1985. *The Greek State at War: Part 4.* Berkeley: University of California Press.

Purcell, N. 1990. 'Mobility and the polis' in O. Murray and S. Price (eds.), *The Greek City from Homer to Alexander.* Oxford: Clarendon Press.

Pye, D. 1978. *The Nature and Aesthetics of Design.* London: Herbert Press.

    1980. *The Art of Workmanship.* London: Royal College of Art.

Quine, W. V. 1981. *Theories and Things*. Cambridge MA: Harvard University Press.

1990. *Pursuit of Truth*. Cambridge MA: Harvard University Press.

Qviller, B. 1981. 'The dynamics of the Homeric society' *Symbolae Osloenses* 56: 109–55.

Raepsaet, G. 1988. 'Charrettes en terre cuite de l'époque archaique à Corinthe' *L'Antiquité Classique* 57: 56–88.

Redfield, J. M. 1975. *Nature and Culture in the Iliad*. Chicago: Chicago University Press.

Renfrew, C. 1969. 'Trade and culture process in European prehistory' *Current Anthropology* 10: 151–60.

1972. *The Emergence of Civilisation: the Cyclades and the Aegean in the Third Millennium BC*. London: Methuen.

1975. 'Trade and action at a distance' in J. A. Sabloff and C. C. Lamberg-Karlowski (eds.), *Ancient Civilisation and Trade*. Albuquerque: University of New Mexico Press.

1989. 'Comments on "Archaeology into the 1990s"' *Norwegian Archaeological Review* 22: 33–41.

Renfrew, C. and Bahn, P. 1991. *Archaeology: Theories, Methods, Practice*. London: Thames and Hudson.

Richman, M. H. 1982. *Reading Georges Bataille: Beyond the Gift*. Baltimore: Johns Hopkins University Press.

Richter, G. M. A. 1970. *Kouroi: Archaic Greek Youths*. London: Phaidon.

Ricoeur, P. 1981. *Hermeneutics and the Human Sciences* (John B. Thompson, trans.). Cambridge: Cambridge University Press.

Ridgway, D. 1992a. 'Demaratus and his predecessors' in G. Kopcke and I. Tokumaru (eds.), *Greece Between East and West 10th–8th Centuries BC*. Mainz: von Zabern.

1992b. *The First Western Greeks*. Cambridge: Cambridge University Press.

Rihll, T. 1993. 'War, slavery and settlement in early Greece' in J. Rich and G. Shipley (eds.), *War and Society in the Greek World*. London: Routledge.

Rissman, L. 1983. *Love as War: Homeric Allusion in the Poetry of Sappho*. Königstein: Hain: Beiträge zur klassischen Wissenschaft 157.

Robertson, M. 1948. 'Excavations in Ithaca V: the geometric and later finds from Aetos' *Annual of the British School at Athens* 43: 60–113.

Robinson, H. S. 1976. 'Excavations at Corinth: Temple Hill, 1968–72' *Hesperia* 45: 203–39.

1984. 'Roof tiles of the early seventh century BC' *Athenische Mitteilungen* 99: 55–66.

Roebuck, C. 1972. 'Some aspects of urbanisation in Corinth' *Hesperia* 41: 96–127.

Rolley, C. 1977. Les trépieds à cuve clouée. Fouilles de Delphes 5.3.

Rosch, E. 1976. 'Classification of real-world objects: origins and representations in cognition' in S. Ehrlich and E. Tulving (eds.), *La Mémoire Sémantique*. Paris: Bulletin de Psychologie.

1978. 'Principles of cognition' in E. Rosch and B. Lloyd (eds.), *Cognition and Categorisation*. ew Jersey: Lawrence Erlbaum.

Roussel, D. 1976. *Tribu et Cité*. Be sançon Annales Littéraires de l'Université de Besançon.

Rowlands, M., Larsen, M. and Kristiansen, K. (eds.) 1987. *Centre and Periphery in the Ancient World*. Cambridge: Cambridge University Press.

Runciman, W. G. 1982. 'Origins of states: the case of archaic Greece' *Comparative Studies in Society and History* 24: 351–77.

Ryan, M. 1982. *Marxism and Deconstruction*. London: Macmillan.

Salmon, J. 1972. 'The Heraeum at Perachora and the early history of Corinth and Megara' *Annual of the British School at Athens* 67: 159–204.

1977. 'Political hoplites?' *Journal of Hellenic Studies* 97: 84–101.

1984. *Wealthy Corinth: a History of the City to 338 BC*. Oxford: Clarendon Press.

Schaeffer, H. 1957. 'Proboulos' *Pauly-Wissowa Real-Encyclopädie der klassischen Altertumswissenschaft* 23: 1221–31.

Schefold, K. 1966. *Myth and Legend in Early Greek Art* (Audrey Hicks, trans.). London: Thames and Hudson.

1992. *Gods and Heroes in Late Archaic Greek Art* (Alan Griffiths, trans.). Cambridge: Cambridge University Press.

Schnapp, A. 1984. 'Eros en chasse' in *La Cité des Images*. Paris: Nathan.

1988. 'Why did the Greeks need images?' in J. Christiansen and T. Melander (eds.), *Ancient Greek and Related Pottery*. Copenhagen: Ny Carlsberg.

Schnapp-Gourbeillon, A. 1981. *Lions, Héros, Masques: les Représentations de l'Animal chez Homère*. Paris: Maspéro.

Schweitzer, B. 1971. *Greek Geometric Art* (P. Usborne and C. Usborne, Trans.. London: Phaidon.

Scoditti, G. M. G. and Leach, J. W. 1983. 'Kula on Kitava' in J. W. Leach and E. Leach (eds.), *The Kula: New Perspectives on Massim Exchange*. Cambridge: Cambridge University Press.

Scully, S. 1990. *Homer and the Sacred City*. Ithaca: Cornell University Press.

Shanks, M. 1992a. *Artefact Design and Pottery from Archaic Korinth: an Archaeological Interpretation*. Unpublished PhD thesis, Cambridge University.

1992b. *Experiencing the Past: On the Character of Archaeology*. London: Routledge.

1992c. *The life of an artefact*. Unpublished paper. Department of Archaeology, University of Wales, Lampeter.

1992d. 'Some recent approaches to style and social reconstruction in Classical Archaeology' *Archaeological Review from Cambridge* 11: 48–53.

1992e. 'Style and the design of a perfume jar from an archaic Greek city state' *Journal of European Archaeology* 1: 77–106.

1994. 'A ruined past: experience and reality' *Archaeological Dialogues* 1: 56–76.

1995a. 'Archaeological experiences and a critical romanticism' in M. Tusa and T. Kirkinen (eds.), *The Archaeologists and their Reality: Proceedings of the 4th Nordic TAG Conference 1993*. Helsinki: Department of Archaeology.

1995b. 'The forms of history' in I. Hodder, M. Shanks, A. Alexandri, V. Buchli, J. Carman, J. Last and G. Lucas (eds.), *Interpreting Archaeology: Finding Meaning in the Past*. London: Routledge.

1996a. *Classical Archaeology: Experiences of the Discipline*. London: Routledge.

1996b. 'Photography and archaeology' in B. Molyneaux (ed.), *Visual Archaeology and the Shape of Meaning*. London: Routledge.

Shanks, M. and Hodder, I. 1995. 'Processual, postprocessual and interpretive archaeologies' in I. Hodder, M. Shanks, A. Alexandri, V. Buchli, J. Carman, J. Last and G. Lucas (eds.), *Interpreting Archaeology: Finding Meaning in the Past*. London: Routledge.

Shanks, M. and McGuire, R. 1996. 'The craft of archaeology' *American Antiquity* 61: 75–88.

Shanks, M. and Tilley, C. 1982. 'Ideology, symbolic power and ritual communication: a reinterpretation of Neolithic mortuary practices' in I. Hodder (ed.), *Symbolic and Structural Archaeology*. Cambridge: Cambridge University Press.

1987. *Social Theory and Archaeology*. Cambridge: Blackwell Polity.

1992. *Reconstructing Archaeology: Theory and Practice* (second edn.). London: Routledge.

Shapin, S. and Schaffer, S. 1985. *Leviathan and the Air-Pump: Hobbes, Boyle and the Experimental Life*. Princeton NJ: Princeton University Press.

Shaw, J. W. 1989. 'Phoenicians in southern Crete' *American Journal of Archaeology* 93: 165–83.

Shelmerdine, C. W. 1985. *The Perfume Industry of Mycenaean Pylos*. Göteborg: Paul Åström.

Shennan, S. 1982. 'Ideology, change and the European early Bronze Age' in I. Hodder (ed.), *Symbolic and Structural Archaeology*. Cambridge: Cambridge University Press.

Shepherd, G. 1993. *Death and Religion in Archaic Greek Sicily: a Study in Colonial Relationships*. Unpublished PhD thesis, Cambridge University.

Sherratt, A. and Sherratt, S. 1991. 'From luxuries to commodities: the nature of Mediterranean bronze age trading systems' in G. N. H. (ed.), *Bronze Age Trade in the Mediterranean.* Göteborg: Paul Åströms.

Sherratt, S. and Sherratt, A. 1993. 'The growth of the Mediterranean economy in the early first millennium BC' *World Archaeology* 24: 361–78.

Shipley, G. 1993. 'Introduction: the limits of war' in J. Rich and G. Shipley (eds.), *War and Society in the Greek World.* London: Routledge.

Snodgrass, A. 1964. *Early Greek Armour and Weapons.* Edinburgh: Edinburgh University Press.

　1965. 'The hoplite reform and history' *Journal of Hellenic Studies* 85: 110–22.

　1980a. *Archaic Greece: the Age of Experiment.* London: Dent.

　1980b. 'Towards the interpretation of the Geometric figure scenes' *Mitteilungen des deutschen Archäologischen Instituts, Athenische Abteilung* 95: 51–8.

　1982. 'Les origines du culte des héros dans la Grèce antique' in G. Gnoli and J.-P. Vernant (eds.), *La Mort, les Morts, dans les Sociétés Anciennes.* Cambridge: Cambridge University Press.

　1983. 'Heavy freight in archaic Greece' in P. Garnsey, K. Hopkins and C. R. Whittaker (eds.), *Trade in the Ancient Economy.* London: Chatto and Windus.

　1987. *An Archaeology of Greece: the Present State and Future Scope of a Discipline.* Berkeley: University of California Press.

　1988. 'The archaeology of the hero' *Annali dell'Istituto universitario orientale di Napoli, Dipartimento di studi del mondo classico e del Mediterraneo antico, Sezione di archeologia e storia antica* 10: 19–26.

　1991. 'Specialised sculpture avant la lettre.' *Classical Review* 43: 376–7.

　1994. 'The growth and standing of the early western colonies' in G. R. Tsetskhladze and F. De Angelis (eds.), *The Archaeology of Greek Colonisation.* Oxford: Oxford University Committee for Archaeology.

Sourvinou-Inwood, C. 1993. 'Early sanctuaries, the eighth century and ritual space: fragments of a discourse' in N. Marinatos and R. Hägg (eds.), *Greek Sanctuaries: New Approaches.* London: Routledge.

Spivey, N. 1988. 'The armed dance on Etruscan vases' in J. Christiansen and T. Melander (eds.), *Ancient Greek and Related Pottery.* Copenhagen: Ny Carlsberg Glyptotek and Thorvaldsens Museum.

Starr, C. G. 1986. *The Individual and Community.* Oxford: Oxford University Press.

　1992. *The Aristocratic Temper of Greek Civilisation.* Oxford: Oxford University Press.

Stewart, A. 1986. 'When is a kouros not an Apollo? The Tenea "Apollo" revisited' in M. A. Del Chiaro (ed.), *Corinthiaca: Studies in Honour of Darrell A Amyx.* Columbia MI: University of Missouri Press.

　1990. *Greek Sculpture: an Exploration.* New Haven: Yale University Press.

Stillwell, A. N. 1948. *Corinth 15.1: The Potters' Quarter.* Princeton NJ: American School of Classical Studies at Athens.

　1952. *Corinth 15.2: The Potters' Quarter. The Terracottas.* Princeton NJ: American School of Classical Studies at Athens.

Stillwell, A. N. and Benson, J. L. 1984. *Corinth 15.3: The Potters' Quarter: the Pottery.* Princeton NJ: American School of Classical Studies at Athens.

Strathern, M. 1988. *The Gender of the Gift.* Berkeley: University of California Press.

Strøm, I. 1971. *Development of the Etruscan Orientalising Style.* Ødense: Ødense University Classical Studies 2.

　1992. 'Evidence from the sanctuaries' in G. Kopcke and I. Tokumaru (eds.), *Greece Between East and West 10th–8th Centuries BC.* Mainz: von Zabern.

Stubbings, J. 1962. 'Ivories' in T. Dunbabin (ed.), *Perachora: the Sanctuaries of Hera Akraia and Limenia. Volume Two: Pottery, Ivories, Scarabs and Other Objects from the Votive Deposit of Hera Limenia*. Oxford: Clarendon Press.

Taylor, T. and Whitley, J. 1985. 'Decoration, description and design' *Archaeological Review from Cambridge* 4: 171–80.

Theweleit, K. 1987. *Male Fantasies. Volume One: Women, Floods, Bodies, History* (S. Conway, E. Carter and C. Turner, trans.). Cambridge: Blackwell Polity.

1989. *Male Fantasies. Volume Two: Male Bodies: Psychoanalysing the White Terror*. Cambridge: Blackwell Polity.

Thomas, J. 1990. 'Archaeology and the notion of ideology' in F. Baker and J. Thomas (eds.), *Writing the Past in the Present*. Lampeter: Saint David's University College.

Thompson, J. B. 1984. *Studies in the Theory of Ideology*. Cambridge: Blackwell Polity.

1989. 'The theory of structuration' in D. Held and J. B. Thompson (eds.), *Social Theory of Modern Societies: Anthony Giddens and his Critics*. Cambridge: Cambridge University Press.

1990. *Ideology and Modern Culture: Critical Social Theory in the Era of Mass Consumption*. Cambridge: Blackwell Polity.

Thompson, W. D. 1936. *A Glossary of Greek Birds*. Oxford: Clarendon Press.

Tilley, C. 1984. 'Ideology and the legitimation of power in the middle Neolithic of southern Sweden' in D. Miller and C. Tilley (eds.), *Ideology, Power and Prehistory*. Cambridge: Cambridge University Press.

1990. 'Michel Foucault: towards an archaeology of archaeology' in C. Tilley (ed.), *Reading Material Culture: Structuralism, Hermeneutics and Poststructuralism*. Oxford: Blackwell.

1996. *An Ethnography of the Neolithic*. Cambridge: Cambridge University Press.

Tomlinson, R. A. 1977. 'The upper terraces at Perachora' *Annual of the British School at Athens* 72: 197–202.

1980. 'Two notes on possible hestiatoria' *Annual of the British School at Athens* 75: 220–8.

1990. 'The chronology of the Perakhora Hestiatorion and its significance' in O. Murray (ed.), *Sympotica: a Symposium on the Symposion*. Oxford: Clarendon Press.

1992. 'Perachora' in *Le Sanctuaire Grec*. Geneva: Fondation Hardt.

Treister, M. Y. 1995. 'North Syrian metalworkers in Archaic Greek settlements?' *Oxford Journal of Archaeology* 14(2): 159–78.

Trigger, B. 1984. 'Alternative archaeologies: nationalist, colonialist, imperialist' *Man* 19: 355–70.

1989. 'Hyperrelativism, responsibility and the social sciences' *Canadian Review of Sociology and Anthropology* 26: 776–97.

1991. 'Post-processual developments in Anglo-American Archaeology' *Norwegian Archaeological Review* 24: 65–76.

Uberoi, J. P. S. 1971. *The Politics of the Kula Ring*. Manchester: Manchester University Press.

Ucko, P. 1969. 'Ethnography and the archaeological interpretation of funerary remains' *World Archaeology* 1: 262–80.

Ure, P. N. 1922. *The Origin of Tyranny*. Cambridge: Cambridge University Press.

Vallet, G. and Villard, F. 1964. *Megara Hyblaea 2: La Céramique Archaïque*. Paris: Boccard.

Van Wees, H. 1994. 'The Homeric way of war: the Iliad and the hoplite phalanx' *Greece and Rome* 41: 1–18, 131–55.

Vastokas, J. 1978. 'Cognitive aspects of Northwest Coast Art' in M. Greenhalgh and V. Megaw (eds.), *Art in Society*. London: Duckworth.

Vaughn, P. 1991. 'The identification and retrieval of the hoplite battle dead' in V. Hanson (ed.), *Hoplites: the Classical Greek Battle Experience*. London: Routledge.

Verdelis, N. 1962. 'A sanctuary at Solygeia' *Archaeology* 15: 185–8.

Vermeule, E. 1979. *Aspects of Death in Early Greek Art and Poetry*. Berkeley: University of California Press.

Vernant, J.-P. 1962. *Les Origines de la Pensée Grecque*. Paris: Presses Universitaires de France.

    1969. 'Le mythe hésiodique des races: essai d'analyse structurale' in *Mythe et Pensée chez les Grecs*. Paris: Maspero.

    1982. 'City-state warfare' in *Myth and Society in Ancient Greece*. London: Methuen.

    1991a. 'A "beautiful death" and the disfigured corpse in Homeric epic' in *Mortals and Immortals: Collected Essays*. Princeton NJ: Princeton University Press.

    1991b. 'Death in the eyes: Gorgo, figure of the other' in *Mortals and Immortals: Collected Essays*. Princeton NJ: Princeton University Press.

    1991c. 'Feminine figures of death in Greece' in *Mortals and Immortals: Collected Essays*. Princeton NJ: Princeton University Press.

    1991d. '*Panta kala*: from Homer to Simonides' in *Mortals and Immortals: Collected Essays*. Princeton NJ: Princeton University Press.

Vernant, J.-P. and Frontisi-Ducroux, F. 1983. Figures du masque en Grèce ancienne. *Journal de Psychologie* 1–2: 56–75.

Veyne, P. 1988. *Did the Greeks Believe in their Myths: an Essay on the Constitutive Imagination* Chicago: University of Chicago Press.

Vian, F. 1968. 'La fonction guerrière dans la mythologie grecque' in J.-P. Vernant (ed.), *Problèmes de la Guerre en Grèce Ancienne*. Paris: Mouton.

Vickers, M. and Gill, D. 1994. *Artful Crafts: Ancient Greek Silverware and Pottery*. Oxford: Clarendon Press.

Vidal-Naquet, P. 1981a. 'The black hunter and the origin of the Athenian Ephebeia' in R. L. Gordon (ed.), *Myth, Religion and Society*. Cambridge: Cambridge University Press.

    1981b. 'Land and sacrifice in the Odyssey: a study of religious and mythical meanings' in R. L. Gordon (ed.), *Myth, Religion and Society*. Cambridge: Cambridge University Press.

    1981c. 'Recipes for Greek adolescence' in R. L. Gordon (ed.), *Myth, Religion and Society*. Cambridge: Cambridge University Press.

Virilio, P. 1986. *Speed and Politics* (M. Polizzoti, trans.). New York: Semiotexte.

von Bothmer, D. 1987. 'Greek vase painting: 200 years of connoisseurship' in *Papers on the Amasis Painter and his World*. London: Thames and Hudson.

von Wright, G. 1971. *Explanation and Understanding*. London: Routledge and Kegan Paul.

Wain, P. 1995a. 'A taste of tradition: the teapots of Yixing' *Ceramic Review* 153: 42–5.

    1995b. *Zisha Teapots: Contemporary Teapots from Yixing, China*. Aberystwyth: Aberystwyth Arts Centre.

Warnke, G. 1987. *Gadamer: Hermeneutics, Tradition and Reason*. Cambridge: Blackwell Polity.

Watson, P., LeBlanc S. and Redman, C. 1971. *Archaeological Explanation: the Scientific Method in Archaeology*. New York: Columbia University Press.

West, M. L. (ed.). 1992. *Iambi et Elegi Graeci* (second edn.). Oxford: Oxford University Press.

    1993. *Greek Lyric Poetry: Translated with Introduction and Notes*. Oxford: Clarendon Press.

Whitbread, I. K. 1986. *The Application of Ceramic Petrology to the Study of Ancient Greek Transport Amphorae, with Special Reference to Corinthian Amphorae Production*. Unpublished PhD thesis, Southampton University.

Whitley, J. 1987. *Style, Burial and Society in Dark Age Greece: Social, Stylistic and Mortuary Change in the Two Communities of Athens and Knossos between 1100 and 700 BC*. Unpublished PhD thesis, Cambridge University.

    1991a. 'Social Diversity in Dark Age Greece' *Annual of the British School at Athens* 86: 341–65.

    1991b. *Style and Society in Dark Age Greece: the Changing Face of a Pre-literate Society*. Cambridge: Cambridge University Press.

    1993. 'The explanation of form: towards a reconciliation of archaeological and art-historical approaches' *Hephaistos* 11/12: 7–33.

    1994a. 'The monuments that stood before Marathon: tomb cult and hero cult in archaic

Attica' *American Journal of Archaeology* 98: 213–30.

1994b. 'Protoattic pottery: a contextual approach' in I. Morris (ed.), *Classical Greece: Ancient Histories and Modern Archaeologies*. Cambridge: Cambridge University Press.

1997. 'Beazley as theorist' *Antiquity* 71: 40–7.

Will, E. 1955. *Korinthiaka: Recherches sur l'Histoire et la Civilisation de Corinthe*. Paris: Boccard.

Williams, C. K. 1980. 'Demaratus and early Corinthian roof tiles' in P. Kanellopoulos, N. Zapheropolos, A. Kalogeropoulou, B. Lambrinoudakis and D. Mirasgezis (eds.), *Stele, Tomos eis Mneme Nikolaou Kontoleontos*. Athens:

1981. 'The city of Corinth and its domestic religion' *Hesperia* 50: 408–21.

1982. 'The early urbanisation of Corinth' *Annuario della Scuola Archeologica di Atene e delle Missioni Italiene in Oriente* 60: 9–20.

1986. 'Corinth and the cult of Aphrodite' in M. A. Del Chiaro and W. R. Biers (eds.), *Corinthiaca: Studies in Honour of Darrell A. Amyx*. Columbia: University of Missouri Press.

Williams, C. K. and Fisher, J. E. 1971. 'Corinth 1970: the forum area' *Hesperia* 40: 1–51.

Williams, R. 1976. *Keywords: a Vocabulary of Culture and Society*. London: Fontana.

Winter, A. 1978. *Die antike Glanztonkeramik. Praktische Versuche*. Mainz: von Zabern.

Winter, F. E. 1971. *Greek Fortifications*. London: Routledge and Kegan Paul.

Wolff, J. 1981. *The Social Production of Art*. London: Macmillan.

1984. *Aesthetics and the Sociology of Art*. London: George Allen and Unwin.

Wylie, A. 1989a. 'Archaeological cables and tacking: the implications of practice for Bernstein's "Options beyond objectivism and relativism"' *Philosophy of the Social Sciences* 19: 1–18.

1989b. 'Matters of fact and matters of interest' in S. Shennan (ed.), *Archaeological Approaches to Cultural Identity*. London: Unwin Hyman.

1991. 'Beyond objectivism and relativism: feminist critiques and archaeological challenges' in N. Willo and D. Walde (eds.), *Archaeology of Gender*. Calgary: University of Calgary.

Yates, T. 1990. 'Jacques Derrida: "there is nothing outside of the text"' in C. Tilley (ed.), *Reading Material Culture: Structuralism, Hermeneutics and Poststructuralism*. Oxford: Blackwell.

Young, R. S. 1942. 'Graves from the Phaleron cemetery' *American Journal of Archaeology* 46: 23–57.

Zinserling, V. 1975. 'Zum Bedeutungsgehalt des archaischen Kuros' *Eirene* 13: 19–33.

INDEX

NEW STUDIES IN ARCHAEOLOGY

Series editors
Clive Gamble, *University of Southampton*
Colin Renfrew, *University of Cambridge*

N

D